Falsely Accused of Islamophobia

My Struggle Against Academic Cancellation

Steven Greer

Falsely Accused of Islamophobia

My Struggle Against Academic Cancellation

Steven Greer

Academica Press
Washington~London

Library of Congress Cataloging-in-Publication Data

Names: Greer, Steven (author)
Title: Falsely accused of islamophobia : my struggle against academic cancellation | Greer, Steven

Description: Washington : Academica Press, 2023. | Includes references. Identifiers: LCCN 2023931831 | ISBN 9781680537192 (hardcover) | 9781680530797 (paperback) | 9781680537208 (e-book)

Copyright 2023 Steven Greer

Dedication

To Aster, Penny and Rowan

"Professor Greer's eye-opening and detailed account of harassment, intimidation and censorship is a must-read for anyone concerned about academic freedom and freedom of expression. *Falsely Accused of Islamophobia* is a sorely needed call to protect our fundamental rights to debate, to discuss, and to disagree without fear – whatever our religion or belief."

- Megan Manson, National Secular Society.

"The piercing clarity of the intellectual spotlight ... (Greer) ... shines on all the dust, grime and fluff of the bogus charges against him makes the University of Bristol management and media organs that amplified Brisoc's complaint ... look like a bunch of amoral amateurs ..."

- Hannah Baldock, Free Lance Journalist.

"Steven Greer's book provides a compelling account of how academic freedom can be imperilled by student complaints and a vicious social media campaign. Universities must do more to protect their academic staff from such unjustified vilification."

- Professor Eric Barendt, University College London.

"... an essential addition to the literature on cancel culture and academic illiberalism...It is to be hoped that more academic victims of cancel culture will write their own stories in future. If they do it half as comprehensively as Greer has, then they will have achieved something extremely important: they will have rebuked – and exposed – their persecutors."

- Daniel Sharp, *Freethinker* magazine.

"A must-read for anyone concerned about academic freedom and freedom of expression. This book is a sorely needed call to protect our fundamental rights to debate, to discuss, and to disagree without fear - whatever our religion or belief."

- Dr Jan Macvarish, Free Speech Union.

"A compelling and cautionary account of the threat to freedom of speech in academia in the age of cancel culture."

- Professor Simon Baughen, Swansea University.

Contents

Preface to the paperback edition ix
Preface to the hardback edition xiii

Chapter 1
Background 1

Chapter 2
Context 21

Chapter 3
Processes 41

Chapter 4
Allegations 99

Chapter 5
Implications 137

Chapter 6
Reflections 181

Chapter 7
Postscript 199

Appendix A
Unit Guide for Human Rights in Law, Politics and Society 2019-20 211

Appendix B
Lecture 3: Islam, China and the Far East 241

Appendix C
Core Differences Between IHRL,
Traditional Political Islam and Traditional 'Asian values' 265

Appendix D
Steven Greer: Evidence Report 267

Appendix E
Lecture 8: Terrorism and counter-terrorism 273

Appendix F
Chronology 303

Preface to the paperback edition

In common with all but the most self-assured authors, having submitted the final manuscript of the hardback to the publishers in the autumn of 2022, some unsettling questions arose – would anybody read it? And, if they did, would they appreciate it? What impact, if any, would it have? Would it get me into further trouble? Or would it contribute to remedying the injustices inflicted upon me, my family and academic freedom by BRISOC and the University of Bristol?

The only objective measure of how well, or how badly, a book has been received is the number of copies sold. But even this is a highly unreliable indicator of its intrinsic interest or value. A good book may not sell for any number of reasons including poor marketing. A single copy, particularly one held by a library or another institution, may also be read and appreciated by many. And sales alone do not reveal whether purchasers were hostile, sympathetic or neutral towards what they bought when they parted with their money, or if they remained so afterwards. Similar issues arise with reviews. The vagaries of the publishing world ensure that whether any given book is reviewed at all is very hit and miss. One with something valuable to say may simply be ignored. Conversely, another with less to commend it, may be widely reviewed largely or entirely because of the profile or connections of the author, or because it chimes with the prejudices (positive or negative) of those who control the relevant process. And, of course, what counts as 'valuable' or 'commendable' is not an objective matter either.

In my case the answers to the first four questions cited above are, however, very clear. Thankfully, this book has not, as yet, added to my woes. In fact, the opposite has so far occurred. I have been reliably informed that publication and my story have been sympathetically reported by media outlets with a global audience/readership of 231 million. This has, of course, resulted in massive world-wide adverse publicity for BRISOC and the University of Bristol. The University appears to have thought that by siding with BRISOC in defiance of the verdict of its own inquiry it could swat me away like an irritating insect and the controversy would be well and truly over. But a sting in the tail has caused considerable discomfort later. No credible defence has yet been offered to any of the central charges including the fact that the University compounded the risk BRISOC's social media campaign posed to my life. In fact, not only is the University's head still stuck deep in the sand at the bottom of a hole of its own making – it just keeps on digging.

I am, nevertheless, deeply satisfied that I did not disappear into defeated obscurity as the University expected. On the contrary. Not only have I survived the travails of the past two-and-a-half years; in the struggle to which the subtitle refers I have triumphed and flourished beyond anything I could possibly have imagined even a few months ago. Of course, some will remain forever unconvinced by the case presented in these pages. A few may even still wish me physical and/or psychological harm. But there can be no doubt that my counteroffensive against the attempt by BRISOC to ruin my reputation, deprive me of my livelihood, prematurely end my career, ostracize me from my colleagues, vilify, victimize and silence me – and the University's active and willing connivance in it – has been unbelievably successful.

The jury is still out with respect to the final question – will the book contribute to remedying the multiple injustices inflicted upon me, my family, and academic freedom? There are, however, encouraging signs that a day of reckoning may be coming. But making it happen lies in the hands of others now. Veteran Labour MP, Barry Sheerman, has already called for the Vice Chancellor and the University's entire senior management team to resign. Alumni for Free Speech (AFFS) is urging alumni and other donors to 'withhold funds' until Bristol 'demonstrates both the resolve to improve its free speech protections and real progress in doing so.' It has also referred the University to the regulator, the Office for Students (OfS). The Oxford Institute for British Islam (OIBI) has done likewise with respect to apparent ongoing breaches by the University of its statutory duty 'to have due regard to the need to prevent people from being drawn into terrorism.' The Higher Education (Freedom of Speech) Act 2023 has also now been passed with

Cambridge philosophy professor and acclaimed academic freedom campaigner, Arif Ahmed, appointed as the OfS's new 'free speech champion.' The prospect of the OfS requiring the University of Bristol to set up an independent inquiry into how it handled the BRISOC scandal has, therefore, significantly improved.

Finally, the publication of this revised and expanded paperback edition presents opportunities not only to report developments since the hardback appeared in February 2023, to update the chronology, and to correct some minor defects in the original text. It also enables me to thank those who provided assistance over the past few months as described more fully in the new Postscript chapter. I would especially like to single out the following: my publishers, Academica Press; my PR agency, Palamedes; Dr Taj Hargey and my other colleagues at the OIBI; the Free Speech Union; the Common Sense Society; the National Secular Society; The Freethinker; AFFS; Eric Barendt, Professor Emeritus at University College London; and of course my ever-loyal and loving wife and family.

Preface to the hardback edition

On 15 February 2021 my world was turned upside down. I had just discovered that the University of Bristol Islamic Society (BRISOC), frustrated by the lack of progress with a formal complaint lodged the previous autumn, had launched a potentially life-threatening social media campaign to have me sacked as Professor of Human Rights at the University of Bristol Law School in the UK. Multiple counts of Islamophobia in my teaching and other public output were alleged. Their online petition, accompanied by my photo, demanded that I apologise 'to all Muslim students.' And if I refused, the University was called upon to discipline me including by dismissal. BRISOC also insisted that the Islam, China, and the Far East module on my Human Rights in Law, Politics and Society (HRLPS) course – which I'd taught without significant alteration or difficulty, including to many Muslim students, for nearly a decade and a half – should be 'scrapped.' Just over a week later, my wife and I were so unnerved by a suspicious incident outside our home, coinciding with the reporting of the controversy by *Al Jazeera*, that I fled Bristol with her to stay somewhere safer for several days.

In July 2021 a University of Bristol inquiry exonerated me completely and without equivocation from all BRISOC's accusations, an outcome unanimously upheld on appeal that October. However, in September, the Law School nevertheless removed the Islam, China and the Far East module from the HRLPS syllabus from 2021-22 onwards, expressly in order to avoid further complaints and to protect Muslims students from being 'othered.' In October, the University publicly announced my exoneration, while at the same time recognising BRISOC's 'concerns,' and acknowledging that the HRLPS course needed to be altered in order to be 'respectful of the sensitivities' of students taking it. It is difficult to regard either of these developments as other than a defiant repudiation of the outcome of the inquiry which found no substance whatever in BRISOC's allegations.

Exhausted and demoralized by the whole experience I was signed off work by my doctor from September 2021 to the beginning of January 2022. But, early in the new year, my fortunes changed dramatically when, as a direct consequence of BRISOC's campaign, I was appointed the first Visiting Research Fellow, and later Research Director, at the Oxford Institute for British Islam, a newly established progressive Muslim think tank and research academy. But, as I write in the early autumn of 2022, the dust has yet fully to settle on the upheaval in my life over a year and a half after the crisis surfaced.

This book is not, however, intended to be an exercise in self-pity, whinging, or in seeking revenge. If it were, it is unlikely anyone would be interested in reading it. Instead, it has the following principal objectives. One is to document my experience both in order to set the record straight and to provide a firm and clear evidential basis for my reflections upon it. A second is to name and shame the institutions and organizations responsible for the injustices I've suffered in an attempt to hold them accountable in the court of public opinion and, if possible, in a court of law. A third is to consider the wider implications of my ordeal in the hope that this might help protect others from suffering a similar fate, or at least offer some encouragement if they do. Finally, I seek to demarcate responsible critical appraisal of Islam from prejudiced hostility to it and to defend the right to the former while deploring the latter. Sadly, although I'm not aware of any comparable false charge of Islamophobia against a British academic, what has happened to me is otherwise far from unique. It is, rather, just another example of rampant academic 'cancel culture,' and the corresponding lack of effective commitment to academic freedom on the part of institutions of tertiary education throughout the English-speaking world and beyond.

My 'lived experience,' and that of many others, raise numerous questions. Why, for example, are so many students and their teachers so easily convinced by prejudiced, manifestly unfounded accusations, and seduced into hunting non-existent witches and virtually burning non-existent heretics? Why do host institutions and close colleagues capitulate so readily to the online mobs rather than rising to the victims' defence? What might be done to tackle these toxic trends and to cultivate a more tolerant and less censorious, hair-trigger, environment? I regret that I don't have definitive answers. But this book seeks to contribute to the expanding literature which attempts to diagnose the problem, and to make some suggestions.

We begin in Chapter 1 with a brief autobiography. Chapter 2 describes the HRLPS unit and the Islam, China and the Far East module. Chapter 3 recounts how the BRISOC controversy unfolded, while Chapter 4 addresses the substantive allegations. Chapter 5 considers the wider implications and Chapter 6 summarizes the core issues and reflects upon the lessons that might be learned.

I was almost broken by BRISOC's complaint-and-campaign. Yet, far from destroying or silencing me, it has ultimately provided fresh, and even more credible platforms including this book, from which to disseminate the views they wrongly regard as Islamophobic. And although demoralized by the negative response of my employer, the overt hostility of a tiny minority of my colleagues, and the apparent indifference of most of the others, many total strangers who have since become treasured friends, rallied to my cause. Rather than canvass those supporters who do and who do not want to remain anonymous, I have decided not to name any here. They know who they are and also how much their sympathy and solidarity are appreciated. I would, however, particularly like to thank the following: the Free Speech Union, which, amongst other things, generously provided free legal assistance to prime my litigation against the University of Bristol; my legal team, Bryn Harris, Luke Gittos, and Nick Stanage; Lucy Greer for expert advice about marketing; Jack Smith for the cover graphic; the Bristol Free Speech Society which hosted a detailed online interview since available on YouTube; Policy Exchange for referring to the false charges against me in the online launch of my book, *Tackling Terrorism in Britain*; Simon and Victoria Baughen, Karolien Celie, Brice Dickson, Susan Greer, Stan Houston, Neil Thin, and Colin Samson, who either encouraged me to put fingers to keyboard and/or read and commented upon earlier drafts; and the staff of Academica Press for bringing the project to fruition. Needless to say, nobody but me bears any responsibility for the views expressed. But, as always, the most steadfast, unconditional and loving support has come from my wife Susan, my daughters, Cara, Lucy, and Hope, their partners, Jack, Joe, and Jake and their families, and my brother Peter, and sister-in-law Elma. Without them things would have been infinitely worse.

Chapter 1

Background

Introduction

On the surface a puzzling conundrum lies at the heart of this book. There is not a scrap of evidence from any stage or department in my life remotely suggesting that I am, or have ever been, guilty of anti-Muslim prejudice. Yet, in 2020, with little warning, I was suddenly accused of Islamophobia. The fact that, by then, I had had an unblemished academic career for nearly four decades compounds the mystery. How could someone like me teach and publish for years without incident in the relevant field, and in such a well-regulated environment, yet suddenly turn unnoticed into a hate-filled bigot until the University of Bristol Islamic Society (BRISOC) called me out? As indicated in the Preface to the hardback these questions raise other issues, deeper and wider than my own personal experience, to be considered later. However, let's begin with a sharp irony at the core of BRISOC's allegations. I stand accused of offences against their Muslim identity. Yet, as this chapter seeks to explain, had they or anyone else bothered to find out, they would quickly and easily have discovered that Islamophobia is utterly incompatible with *my* identity, my background, what I think and believe, my 'lived experience,' and in particular how I've conducted my professional life.

Childhood

I was born in Belfast in September 1956 to very ordinary Ulster Protestants, devout Methodists by conviction and choice, and uncommonly anti-sectarian. My father was an electrician and my mother, a secretary and typist. In later life I often claimed to be working class. I had, after all, arrived when my father worked on the production line of a computer factory, often on strike for better pay and conditions. But my family circumstances were probably more lower-middle class. We lived in a quiet suburb of south Belfast with my maternal grandfather, a widower, and former blacksmith and farrier, in a 1920s bungalow surrounded on three sides by a large corner garden. We were neither rich nor poor. Just content. Indeed, my parents, who grew more prosperous as they aged, managed to sustain this, and their marriage, until they died a few years apart in their 80s. Each of them also finished their working lives at Queens University Belfast (QUB). My father was Senior Technician in the Department of Electrical Engineering. I fondly remember him taking me and my younger brother, Peter, to the multi-story Ashby Building, then one of the tallest in Belfast, on an occasional Saturday morning. Peter and I ran up and down the long corridors with their polished floors, past gleaming stainless-steel display engines smelling vaguely of lubricant, pestering our dad for a bottle of Coke from the dispensing machine, a rare treat. I suppose that was one of the early subliminal positive impressions I had of University – like a medieval cathedral, an imposing in-your-face statement of knowledge and power, with the added attraction, in the case of the Ashby Building, of easy access to Coca-Cola. But only if your dad was in an obliging mood and had the correct coinage for the dispensing machine. No change was given in those days.

My mother ended her working life as PA to the Head of the Department of Aeronautical Engineering. My brother also graduated in Electrical Engineering from QUB. But, for some unknown reason, the engineering gene totally passed me by. In mid-career, mum also formed a life-long friendship with a Catholic colleague when they shared an office as secretaries in Civil Engineering. This was unlikely, less because of the different religious affiliations, and more because of their sharply contrasting lifestyles. My family was strictly teetotal and non-smoking. By contrast, mum's friend was a heavy smoker and a committed social drinker. My mother was also an astute judge of character, including of the academic staff at her workplace. At home she mercilessly mocked the charlatans, posers, and wasters she encountered, heaping praise upon the quiet, diligent hard workers. A junior Indian academic was one of her favourites. I think this rubbed off on me too.

Northern Ireland in the 1960s was very parochial, insular, ethnically homogenous, and monocultural. The distinction which mattered most to nearly everybody was that between Protestants and Catholics. For historical reasons, fully explained in the extensive literature, this was and remains, as much political as religious. Although we were all from the same northern European ethnicity, spoke English,[1] and virtually all adhered to different versions of the Christian faith, this difference was widely considered to be of monumental, even for some of cosmic, importance. Class and other differentials also split largely along these sectarian lines. Almost everybody was connected with a specific church. For some this was nominal, and only invoked when it came to christenings, marriages and funerals. Religious observance was, nevertheless, very high, particularly amongst Catholics.

Unlike the industrial towns of northern England, Belfast received virtually no post-war migrants from the Commonwealth. As a result, there were no non-white minorities of any size, and hardly any adherents to non-Christian religions, including Islam. Indeed, the few non-whites there were tended to be in prestigious positions as hospital doctors or academics at QUB, some on short-term stays. My parents' dinner table accounts of the fascinating people from foreign parts they met in their workplaces may also have been positively subliminal for me. Nevertheless, society was not free from racism. In my experience, at the time, this largely took the form of jokes and insults referenced to abstract, absent 'others,' such as calling anyone tight with money, 'Jewish.' There were in fact, very few Jews in the city and I never knowingly met any. An amusing story, possibly apocryphal, illustrates Belfast's one-dimensional sense of religious and political identity. Barricades went up in working class Protestant and Catholic districts during the early days of 'the Troubles,' the civil conflict which began in the late 1960s with street disorders and rapidly degenerated into terrorism. Access was strictly controlled by residents. According to the tale, approaching one of these, a Jewish man sought permission to enter.

---

[1] According to the 2021 Census, English was the main language of 95.4% (1,751,500) of the population of Northern Ireland, as compared with 0.3% who claimed Irish was their main language. Just over 12% claimed some ability in the Irish language.

He was asked: 'Are you a Catholic or a Protestant?' He replied that, as a Jew, he was neither. 'But are you a Protestant Jew or a Catholic Jew?' came the reply. In other words, everyone must choose a side. But I cannot recall a single instance of anti-Muslim prejudice in those days. The general view, which I then shared, was that Islam was simply a distant 'false' faith like Hinduism, Buddhism and every other foreign non-Christian religion.

For most people from my background, the late-1950s and most of the 1960s was also a 'golden age' characterised by a strong sense of community, security, increasing prosperity and opportunity. My own childhood was blissfully happy. My family was the quintessential 'safe space.' My paternal grandmother lived round one corner. My aunt and uncle and their children lived round another. Other aunts and uncles, and their families, were but a short car drive away. Nobody died before their time. Nobody contracted a debilitating illness. Nobody flounced off with a fancy-man or fancy-woman. My mother didn't get on very well with her only sibling, a brother. But, nevertheless, they occasionally met and talked. Aside from this, there were no vicious interminable family feuds. And no adult did anything to hurt me. Apart that is from the occasional walloping from my mum, which I usually richly deserved, and a public 'slippering' (caning with a gym shoe) at secondary school. The teacher in question caught me in an audio-visual French lesson looking at the slides down the tube of a rolled-up piece of my own artwork. This was clearly a miscarriage of justice. I had, after all, been paying attention with even more intense concentration than anybody else in the class. Nevertheless, I took my punishment with fortitude, almost cried but held it together, and as a result gained some street cred with my peers. I wasn't pleased to find out, years later that, following the transference of this particular teacher to her school, the young woman I married had had a crush on him. I don't believe in corporal punishment, especially when the recipient is a child. But, to be honest, my slippering did me no lasting damage. It certainly didn't deter me from any future misconduct either. I wasn't inclined in that direction anyway.

Although I was generally a serious, well-behaved, shy little boy, deeply immersed in Christianity, who liked and did well at school, I nevertheless had a few other brushes with the school authorities, including being sent out of the Latin class on the last day one summer term because I hadn't brought my books. I thought we were going to play snakes-and-ladders as in other lessons that day. *Vita sic est.* In defiance I sauntered up and down the playing fields outside the classroom to the amusement of the rest of the class who could clearly see me out of the almost wall-length windows. Not long after, on the school trip to Paris, I was confined to barracks for the evening having missed the coach back from Versailles. I simply hadn't paid sufficient attention to the time of departure. As it happened, I was retrieved by the same teacher, more relieved than angry, who'd slipped me a year or two before. '*Je voudrai signaler un enfant perdue*' is not a phrase anyone wants to have to use for real. Luckily, I was not only found before I even knew I was lost; nobody had brought their gym shoes on the trip.

In those days the winters were always cold and snowy, and the summers long, sunny and warm. Or so I remember. For us kids, the Big Freeze of 1963, which paralysed the UK for two months, was particularly wonderful. My brother, our friends, and I rolled around in the snow, jumped over a small snowman our parents made in the garden and threw snowballs at each other, all lovingly recorded by my father on his cine camera. As often observed, children then had much more freedom than today. For example, during the two-month-long summer holidays, if the weather was fine, the kids would leave home just after breakfast, return briefly for lunch, and not be seen again until teatime.

Our neighbourhood was predominantly Protestant. But it also had a few Catholic families. Everyone knew who they were. But for us boys this was of little interest. All that mattered was that their offspring weren't girls, and that they were willing to join in riding bikes, climbing trees, playing street cricket, rounders, and football, and, of course, throwing stones – a Belfast pastime in which, we later discovered, even adults participated on certain occasions. But the enemy for us wasn't the Catholics. Nor could it have been the Muslims, the Jews, the blacks, the Asians or any other minority. For one thing there weren't any. It was the kids from Aylesbury Crescent, an entirely confected local enmity based on proximity, and targeting boys exactly like ourselves. It could just as easily have been the ones from Haypark Avenue.

In addition to the family, the neighbourhood, and the school, the fourth pillar of my childhood was the local Methodist church. We went there every Sunday morning, and my father again in the evening. On Sunday afternoons my brother and I attended Sunday School and, when we were a bit older, Boys' Brigade and, in my case, the mid-week Bible study and prayer meeting. As a child, I thought anyone in Northern Ireland who was not a practicing Christian was simply a 'bad person,' bent on God-defying wrong-doing and hedonistic self-indulgence, and likely to pay dearly for it on the Day of Judgment. I well remember for example, over-hearing a hushed and horrified conversation between my mother and a neighbour about the funeral of a young BBC Northern Ireland presenter, held without clergy or any religious element whatsoever. To reject God just when you were about to meet him – the ultimate blasphemy!

Youth

In 1967, I passed the '11-plus' exam and went to the local all-boys state school, Annadale Grammar. Named after Anna Wellesley, the mother of the first Duke of Wellington the victor of the battle of Waterloo, it was built in a dip in the landscape on what had once been her estate. Hence 'Anna-dale.' As a boy I used to imagine the young Duke-to-be cantering on horseback over the gently undulating terrain. They say the battle of Waterloo was won on the playing fields of Eton. But maybe it was really won on what would become the playing fields of Annadale. However, it is well-known that Wellington and his mother didn't get on. And, to be honest, I'm not even sure if he ever visited.

Although Annadale was based on an English public school – with houses, prefects, and Latin (for the more academic boys) – the pupils were, like me, predominantly the working and lower-middle class beneficiaries of post-war UK education reforms. In fact, I would have preferred to have gone to the much posher Methodist College ('Methody'). But, although I applied, I wasn't offered a place. This was because, my father said, I'd had 'nobody to speak for me,' an early demoralising introduction to the principle of 'who' rather than 'what' you know. Annadale's buildings had been hastily erected from cheap, prefabricated panels just after the Second World War. The double-skin walls were so thin that quite a few holes were punched in the inner layer by some of the stronger, older, and less well-behaved boys, just because they could.

But, apart from the rather shabby fabric, I benefited hugely from Annadale. I was never really bullied, although I did experience some oblique and misdirected 'guilt-by-association' homophobia stemming from my friendship with the school's musicians some of whom were gay and very camp. Otherwise, I felt respected and valued. I learned the violin and the viola (playing the latter in the City of Belfast Youth Orchestra), was briefly in the school's 2nd fifteen rugby team, won the third-form high jump, represented the school in a debating competition, sang in the choir, and played Bob Cratchit in the school production of *A Christmas Carol*. I also remember, but not quite when, being very impressed by the scientific method – the systematic, non-prejudiced testing of hypotheses against comprehensively assembled and neutrally analysed data – and by scientific language – the cautious, measured, and often circumspect admission that only conclusions supported by the data are justified and that these may be, as yet, limited and unclear, and will always be provisional until they are repeatedly confirmed or disproved. But, in retrospect, what I appreciate most was being encouraged to think for myself.

Politics hardly featured at all at home. Indeed, within the extended family they were taboo. This was not least because the aunt and uncle who lived round the corner were, in the mid-1960s, amongst the first followers of the Rev Ian Paisley, then an obscure firebrand, anti-Catholic, evangelical preacher who later founded his own Free Presbyterian Church and the ultra-loyalist Democratic Unionist Party (DUP). But I well remember a few casual remarks that probably helped frame my own political orientation. For example, I once heard my mother saying that she thought the partition of Ireland had been a mistake, and my father reporting with great disdain, a remark to which he had been privy that 'the only good Catholic is a dead one.' The fact that it had been made by another member of the extended family struck him as particularly reprehensible.

On another occasion, when filling in an application form, I asked my parents what I should put down for nationality. My dad unhesitatingly said 'Irish.' My mum thought 'British' was technically more accurate. In fact, they were both right. British/Irish or Irish/British is how I've thought of myself for as long as I can remember. And I've had both passports for decades to prove it. As the Troubles took off, my mum stopped voting altogether on the grounds that all politicians were rotten and kept the conflict going rather than genuinely seeking to resolve it. The family was amused, however, when not long before she died in her 80s, she voted DUP. Had it not been for her age and the idiosyncratic reason – their urban fox policy, one of her bugbears at the time – this would have been a huge repudiation of everything she'd previously stood for. But, to be fair, the DUP had also mellowed quite a bit by this stage and were even in government with their once sworn enemies, Sinn Féin.

My happy carefree childhood came to an abrupt end in 1969. Coupled with the onset of teenage angst, I suffered two interconnected crises. First, I was deeply upset by the onset of the Troubles. On the family holiday in Scotland that summer, a month or so before my 13th birthday, I was afflicted by a bout of teenage depression. I couldn't rid my mind of the fact that violence and killing had broken out in what, to me, had been the most tranquil of places. It was my first thought when I woke every morning, the last at night, and it dominated my thinking all day. But it was much less a fear of being, or of my family being harmed, and much more a sense of acute bewilderment about why it was happening, profound sorrow that it was, and a deep concern about what could be done to stop it. The phenomenon of compulsive thinking is, of course, well understood in psychology and psychiatry. But not so much by my parents. Their solution was briskly to instruct me to put what was bothering me out of my mind, not to worry, and to think about something else. This came very easily to them. But I couldn't make it happen at all. I was grateful later, however, as this preoccupation primed my first forays into research, a silver lining I've also found in other life crises including the one this book is about.

The obsessive thoughts gradually subsided as the challenges of living through the Troubles became more immediate. Life was grim, particularly in the early 1970s. No-warning bombs were exploding regularly, including a fatal one at a pub a few streets away from our home. Shootings were also frequent. Late one summer evening, for example, preparing for exams with my bedroom window open, I heard the sounds of a fierce gun battle being waged on the other side of the city. Riots could also erupt with little warning. Gangs of Protestant/loyalist and Catholic/nationalist youths roamed the streets looking for trouble. I was also (briefly) detained at Heathrow airport to have my arms checked for tattoos. And, like everybody else in Belfast, I was often stuck in traffic jams caused by mobile army patrols, subjected to the minor day-to-day indignities of body and bag searches by the security forces, and delayed in long queues disembarking from Irish Sea ferries on the British mainland while counterterrorist formalities were completed.

The early 1970s were also a time of great political and cultural ferment across the west. Many of us, including me, grew our hair long (imagine a dishevelled ginger-haired Louis XIV) and professed hostility to bourgeois, capitalist, imperialist society. However, there wasn't a single student from any ethnic minority in the entire school. Although my class was virtually 100% Protestant (there was one Catholic boy), a tiny minority had nationalist sympathies. In those days, this could get you into serious trouble. For example, a pupil in the year above was murdered by loyalists for 'being in the IRA.' But the truth was that he'd simply befriended other Catholic teenagers. And, while most came from church-going families, some were atheist or agnostic. We had many vigorous formal debates in English lessons about these and other topics. But Islam was not one of them.

In fact, I have no recollection of when I first heard about Islam. It probably occurred in my childhood with the characters and stories from the familiar 'orientalist fantasy' about the 'exotic east' – Ali Baba, Sinbad, the Arabian nights, Aladdin, magic carpets, genies in bottles, and so on. Although, to be honest, I wasn't particularly aware then that they belonged to an Islamic cultural context. Later, my interest in history, especially the collapse of the Ottoman empire, led to a more informed understanding. For several reasons I also became more conscious of the middle east in my teens. There was a series of wars between Israel and its neighbours. The Palestinian cause, then framed in secular terms, also became better-known. The oil crisis of the early 1970s brought another facet to the fore. But it was the Islamic revolution in Iran in the late 1970s which signalled that something very significant was happening in the Muslim world.

The second challenge in my early teens was a profound religious crisis triggered by my first encounters at Annadale with boys who had either never had my kind of religious upbringing, or having had it, had rejected it. I sought resolution by burying my head as deeply as I could in evangelical Christianity which, as the most confident, uncompromising and reassuring perspective available, seemed to offer a solution. Looking back, all these problems from 1969 onwards were almost certainly symptoms of an underlying depressive condition from which I've suffered, off and on, most of my adult life. But I'm glad to say this is now much more effectively managed than before by a mild dose of anti-depressants, meditation, and my own DIY brand of Buddhism. In a nutshell, the last of these amounts to this: we will be better able to reduce and to manage suffering (our own and that of others) if, privately and in the company of those similarly inclined, we lighten our grip on aversion and desire, avoid hatred, greed and delusion, are mindful of the impermanence, insubstantiality, and interconnectedness of all things, and if we strive earnestly to avoid harming and to promote the well-being of all, including ourselves. I can't honestly say that I've always lived up to this ideal. But it certainly expresses some of the core values I hold.

Luckily none of my family or close friends was killed or maimed in the Troubles. But I knew plenty of people who were murdered by either loyalists or republicans. These include Pat Finucane, the solicitor killed at his own home by loyalist gunmen allegedly acting in collusion with elements of the security forces. I was also deeply ashamed when, during the Ulster Workers Council strike in 1974, loyalist mobs burned Catholic shops on the Ormeau Road where I lived. But one of the most shocking incidents for me was seeing the body of a prominent Unionist colleague lying on the street outside the QUB Law Faculty, shot in the head by the IRA ostensibly for publicly supporting the supergrass process – mass counterterrorist trials on the evidence of informants – which I and others criticised on civil liberties grounds. Not only had we each just debated the pros and cons in a local current affairs journal, but the week before his murder we'd also had an unusually friendly chat on the very spot where he was killed.

I could recount many other harrowing tales. One concerns a friend. When the kids in our neighbourhood went to secondary school, the Catholics to their Church-run establishments and the rest to the state equivalents, we no longer played in the street and, therefore, lost touch with each other. However, one evening in the early 1970s, my mother discovered a former Catholic playmate, now a teenager, hiding in our cloakroom to escape a gang of loyalist thugs bent on giving him a thrashing or worse. While mum called the police, my dad confronted the gang as they came down the garden path. They quickly scarpered, denouncing us as 'Fenian lovers' and threatening reprisals which didn't materialize. I've never been more proud of my parents. They would have done the same whatever the minority identity of the fugitive, including if they'd been Muslim. One dark evening some weeks later I was crossing the school playing fields on my way to a rehearsal when I encountered another gang. A much smaller teenager, brandishing a knife, asked if I would like my throat cut. Not remotely intimidated on account of the disparity in our sizes, I politely declined. Just then, out of the darkness a voice, which I didn't recognise, said: 'Leave him alone! He's a good taig!.' The term 'taig' is loyalist slang for Irish Catholic, sometimes co-opted, as in this case, by Catholic youths themselves. I never found out for sure whose the voice was, or why they'd said this. But I like to think my former Catholic playmate had something to do with it.

An issue from my past also puts a different complexion on another of BRISOC'S accusations, that as an elderly white male I have benefitted from 'white privilege.' I certainly don't deny that, by comparison with most other people on the planet, I'm privileged in terms of race, gender, and many other accidents of my birth. But not every white male is more privileged than every non-white male or female. It is difficult, for example, to see how a white boy, on free school meals, being raised on a deprived council housing estate by an alcoholic mother, is more privileged than a black girl from a stable and supportive family educated at an expensive private school. Another problem with the 'white privilege' label is the fact that it ignores, overlooks, or downplays complex hierarchies and subordinations within the white race itself. For one thing, white males are generally more privileged that white females and not every white male is equally privileged by comparison with his white male peers. The same is true of non-whites. In both cases there are, in other words, significant differences deriving from language, religion, political or other opinion, nationality, property, birth, sexuality, disability, social class, and other status. Furthermore, neither 'white' nor 'non-white' are binary categories. Some people are of mixed heritage. And the further back in history we go the more this is the case. It has recently been discovered, for example, that a small percentage of the DNA of every homo sapiens is in fact Neanderthal – making us all not just mixed race, but mixed species.

Of more direct relevance to the issues in this book is that fact that insulting 19th century media stereotypes depicting the Irish as drunken, stupid, ugly, barbarous, pugnacious, unkempt, fractious, and treacherous, were revived during the Troubles, often with no distinction between northerners and southerners or between Protestants, Unionists, Catholics or Nationalists. In my lived experience anti-Irishness manifested itself on trips to England, and later studying at Oxford, in a few 'micro-aggressions.' And then there were the 'No blacks. No dogs. No Irish.' signs on various private premises in English cities. I never saw any of these myself. But, in the early 1970s, a friend, then a student, tried to talk his way around one obstructing his summer employment on a building site in London. The careful explanation that, as a Protestant from Northern Ireland, he was British not Irish, was given short shrift by the foreman and his workmates.

However, in spite of all these challenges, I continued to do well at school and considered careers in medicine, archaeology, and teaching, amongst others. One ambition in my early teens was to be a medical missionary bringing Christianity and healing to Africa – an innocent boy's do-good fantasy which today would be quickly condemned by many as 'colonialist white saviourism.' Being in a dither about which way to go, and observing that I enjoyed the cut and thrust of debate, parents and others encouraged me to apply to university to study law. So, post A-level I joined the Oxbridge stream at Methody (got there in the end!), took the entrance exams for Oxford, and ended up with an Exhibition (a kind of scholarship) at Keble College.

But, things didn't go too well, at least to begin with. When Thomas Carlyle, the famous 19th century polymath, described economics as a 'dismal science,' he'd obviously overlooked law. I found it, not only very difficult, but also incredibly boring and depressing, and Oxford itself very alien and overwhelming. Within a few days of my arrival, I was banging on my tutor's door, pleading to be allowed to transfer to another discipline. But he, probably wisely, cautioned against it, attributing my difficulties to settling-in problems. So I stayed, hoping to exit after my first-year exams. But since my results were poor, I was not a particularly attractive candidate for tutors in other subjects. So, I'd little alternative but to knuckle down, work as hard as I could, get a good degree, and then consider doing something else.

So, after Oxford, I obtained a Masters in Sociology at the London School of Economics and Political Science, followed by a PhD at QUB. The last of these, in particular, gave me the opportunity for which I'd long yearned – to study the Northern Ireland problem, to find out why the Troubles had happened, how they might have been prevented, and how they could now be solved. In 1983, running out of public funding for my PhD, I was appointed part-time Cobden Trust Research Student in Emergency Laws and Human Rights at the Faculty of Law at QUB. The Cobden Trust, then the research wing of the National Council for Civil Liberties (now *Liberty*), sponsored the studentship which enabled the recipient to spend half their time on their thesis and the other half researching topics as directed. In my case, there were two of the latter – the case for the restoration of jury trial to terrorist offences in Northern Ireland,[2] and the emerging 'supergrass' system, to which reference has

---

[2] S. Greer and A. White, *Abolishing the Diplock Courts - The Case for Restoring Jury Trial to Scheduled Offences in Northern Ireland* (The Cobden Trust, 1986).

already been made. My PhD began as a study of the law governing the use of the army as an 'aid to the civil power.' But it was eventually replaced by the supergrass issue. Taking full advantage of the now-obsolete, 'write-as-much-and-take-as-much-time-as-you-like' regime, I didn't present my thesis until 1990. It was later published as a book and 'commended,' ie declared runner up, in the Socio-Legal Studies Association/Oxford University Press Socio-Legal Book Prize 1995.[3] My perspective on counterterrorism, which grew out of this project, crystalized around two core conclusions. First, domestic terrorism has to be addressed effectively and humanely, not least because if the response is not humane it is unlikely to be effective. The second is that domestic counterterrorism should not prejudice the chances of whatever deeper and wider political and social settlement might be required.

During my return to Belfast from 1981-85 I was also active in the Committee on the Administration of Justice (CAJ) and the Northern Ireland Association of Socialist Lawyers (NIASL), each of which monitored the compliance of law and policy in Northern Ireland with civil liberties and the rule of law. The CAJ was more politically neutral than NIASL which, as the name suggests, argued for socialist solutions to then current challenges. It was also unusual, however, in that it embraced a range of opinion over very contentious issues such as the legitimacy of the IRA's campaign and sympathy for the USSR, to each of which I and others were opposed.

Having tutored part-time in 1984-85 at QUB, I was appointed, in 1985, to a one-year lectureship at the University of Sussex, and in 1986 I took up another temporary appointment at, what was then the Faculty of Law in the University of Bristol. I became a permanent member of the academic staff a few years later. Over this period, I'd also married and drifted away from evangelical Christianity, through Anglicanism, into Quakerism. I've never been wholly convinced by pacificism, the hallmark of the Quaker 'brand.' Much less so now. But the Quakers seemed decent people determined to do good in a wicked world. The South Belfast Meeting also offered a rare opportunity for what, to me,

---

[3] S. Greer, *Supergrasses: A Study in Anti-Terrorist Law Enforcement in Northern Ireland* (Clarendon Press, 1995).

seemed like authentic spirituality only loosely connected with mainstream Northern Irish Christianity. Relief work in the Irish potato famine of the 1840s had also earned the Quakers enduring respect across the sectarian divide. I felt privileged to be involved. And I loved the meetings for worship, particularly the ones where 'the spirit' didn't 'move' anybody to say anything. These turned out to be a primer for the Buddhist mediation sessions towards which I gravitated in Bristol much later. Not long after having returned to England, I joined the British Labour Party. But I left in 2013 disillusioned by the party's leftward drift, a decision later reinforced by the conviction that Jeremy Corbyn was a disaster who would lead the party into the political wilderness. Which he did.

Career

I should probably explain how such a reluctant law student became a Professor in a Law School. The truth is that, although I'd started off hating the study of law, by the time I'd finished I'd invested a huge amount of time and effort in, and had also gradually made my peace with, it. I'd also realised that I'd learned a great deal from it, particularly about how to organize information and how to think systematically. And, in spite of a rather less than stimulating experience from my formal studies at Oxford, I never lost faith in the modern western university's then rock-solid dedication to learning and to the spirit of free inquiry and open debate which I'd acquired in my early teens.

After QUB, my intention had been to build an academic career straddling law and sociology. But there were more jobs in the former than the latter, so this is where I ended up. In the mid-1980s the Faculty of Law at the University of Bristol was a fuddy-duddy place, dominated like most other UK law schools then, by 'legal positivism' – the largely descriptive study of law as a system of self-contained institutions, rules and procedures, with little or no reference to any 'external' context including social science, public policy, morality, justice, economics, philosophy, and the like. But change was in the air as other paradigms which approached the subject with much more thorough attention to such other issues began to gain traction. Having studied both law and sociology, this was grist to my mill. However, for quite a few years and for various reasons, I taught a variety of subjects, little of the content of which I found inspiring, or of which I quickly tired. But, nevertheless, this was all useful experience. Gradually I moved into areas which interested me more, and also up the status hierarchy, eventually being promoted to a personal chair. This enabled me to choose my own title. I opted for 'Professor of Human Rights' because, by this stage, this best reflected the primary focus of my professional interests.

My research has also enabled me to travel the world, from Minneapolis to Kathmandu, including Australia, China, the middle east, Mexico, Harvard Law School, other major US universities, and many parts of Europe. I have also worked with several Arab and Muslim organisations in the UK and abroad.[4] It is unlikely in the extreme that I

---

[4] 'Human Rights, Democracy and the Rule of Law: the European Experience,' Public Lecture, Malé, The Maldives, 13 July 2006, at the invitation of Hama, a Maldivian human rights organisation; 'Human Rights Realism: the Challenge for Legal and Political Systems,' *International Seminar on Comparative Law (ISCOM 2008) - Towards Interaction and Convergence of Legal Systems*, Faculty of Syariah and Law, Islamic Sciences University, Kuala Lumpur, Malaysia, 18-20 November 2008; Member of a four-person team of international advisors to the Palestinian Centre for the Independence of the Judiciary and the Legal Profession – MUSAWA – on 'Legal Mechanisms Available to Settle the Palestinian Internal Crises and the Palestinian Case under International Law,' Limassol, Cyprus, 25-27 January 2009; 'Have the UK's anti-terrorist laws violated basic human rights and turned Muslims into a 'suspect community'?,' public lecture to Dialogue Society (a Muslim organisation with Turkish origins), London, 26 March 2009; Three seminars on 'Women's rights and international human rights law' to training course on *Access to Justice for Poor Women*, hosted in Jericho by MUSAWA and Relief International, 22-23 May 2009; Discussant (with author) at launch of H. A. Hellyer's, *Muslims of Europe: The 'Other' Europeans* (Edinburgh University Press, 2009), Dialogue Society, London, 13 October 2009; 'Constitutional courts and international human rights law,' paper *to Third Conference on Palestinian Justice, 'A Suitable Constitutional Judicial System for Palestine and the Need for a Constitutional Court as a Requirement to Build a Palestinian State,'* Video Conference with Ramallah-Gaza-Cairo-Amman, organized by the Palestinian Red Crescent Society and MUSAWA, sponsored by the European Union and the International Bar Association, Ramallah, 13-14 December 2009; 'Human Rights and Islam: Muslim and Non-Muslim Perspectives,' panel discussion with Professor Mashood Baserin (SOAS), Dialogue Society, London, 19 January 2010; 'The international protection of human rights in Europe and its effects upon Muslims,' *Conference on Islam and Human Rights*, Al-Mahdi Institute, Birmingham, 13 March 2010; 'The Arab Revolutions: Towards Democracy, Human Rights and the Rule of Law?' Fellowship Dialogue Society, University of Bristol Chaplaincy, 16 May 2011; Interview on *Salaam Shalom Radio*, Bristol, in response to lecture 'Have Muslims become a 'suspect community in post-9/11 Britain?,' 1 September

would even have been considered by any of these had there been the slightest whiff of Islamophobia in my outlook. Nor would I have received invitations from some on several occasions. I've also published numerous pieces about Islam and Muslims in various places including several papers in journals and a collection of essays, all peer-assessed,[5] plus a number of blogs on the University of Bristol Law School Blog site,[6] and on several others.[7] The most recent is my book, *Tackling Terrorism in Britain: Threats, Responses, and Challenges Twenty Years After 9/11*,[8] which, amongst other things, rehearses virtually all the arguments to which BRISOC object. Together these represent the core of my thinking about Muslims and Islam. If they're Islamophobic – which of course they're not – this would also be true of the organizations and

---

2011; 'Counterterrorism and Muslims in Britain: What's the problem? What's the solution?,' *GW4 Understanding Religion and Law Workshop*, Institute of Arab and Islamic Studies, University of Exeter, 10 December 2015.

[5] 'Anti-Terrorist Laws and the United Kingdom's "Suspect Muslim Community": A Reply to Pantazis and Pemberton' (2010) 50 *British Journal of Criminology* 1171-1190; 'Have Muslims become a "suspect community" in post-9/11 Britain?,' University of Bristol Twilight Talks/Bristol Festival of Ideas, the Watershed, Bristol, 20 July 2011; COMMENT AND DEBATE – 'Reply to Marie Breen-Smyth, "Theorising the 'suspect community': counterterrorism, security practices and the public imagination"' (2014) *Critical Studies on Terrorism*, 1-4; 'The myth of the "securitized Muslim community": the social impact of post-9/11 counterterrorist law and policy in the west' in G. Lennon & C. Walker (eds.), *Routledge Handbook of Law and Terrorism* (Routledge, 2015), 400-15.

[6] 'Tackling Terrorism in Britain: What are the Threats, Responses, and Challenges Twenty Years After 9/11,' 29 November 2021; 'Counter-terrorism was ignored in the UK general election – it must not be forgotten in 2020,' 14 January 2020; 'De-radicalisation and the London Bridge attack of 29 November 2019,' 9 December 2019; 'Know Your Enemy: Racism and Islamophobia,' 22 August 2019; 'Three cheers for the independent review of Prevent' (co-authored by L. Bell), 6 February 2019; 'Six myths about the "Prevent duty" in universities' (co-authored by L. Bell), 22 January 2018; 'Challenge to "Prevent duty" in universities rejected in judicial review proceedings,' 21 August 2017; 'Universities and Counter-Terrorism in the UK: "Educators Not Informants!," "Boycott Prevent!"?,' 23 May 2016; 'The myth of the "securitized Muslim community": the social impact of post-9/11 counterterrorist law and policy in the west,' 9 March 2016.

[7] 'Taking the sting out of anti-terrorist laws,' Dialogue Society, 17 February 2011, http://www.dialoguesociety.org/articles/381-taking-the-sting-out-of-anti-terrorist-laws.html#.VyOEia0UW70.

You Tube video, 'Prevent Duty: myths and misconceptions with Professor Steven Greer, 14 December 2017, https://www.youtube.com/watch?v=pU0qwm9FiPUS.

'Six myths about the 'Prevent duty' in universities' (co-authored by L. Bell), *Times Higher Education Blog*, 9 April 2018, https://www.timeshighereducation.com/blog/six-myths-about-prevent-duty-universities

[8] Routledge, 2022.

publishers which published or otherwise accommodated them, and the assessors who recommended them for public consumption.

Conclusion

BRISOC's claim that I am an Islamophobe is incomprehensible in the first instance because it is so incompatible with my identity. My parents raised me not to hate anyone, certainly not whole classes of people defined by their race, ethnicity, gender, religion, nationality, ideology, or by any combination of these variables. In fact, trying to be positive about 'the other,' in spite of how misguided or difficult they might seem, has remained the lodestone of my life ever since. As I grew from boyhood to manhood I embarked on a not-always welcome or comfortable, spiritual, intellectual and ideological journey to find, for me, the best fit for this outlook and its implications given the conditions of the late 20th and early 21st centuries. Eventually I arrived at a modus vivendi based on a fluid fusion between commitment to agnosticism, humanism, western rationalism, the scientific method, democracy, human rights, the rule of law, open markets, peace, justice, the centre-left, and my own interpretation of eastern mysticism. Honouring the imperative to 'Know Thyself,' this is who I believe I am.

'Knowing the Other' is also of critical importance for me, as it should be for everyone. Each of these two knowledge-quests should be open to constructive critical, including self-critical, scrutiny. They should also be infinitely revisable. As a student of ideas, I've long been interested in all ideologies and belief systems. I acknowledge that our deepest and most fundamental values are ultimately held intuitively – for example the notion that deliberately harming another is prima facie wrong and, at the very least, requires a compelling justification. But I am, nevertheless, sceptical about systems of revealed truth which tell us to 'do X but not Y because God requires it.' This is a conscious rather than an 'unconscious bias.' But it does not, of course, make me an Islamophobe, an antisemite, a Christianophobe, Hindu-ophobe, or any other kind of 'phobe' because I don't hate any of the faiths concerned or those who adhere to them. Doubting what they claim and why they believe it, is one thing. Hatred is another entirely. And I also remain open to persuasion that I may be wrong.

I chose to enter the academic profession, rather than to practice law, because I wanted to keep on learning, to pass on the baton of intellectual curiosity and free inquiry to others, and to do my best to make the world a better place for all. Maybe this is just a more mature version of my boyhood aspiration to be a Christian medical missionary. If so, I make no apology for it. But I certainly did not become an academic in order to persecute or insult minorities. Like everybody, I am a product of my upbringing, my 'lived experience,' and my time. The bitter irony is that, while claiming to be rooting out prejudiced hatred, BRISOC's complaint-and-campaign is itself an exercise in hatred and prejudice precisely because of its monumental lack of insight into who I am and what I think. The rest of the book seeks to explain this further and to explore its implications.

Chapter 2

Context

Introduction

Pick up any serious newspaper any day of the week and it's likely to be full of items relating to human rights. These tend to fall into one of two categories. The term, 'human rights,' may expressly appear in the headline. Yet, even without it, the issue in question – war crimes, immigration, counterterrorism, freedom of speech, health care, world poverty, or whatever – could, nevertheless, have a human rights dimension. In other words, interest in and the relevance of, human rights have spread far beyond the international legal environment where they first formally appeared in the middle of the last century. Any given news item is also likely to belong to one of two other categories. It will either seek to highlight a violation, allegedly perpetrated in the present or the past at home or abroad, typically by the state or the powerful. Or it will criticise the human rights ideal itself, or the way in which it allegedly operates, for obstructing a more robust and appropriate solution to a perceived problem.

But it has not always been so. In fact, human rights have achieved their current public profile only comparatively recently. Opinions differ about precisely when this happened and about the significance of deeper historical precursors. And although particularly visible, news is not the only indicator. Increasingly, the human rights ideal has made its presence felt in many other places, including constitutions, legislation, courtrooms, parliamentary debates, university seminars, school classrooms, think tanks, the pub, and at the dining tables of the chattering classes.

Since the mid-1980s, I've taught various human rights courses/subjects/units, including at the University of Sussex, the University of

Wollongong in Australia, the School of Law at the University of Connecticut in the US, and the International Institute of Human Rights in Strasbourg. But until about 15 years ago, those in the University of Bristol Law School were, perhaps not surprisingly, very law-oriented. Then, around 2005, I had the opportunity to design and to teach, an optional unit which sought to integrate my interest in human rights with my backgrounds in law and social science. What emerged was Human Rights in Law, Politics and Society (HRLPS).

Human Rights in Law, Politics and Society

BRISOC has claimed that human rights units in Law Schools should stick to describing the objective legal truth and should not stray into parallel disciplines such as politics, philosophy or religion. This betrays both shocking ignorance and arrogance. For one thing, there is no such thing as the 'objective legal truth' about human rights. And, as already indicated, relevant debates have long escaped the confines of legal paradigms. The clue that HRLPS is not limited to 'law' also, of course, lies in the title. All of this has been clearly explained to students in advertising for the unit, the Unit Guide as found in Appendix A, and in the introductory lecture.

Broadly speaking, when I designed and taught it, HRLPS sought to address three principal questions: What are human rights? How and why have they acquired the profile they have in the contemporary world? And what have been the consequences, including pros and cons? Amongst other things this involved identifying norms, institutions, processes, trends, and debates, and critically exploring the many ambiguities and challenges each presents. Of critical importance for me was the attempt to cultivate and to encourage critical appreciation of the paradigm itself, moving beyond the crude binary distinction between 'human rights good guys' and 'anti-human rights bad guys,' to fostering an awareness of the complexity, multidimensionality, and paradoxes contemporary issues raise.

The unit was originally introduced to the sociology curriculum in 2006-07 and then to law the following year. Not long afterwards there were both undergraduate (LLB), and postgraduate masters (LLM) versions. In the interests of economies of scale, each had similar content but different assessment regimes. While the Law School permits some overlap between units on the same degree programme, these must obviously be kept to a minimum. One consequence was that, since Africa already had a high profile on the LLM unit in International Human Rights Law, it was included on the LLM in HRLPS only as a 'horizontal' theme – ie not a module (a component of a 'unit'), or part of a module, in its own right – but one which appeared across the syllabus. Since BRISOC's complaint seems entirely concerned with the undergraduate version, the remainder of this book focuses upon it alone. Indeed, it is not clear if those who brought the complaint against me even know that there was and remains an LLM equivalent.

The University of Bristol, like universities throughout the UK, tries to ensure that degrees involve roughly the same amount of work for students and staff no matter what the discipline, that this is kept within manageable limits, and that broadly standardized ratios between contact time with academic staff and private study are maintained. It is generally assumed that postgraduate units will, and should, involve more effort on the part of students themselves. While content is a matter for negotiation between teaching teams, their departments and Schools, delivery must also conform to certain specifications. In law this has involved a limited choice between different mixes of lectures to the whole cohort taking the unit supported by either small group tutorials of 8-10 students or larger seminar groups of 16-20. The number of modules or topics in an given course/unit is also controlled. Although they had their own separate seminar series, LLM students were, and remain, permitted to attend undergraduate lectures.

Given this framework, HRLPS had nine topics or modules, each involving a highly schematic 50-minute lecture which mapped the landscape, but without going into much detail or citing sources. Each module also had a seminar lasting an hour and 50 minutes where the issues could be explored in more depth. In these, students were typically broken into small discussion groups of two or three, asked to reflect upon a particular question, and to report back to the plenary session. I wrote their responses on a whiteboard and then, together with the class, we reconstructed them, also on the whiteboard. In 2020-21 the challenges of the Covid pandemic resulted, not only in 'blended' online and face-to-face delivery, but also in significant streamlining with, for example, the number of modules reduced from nine to six. The one on 'Islam, China and the Far East,' already narrowed to 'Islam and China' on the LLB unit, survived the cull, unchallenged and unchanged, without objection or discussion.

The undergraduate Unit Guide, found in Appendix A, indicates how the pre-Covid unit was structured, including the recommended literature for each module and questions for discussion in the seminars. In the interests of deflecting the fashionable demand to 'decolonize the university curriculum,' considered further in Chapter 4, it should also be noted that there are plenty of citations to authors with names which appear to indicate non-European backgrounds, and that the inclusion of any given source does not mean that it was simply being offered for uncritical endorsement. In fact, some may have been listed for quite the opposite reason.

Up to the Covid crisis, the following themes were covered: the origins and history of the human rights ideal and its contested status in western debates about law, politics and society; the internationalization and globalization of human rights; arguments about the universality and cultural limits of human rights particularly with respect to Islam, Asia, China, and multicultural societies; attempts to sanction human rights violations through legal and especially judicial processes, particularly by the European Court of Human Rights and the International Criminal Court; and some sharp contemporary debates, including about the relationship between human rights and democracy, poverty and economic development, counterterrorism, and armed conflict. Some of these were 'foundational' or 'horizontal' in the sense that they pervaded the entire unit. Others, for example human rights and counterterrorism, were 'vertical' or relatively self-contained. Yet others, for example the International Criminal Court, were both 'vertical' and 'horizontal' because, although they had a high profile in at least one module, they were also relevant to others. This was all carefully explained to students.

HRLPS could have been described as a 'socio-legal' or social science unit. But my preference was to refer to it as a 'sustained critical reflection upon global current affairs through a human rights lens,' or vice versa. Needless to say, it had to be approved by the Law School and the University of Bristol before it found its way on to the curriculum. And, as with every other unit, the content was described in annual advertising. It was also audited every year, including by several colleagues who sat in on specific seminars. The one on Islam, China and the Far East proved consistently popular for this purpose. The unit was never found to be anything other than intellectually rigorous, well-resourced, and appropriately challenging, nor has anything of significance ever been criticised about it. External examiners have also unanimously praised it, often commending the exemplary student performance in assessments, amongst the highest in the School, with about a third obtaining first class marks including several outstanding results.

In 2019-20 the Law School conducted a thorough review of the entire undergraduate curriculum. HRLPS was one of the few units, the continued inclusion of which, generated no discussion or query. Had there been any suspicion that I, or any part of it, were remotely 'Islamophobic,' this would have been the ideal opportunity for its future to have been considered. The numbers opting to take HRLPS also indicate that it was consistently one of the most popular units on the law curriculum. Every year it also attracted the more reflective and thoughtful students, including a significant proportion of Muslims.

When designing HRLPS and considering its content one thing was crystal clear – the end of the Cold War meant that debates about law, politics, economics and society could no longer credibly be conducted within the standard framework which assumed the dominance of competing western and Soviet models. As already indicated, Africa was covered on another LLM human rights unit. So, this left the Islamic world, China and the Far East as the principal non-western perspectives on relevant debates. In the post-Cold War world, the global political significance of Islam has also greatly increased, as reflected in, amongst other things, a mushrooming of relevant literature, including about human rights, an issue discussed in Chapter 4.

The Islam, China and the Far East module

At the heart of BRISOC's complaint-and-campaign is the HRLPS lecture on Islam, China and the Far East and how I taught the associated seminars. In 2019-20 the lecture was delivered from a PowerPoint template reproduced in Appendix B. An abbreviated version, subsequently made available to students via the unit's online notice board (Blackboard), was displayed on the screen. What follows in the remainder of this chapter is not an exact transcript of what I said. None is available. But I have edited my remarks only to improve grammar and readability. These can be double checked by cross referencing to Appendix B.

It should be remembered that, as a component of a human rights unit, the module is not, of course, 'Islam, China and the Far East' as such, but '*Human Rights* in Islam, China and the Far East.' It should also be noted that, as the literature about human rights in China expanded over the past few years, the scope of the module on the undergraduate unit shifted from 'Islam, China and the Far East' to 'Islam and China.' But, because it remained 'Islam, China and the Far East' on the postgraduate unit – and because the Chinese element in the undergraduate unit needed to be situated in a wider far-eastern context in any case – the lecture to both undergraduates and postgraduates retained the broader focus. So, in the interests of clarity and consistency, the module is referred to as 'Islam, China and the Far East' throughout this book.

The lecture began by referring students to a document on Blackboard summarising the core differences between international human rights law, traditional political Islam, and traditional 'Asian values.' This is reproduced in Appendix C. From there it proceeded as follows. We should begin by considering three questions. First, why Islam, China and the Far East? The answer is that, although the existence and identity of 'Asian values' is disputed, these are the only self-consciously asserted alternatives to western liberalism with significant political implications for the contemporary world. Second, what challenges are posed by the international human rights ideal for Islam, China and the Far East? This pertains to the putative universality of human rights. Third, what challenges are posed by Islam, China and the Far East to the international human rights ideal? This raises questions about the relativity of human rights. The lecture is in three parts. Part One considers Human rights and Islam. Part Two explores Human rights, China and the Far East, and Part Three draws some conclusions.

Human rights and Islam

In this section I considered four key issues: what is Islam; the political history of Islam; the contemporary political profile of Islam; Islam and human rights, particularly key human rights challenges; and the Arab Charter on Human Rights 2004.

The term 'Islam' means 'submission to the will of the one true God.' One of the three monotheistic Abrahamic faiths, the religion was founded in Arabia by Mohammad (570-632 CE). Judaism and Christianity were regarded as authentic, though less complete and less final, sources of fundamental truth than this new revelation and their adherents as 'people of the book.'[9] The key elements of Islam, as traditionally understood, are the Qur'an, the hadith, sunnah, the sharia, and the five pillars. The Qur'an, or 'the recitation,' is said to have been dictated by God to Mohammad, between 610 and 632 CE, via the Archangel Gabriel. Muslims traditionally believe it contains God's final, flawless revelation to humanity. It is non-narrative, non-chronological and non-systematic in form. The message is also addressed, in an allusive and elliptical style, to people already familiar with it. Like all texts, it is open to interpretation. And understanding what it means requires any given part to be referenced to the rest and to other sources. For example, a question arises about whether the prohibition against alcohol is confined to fermented grape and date juice or includes all intoxicants. While each is possible, the former would be arbitrary.

The *hadith* refer to traditions about the life of Mohammad, especially things he allegedly did and said. The authenticity of some is disputed, others are unclear, and some are reputed to be mutually contradictory. By and large, the *sunnah* are rules or norms derived from hadith, but not straightforwardly. Some hadith, for example those concerning

---

[9] This was later extended to include Hinduism, Buddhism, and other faiths with a sacred text or texts.

Mohammad's tastes in food, that he allegedly spent more on perfume than on victuals, and that he mended his own clothes, do not have any normative implications for other Muslims.

The *sharia* – 'path,' 'way,' 'well-trodden path,' 'the way to a watering place' – is the corpus of Islamic law deriving principally from the Qur'an, hadith, sunnah, 'ijma' (consensus amongst Muslims) and 'qiyas' (reasoning by analogy). There is some debate about whether it consists of general principles or prescriptive rules, and whether it is a form of 'natural' or 'positive' law. The former refers to abstract legal principles ostensibly built into the structure of 'the way things are,' while the latter concerns more concrete rules derived from the former for the effective regulation of human life. The sharia applies to such things as social order, eg crime, business, marriage, trial procedure etc, and also to personal religious observance, eg food and drink, worship, rites of passage etc. It is uncompromisingly individualistic and there is no sense of corporate entities being subject to it. However, no Islamic society has ever been governed by the sharia alone. Political expediency, supplemented by local law and custom, and delivered by tribal and patron-client systems, have also typically been included in the mix. Tension between leadership based on tribal allegiance and religious scholarship has also been exacerbated in the Muslim world by the lack of any institution with ultimate authority, other than the Caliph, to interpret the faith. At the devotional heart of Islam are the 'Five Pillars': the Shahadah, or the two testimonies – that 'there is no God but Allah and Mohammad is his Prophet;' Salat – praying 5 times a day; Zakat – alms giving/taxation; Sawm – fasting during Ramadan; the Hajj – making pilgrimage to Mecca during the month of Dhu-al-Hijah at least once in any given lifetime if it can be afforded.

Mohammad was simultaneously a religious, political, and military leader. Following his death in 632 CE a dispute about who should become 'Caliph' – a word derived from the Arabic for 'successor' – caused a rift between Sunnis and Shias which has never been resolved. This reached the point of no return when, in 680 CE, Husayn ibn Ali, Mohammad's grandson, was killed by the forces of the Umayyad empire at the battle of Karbala in what is now Iraq on his way to being installed as Caliph in Baghdad.

In the quest for Mohammad's successor, the Sunnis favoured 'succession by acclamation' of the Muslim community (the 'ummah'), a form of 'charismatic' rather than democratic authority. Amongst other things, Sunnis also accord a central place to the traditional sunnah and recognise four legal traditions. The latter differ from those of the Shia – who favour a hereditary succession from Mohammad's blood line and regard the first three Caliphs post-Mohammad as illegitimate – concern mainly marriage and guardianship. Sufism, which emphasises the subordination of the ego to the will of God, is a mystical and peace-loving Islamic tradition followed by some Sunnis and Shias. It is much less dogmatic than other traditions and more sympathetic to modernization and inter-faith dialogue. There are also many other sects and traditions both within and outside the principal ones.

In considering the geopolitical spread of Islam since the 7th century it is useful to distinguish between core and periphery. In what became the core, the faith spread rapidly through war, conquest, trade, and conversion. Within a century of Mohammad's death, the first Caliphate (the territory governed by a Caliph) extended from the Iberian peninsula to the Himalayas, the rival Byzantine and Persian empires having been defeated in the process. A succession of Muslim empires followed, including (with their capitals/centres in parentheses) the: Umayyad (Damascus, 661-750); Abbasid (Baghdad, 750-1258); Ottoman (Istanbul, 1299-1920); Mogul (Northern India, 16th-19th centuries,); Seljuk Turks (Turkey and middle east, 11th-14th centuries); Safavid (Persia, 16th–18th centuries). However, the spread of Islam in the periphery, ie mostly south-east Asia, was more gradual, complex, and less imperialistic. A third contemporary Islamic realm is the diaspora in the modern west. This is considered, amongst other things, in the lecture on universalism, relativism and multiculturalism.

To understand the relationship between Islam and human rights we need to appreciate that, throughout history, the dominant Islamic political theory in the core has been 'imperial authoritarianism.' The Caliph exercised absolute power, delegated by God on sacred trust for the welfare of all (particularly Muslims), legitimized by, and subject only to, the Qur'an and Sharia. The core normative concept was obligation not rights. There was also no separation of religious from other spheres of interest and authority, and little room for the distinction between civil society and the state, or for the western idea of formal constitutional limits on executive power. Theoretically the key sites/contexts for the exercise of the Caliph's power were the 'ummah,' the 'community'/ 'nation' of Muslims, rather than race, ethnicity, or territory.

To understand the Muslim world today, a vital point of reference concerns the collapse and fall of the Ottoman empire. Known in the 19th century as the 'sick man of Europe,' having sided with Germany and its allies, the empire was dismembered following defeat in the First World War. Under the League of Nations mandate system, former Ottoman provinces were allocated to France and Britain, ostensibly for the purpose of modernization. Many in the global Muslim ummah regarded this as a humiliating form of colonization. Two main choices emerged in the debate this provoked. One was to modernize and to become more like the west. The other was to return to tradition on the assumption that defeat was a form of divine punishment for impiety. In addition to the colonization-decolonization issue and increasing pressures to modernize, other developments occurred in the aftermath of the Second World War. These included, materialism, Israel, oil, secular 'nationalist' pan-Arabism dominant from the 1950s to 1970s, the Iranian revolution of the late 1970s, the Soviet invasion of, and war in Afghanistan from 1979-89, and religious Islamist internationalism, including jihadism, particularly from the 1980s onwards.

Today there are 1.4 billion Muslims worldwide. Islam is the second largest religion in the world at 20% of the global population after Christianity at 33%. It is also the second largest religion in the UK and in many other European countries. Eighty-five per cent of Muslims are Sunnis and 15% Shia. Twenty per cent are Arabs. Types of state with Muslim majorities include 'secular' republics/democracies with no sharia, eg Turkey, the Caucasian and central Asian republics; secular dictatorships with no or limited sharia, eg Egypt, Syria, Iraq (pre-2003) and Libya (pre-2011); constitutional monarchies with no or limited sharia, eg Malaysia, Morocco; 'hybrid republics/democracies' with some sharia, eg the Islamic Republic of Pakistan; traditional authoritarian kingdom(s) with 'full' sharia, eg Saudi Arabia; Islamic republic(s) with 'full' sharia, eg Iran and ISIS (pre-2018).

Since the source of political values in traditional Islam is revelation not reason, two principal questions relevant to the issues in the module, and also in this book, arise: how open are the Qur'an and sharia to 'human rights interpretations,' and which ones are appropriate – 'global, 'western,' 'Islamic'? The interpretation of what postmodernists call 'grand narratives' – comprehensive explanations of the human experience, including liberalism, Christianity and Islam – is driven by both internal and external factors. The 'internal' involve technical debates amongst scholars within any given paradigm, while the 'external' concern economic, political, and military pressures driven, for example, by globalization, westernization and modernization.

In the extensive literature on the relationship between human rights and mainstream Islam a handful of core challenges is commonly recognised. Insults to Islam have traditionally been punishable by death – arguably demonstrated by the Charlie Hebdo massacre in Paris in January 2015[10] – a fact difficult to reconcile with freedom of expression. The punishment for apostasy, including the death penalty, is also difficult to square with the right to freedom of thought, conscience and religion. In Islamic states, ie those governed by the sharia in which the official religion is Islam, only Muslims can be full citizens. Some rights are also limited to citizens, a fact prima facie incompatible with the right not to be discriminated against on the grounds of minority identity. Scholars are agreed that, when it first appeared, Islam improved the position of women in the Arabian peninsula. However, formal gender equality has traditionally not been recognised in all respects. For example, in mainstream Islam, men are permitted more than one wife, but women can only have one husband. Muslim men may marry Muslim, Christian or Jewish wives, but women can only marry a Muslim husband.

---

[10] On 7 January 2015 Islamist gunmen killed 12 people and wounded 11 others in an attack on the offices of the French satirical magazine, Charlie Hebdo, which had previously printed cartoons of the Prophet Muhammad the killers deemed blasphemous.

Husbands are permitted physically 'to chastise' their wives but not vice versa. A husband can divorce his wife much more easily than a wife can divorce her husband. The custody of children on divorce typically goes to the husband. A woman's testimony is equivalent to half that of a man's, at least in the sharia courts. Women who wear the hijab are also less likely to work outside the home or to be involved in higher education.[11] The harsh Hadd punishments apply to a range of offences strange to the western mind – unlawful intercourse, false accusations of unlawful intercourse, highway robbery, and drinking alcohol.

Finally, we turn to the Arab Charter of Human Rights 2004, the most recent in a series of formal statements from the Muslim world regarding human rights. This document, which is less conservative than its two predecessors – the Universal Islamic Declaration on Human Rights 1981 and the Cairo Declaration of Human Rights in Islam 1990 – is, of course, 'Arab' rather than 'Muslim.' But some of its distinctive characteristics derive from the influence of the faith. Several achievements have been widely recognised. It is a milestone in the formal recognition of human rights by at least one branch of Islam. Internationally respected experts and NGOs were consulted. It faithfully reproduces many international human rights and establishes monitoring processes similar to those found in UN human rights treaties.

Commentators nevertheless attribute most of its alleged shortcomings to its Islamic influence. These include the following. It omits several central international human rights or reproduces them in a manner which conflicts with international standards. For example, there is no obligation on states to provide effective national remedies. Some core economic and social rights are limited to citizens. States are obliged to protect from torture, inhuman or degrading treatment, but not

---

[11] This also got me into a lot of trouble with BRISOC, all of it beside the point. The relative proportions are likely to vary from place to place and over time. The statement does not make any claims about the reasons, or about cause and effect. These may include various mixtures of personal choice, family pressure, and the attitude or perceived attitude of others including employers and/or universities. See, eg E. Abdelhadi, 'How wearing the hijab may influence labor market outcomes,' http://www.wipsociology.org/2020/08/25/how-wearing-the-hijab-may-influence-labor-market-outcomes/. In any case raising the issue for discussion, whatever the truth of the empirical claim, is not Islamophobic.

punishment, and there is no prohibition on the use of statements extracted by torture. Gender equality is subordinated to the sharia and to national legal limitations, with the result that women's freedom of movement can be significantly limited as, for example, in Saudi Arabia.

Human rights in China and the Far East

A religious map of Asia was presented at the halfway point in the Islam, China and the Far East lecture. However, for copyright reasons, this has not been included in Appendix B. Otherwise, this section of the lecture had three elements: the 'Asian values' debate; Confucianism; and human rights in post-Maoist China. In some ways the first of these issues reprises an older debate between 'Orientalists,' mostly westerners stereotyping the east, and 'Occidentalists,' both easterners and anti-western westerners stereotyping the west. The controversy was revived in the 1990s when several high-profile Asian figures, such as Mahathir bin Mohamad (Prime Minister of Malaysia) and Lee Kuan Yew (Prime Minister of Singapore), argued that Asia, or at least south-east Asia, should have its own distinctive non-western path to modernization, industrialization, capitalism, and economic growth, where primacy would be accorded to the collective good over individual rights. This model also features in the Bangkok Declaration on Human Rights 1993.

Core 'Asian values' are said to include willing subordination of personal freedom to the interests of family, corporation and nation; social prioritization of public order/social harmony over individual fulfilment; respect for hierarchy, tradition, authority, and obligation; and the work ethic, thrift, and the pursuit of academic and technological excellence. A key issue in the debate concerns the influence of Confucianism, an ancient Chinese philosophy currently undergoing a global revival, turbo-charged by the Chinese party-state. There is also some confusion over whether relevant values pertain to Asia, south-east Asia, to China, or to 'societies with a Confucian culture,' such as China, Japan, Korea, Taiwan, Singapore and Vietnam.

Leading Asian critics of 'Asian values' – such as Lee Teng-hui (former President of Taiwan, Kim Dae Yung (former President of South Korea) and Amartya Sen (a Nobel prize-winning Indian economist) –

have argued, amongst other things that, in addition to Confucianism, Asia has many indigenous value systems, including Islam, Daoism, Buddhism, Hinduism, Shintoism, and Christianity. They note that pre-modern precursors to the modern idea of human rights – such as the ideas and policies advocated and implemented by Kautulya (4th century BCE), Asoka (3rd century BCE), and Akbar (1556-1605) – can be found in the east as well as the west. Many of what are said to be Asian values also characterised the pre-modern west. These commentators also point out that aggregate economic growth, advocated by exponents of Asian values, does not necessarily result in fair distribution and, in fact, typically benefits elites in Asia as elsewhere. There is also no evidence that authoritarianism is more conducive to national economic success than liberal constitutionalism. As Sen, in particular, has observed, core liberal freedoms can also be functional for economic success. For example, the absence of a free press, capable of identifying and publicizing the warning signs, was one of the factors critical in the failure to prevent the catastrophic famines in China and Russia in the 20th century.

But what of Confucianism and how is it relevant to the debate about human rights in the east? Confucius (K'ung Fu Tzu), was a sage, teacher, and middle-ranking government official who lived between 551 and 479 BCE. He is most remembered for a collection of bland, vague, and often obtuse aphorisms, typically between a single sentence and a short paragraph, assembled in no particular order by his disciples in *The Analects of Confucius*, which, he claimed, enshrined wisdom derived from already ancient sources. Primarily concerned with politics, morality, duty, etiquette, and familial responsibility, these seek to cultivate moral character by offering a non-dogmatic, flexible, political/moral/legal method, rather than prescribing a code of fixed rules. Not only are *The Analects* widely regarded as embodying the 2,000 year-plus essence of Chinese culture, and those of other cultures to which it is related, they were also, without significant interruption, the basis of the Chinese civil service exam from 165 BCE to the early 20th century.

The primary goals of Confucianism are: to identify the qualities of good personal and public conduct; to maintain social equilibrium by preserving 'natural' social hierarchies – particularly the five cardinal social relationships, between ruler and subject, father and son, husband and wife, elder and younger brother, and between friends (the only one which is non-hierarchical); to cultivate loyalty and deference expressed in highly formalized and ritualized conduct ('rites' not 'rights'); to encourage the discharge of obligations appropriate to each social tier; and, by affirming the centrality of virtue and benevolence, to cultivate with respect to all relevant individual and public decisions, an instinct to act for the common good rather than for personal advancement. The last of these is illustrated by the distinction between the 'junzi' or 'exemplary person,' who acts intuitively for the common good, and the 'xio-ren' or 'petty person,' who acts solely on the basis of self-interest.

Like its Islamic counterpart, the Confucian conception of political authority is essentially a theory of imperial stewardship. While the power of the emperor is formally absolute, it is nevertheless conditional upon benevolent governance. As long as the emperor fulfils this obligation, he enjoys the 'mandate of heaven' expressing harmony between the social, political and natural realms. This is evidenced, amongst other things, by the absence of portents of doom, such as unexplained celestial phenomena or natural disasters, and by popular acquiescence in imperial governance. Rebellion is one of the key indicators that the mandate of heaven has been lost. And the more serious and widespread this becomes, the more this is the case.

There are certain similarities between the Confucian ethic and the modern idea of human rights. Each recognises that everyone is entitled to respect for their dignity and that this should limit both the exercise of public power and the pursuit of individual self-interest. But there are also significant differences. Confucianism addresses the duty-bound agent whereas the human rights ideal focuses upon the individual rights-holder. For Confucianism, the exercise of public power should be controlled through vague general principles applied by ritual-observant officials with a highly-cultivated moral character. By contrast, for the human rights ideal, it should be sought through the separation of powers and the specification of clear, detailed, formally enunciated, human rights norms. As for remedying injustice, Confucianism relies upon appeals to the moral sensibilities of bureaucrats, while the human rights ideal entrusts this responsibility to independent rights-conscious courts. For Confucianism, human dignity stems from the willing performance of ritualized obligations appropriate to a given social tier, whereas for the human rights ideal it is grounded in our universal humanity. Finally, Confucianism is deeply hierarchical, while the human rights ideal is formally egalitarian.

Since the advent of the Han dynasty in 206 BCE, to the early 20th century, Confucianism was the official ideology of the Chinese state, mingled at various points with, and at others repudiating, Buddhism and Daoism. But from the beginning of the 20th century onwards, things changed dramatically. Following imperial decline and western intervention in the late 19th century, in 1912 the first Republic of China declared the formal end of the more-than 2,000 year-old Chinese empire. This was followed by decades of chaos, fragmentation, Japanese occupation, civil war, and competing models of modernization, culminating in the establishment of the People's Republic of China in 1949. In spite of these upheavals, the Chinese, nevertheless, made a significant contribution to the Universal Declaration of Human Rights in 1948.

Maoist China (1949-1976) was based on a distinctive interpretation of Marxism coupled with visceral hostility to 'bourgeois imperialism,' its values including human rights, and to every manifestation of Chinese tradition, especially Confucianism. Following Mao's death in 1976 the Chinese party-state has, however, sought legitimacy in an alternative ideology blending communism, state-controlled capitalism, nationalism, a revival of the three most prominent traditional Chinese belief systems (Confucianism, Daoism, and Buddhism), a strong commitment to national sovereignty, economic development, political and territorial stability, collective over individual rights, and an enhanced formal commitment to the rule of law.

Since then, there have been inconsistent trends in the attitude of the Chinese party-state towards human rights. Positive developments have included the formal, official commitment to 'human rights with Chinese characteristics,' plus increased engagement with the international human rights system, as evidenced for example by the ratification of a number of human rights treaties. Article 33 of the Chinese Constitution was also amended in 2004 to provide that the state 'respects and safeguards human rights.' However, amongst other things, this is formally conditional on not impinging upon 'interests of state.' Official white papers on human rights and Human Rights Action Plans, albeit tending to defensive self-congratulation, have also been published. Scholarly interest in human rights has also increased and there have been some improvements in due process rights, for example attempts to curb confessions induced by torture, better access to defence lawyers, the correction of miscarriages of justice, and limitations upon pre-trial detention and the scope of the death penalty. However, arguably most significantly of all, in the past three decades, 600 million people have been taken out of poverty.

Nevertheless, on the negative side, since 2015, the party-state has become increasingly authoritarian. There has been a crackdown on human rights lawyers, academics and activists. Since 2017 the personal power and personality cult of President Xi Jinping have also been significantly strengthened. That year, the 19th Congress of the Communist Party of China endorsed 'Xi Jinping Thought on Socialism with Chinese Characteristics for the New Era' as the cornerstone of the new official ideology. Since 2018 at least a million Uighurs, a Muslim minority in Xinjiang in western China, have also been detained in counterterrorist 're-education camps,' a policy almost universally condemned as grossly in violation of human rights and possibly genocidal. The gap between the formal commitment to human rights standards and their effective implementation also remains huge. This is particularly because, though improved, the commitment to the rule of law remains weak and most human rights violations, such as systematic arbitrary detention and the use of torture in the criminal justice process, remain beyond effective judicial control. Official protection of civil and political rights, particularly those concerning expression, belief, protest, and dissent, is also weak. For example, while Christianity is now encouraged, the mild, contemplative Falun Gong movement has been ruthlessly persecuted.

Summary of lecture

The Human Rights in Islam, China and the Far East lecture ended with the following summary and conclusions. As pre-modern ideologies, Islam and 'Chinese/Asian values' emphasise obligations rather than rights. The question of whether they can accommodate human rights is, therefore, not straightforward. They are certainly open to interpretations hostile to human rights. Anti-human rights policies and practices have also been pursued by the Islamic State, against the Muslim Rohingya in Buddhist Myanmar, and in increased repression in Turkey, for example.

Yet over the past decade-and-a-half or so, there have been countervailing trends. For example, on the intellectual front, hostility towards human rights has increasingly lost ground to other viewpoints which take international human rights standards more seriously, though selectively. This can be interpreted either as a form of 'human rights scepticism' – a highly qualified commitment to human rights considered in the first lecture – or a weak form of 'cultural relativism' – the full commitment to human rights but with legitimate emphasis on adaptations to specific cultural contexts considered in lecture 4. It is important to bear in mind, however, that human rights-sensitive interpretations of Islam and Chinese/Asian values have emerged more because of global social and political processes and much less because of the logic of 'internal' debates.

As a result of all these developments, multi-layered discourses have emerged between, and within, both the western and non-western paradigms. These raise the following, amongst other, key questions: are distinctive 'Islamic,' 'Chinese/Asian' models of human rights possible/desirable and according to whose judgment? Will further modernization close the gap between them and western/international models? Is accommodation on specific human rights issues between Islam/China/Asia and international human rights standards, a matter of principle or pragmatic compromise, by what criteria, and according to whose judgment? And finally, what tends to happen in practice? Clear, authoritative and conclusive answers cannot be found in the literature or anywhere else because none exist. Nevertheless, reflecting upon them can only deepen and enrich our understanding of the core challenges.

Conclusion

The next two chapters will consider BRISOC's complaint-and-campaign. But, in anticipation, it is enough for now to observe that every assumption it makes about HRLPS, and the Islam, China and the Far East module, is false. The unit does not seek to offer the 'objective legal truth' about human rights because there is no such thing and, as the title clearly indicates, its remit is not limited to law. Since many disciplines in the arts, humanities, and social sciences now engage with human rights it is also perfectly legitimate for any unit with the objectives of HRLPS to do so as well. And, with more than adequate credentials in law and social science, I am at least satisfactorily equipped to rise to the challenges this presents.[12]

Nor was Islam singled out for 'Islamophobic bigotry' as BRISOC allege. It had the profile assigned to it because of the geo-political significance mainstream Islam has acquired in the contemporary post-Cold War world. Islam was not the only ideology, religious or otherwise, to be exposed to critical appreciation. Amongst others, Christianity, liberalism, communism, and Confucianism did not escape either.

BRISOC's complaint-and-campaign has caused a great deal of harm, not just to me personally, but to academic freedom generally. One of its most regrettable consequences is that, as the following chapter describes, by 'scrapping the module,' precisely as BRISOC demanded, the Law School and the University of Bristol have now ensured that serious critical scrutiny of the relationship between Islam and human rights is now formally off any part of the university curriculum for the foreseeable future. And this is in spite of the fact that there is a substantial, and rapidly expanding, literature on the subject. The detrimental consequences, considered particularly in Chapter 5, are also likely to spread much further.

---

[12] As the following Muslim commentator observes: A. Alam, 'Controversy over Bristol University Professor Steven Greer's "Islamophobia": Why Critical Discussion of Islamic Tradition Should Not Be Snubbed,' *New Age Islam*, 26 February 2021.

Chapter 3

Processes

Introduction

This chapter primarily concerns the six processes arising from the BRISOC controversy – their complaint-and-campaign, the University's inquiry into my alleged Islamophobia, two separate police investigations (one into my conduct and the other into BRISOC's), my return to work following sick leave from 16 September 2021, and my litigation against the University of Bristol. These are of particular importance because, the police investigations and the litigation aside, each suffers from significant flaws, the identification and discussion of which, are vital if BRISOC's misconduct, and that of others, is to be dealt with effectively.

We need to begin, though, by observing that the events of mid-February 2021, and thereafter, did not appear entirely out of the blue. They were, in fact, preceded by a series of other attempts to censure lawfully expressed contributions I sought to make to several legitimate academic debates, some, though not all of which, were related in content to BRISOC's complaint-and-campaign. There is also evidence that, some years before it surfaced, what became the BRISOC controversy was primed by a handful of students and Law School colleagues, determined to orchestrate a smear campaign in order to silence and discredit me simply because they disagree with my publicly expressed views, particularly about the Prevent counterterrorist programme.

Pre-cursors

The precursors to BRISOC's campaign include the allegation that to deny the Prevent counterterrorist programme is racist and Islamophobic is itself racist and Islamophobic, the 'Confucian confusion,' what Universities should do about historic wrongs, the 'child born in an

African village' complaint, a dispute about the Charlie Hebdo massacre, and being named as an Islamophobe at a public rally in Bristol.

Denying that Prevent is racist and Islamophobic is itself racist and Islamophobic

The first, and most relevant, of the precursors occurred in the late spring of 2018. It began when colleagues at other institutions denounced a Bristol colleague and me on social media as 'racist' and 'Islamophobic.' Our offence was to have argued, in articles in the academic journal *Public Law* and in the *Times Higher Education*, that the UK's counterterrorist Prevent strategy (considered more fully in the following chapter) is neither racist nor Islamophobic. They also demanded that we be sacked on the grounds that these views made us unfit for any academic appointment.

Another University of Bristol Law School colleague, since promoted, approvingly re-tweeted these denunciations, including by circulating them to the entire University of Bristol twitter sphere. She also accused us of suffering from 'white psychosis,' itself a racist and 'ableist' slur. Such conduct is, of course, clearly and flagrantly in violation of the University's *Acceptable Behaviour at Work Policy and Guidance*.[13] Amongst other things this provides: 'We will not tolerate bullying or harassment of any kind including ... victimisation ...' and that 'unacceptable behaviour may involve ... words ... that could reasonably be perceived to be the cause of another person's distress or discomfort' and 'may take many forms (including) ... social media.' Examples of unacceptable behaviour cited include: '... personal insults; spreading malicious rumours or gossip, or insulting someone ... offensive comments ....' These laudable sentiments are commonplace throughout the tertiary sector in the UK. But as my experience and that of others indicate, they are not easy to enforce.

An informal approach to the resolution of such problems is also recommended. My co-author and I, therefore, referred the matter to

---

[13] https://www.bristol.ac.uk/media-library/sites/equality/documents/Acceptable-Behaviour - Policy.pdf. See also Equality, Diversity & Inclusion Policy Statement, http://www.bristol.ac.uk/inclusion/governance-policy-and-guidance/edi-policy-statement/.

senior Law School management. Some arms-length-mediation followed. But there was no meeting between the two parties, not least because we were told the culprit was too busy 'breaking in a puppy.' Eventually we were informed that she wished to apologise, but refused to do so in person or in writing. She also declined to take down the offending tweets. Senior Law School management issued a veiled threat that, if we chose to pursue the matter as a formal grievance, the colleague in question would retaliate claiming I'd harassed her by pointing out that she'd completely misunderstood the relevant legislation. Apparently, to ask which provision imposes a personal duty on academic staff to spy on their students, as she alleged, constitutes bullying. There isn't such a provision by the way. Not long afterwards new senior management came into office. They were also informed of the controversy but declined to do anything about it. Reckoning we were likely to get nowhere, we decided to drop the matter. An act of libellous misconduct was, therefore, committed by one of our own colleagues with impunity, bolstered by a threat of retaliation on the part of the very authorities from whom we had every right to expect effective protection.

The Confucian confusion

The pace began to quicken a year later. In March 2019 I was interviewed by two middle-management Law School colleagues following a complaint made by some Muslim students who claimed that, in a Human Rights in Law, Politics and Society (HRLPS) seminar, I 'laughed at the Qur'an.' It turned out that my amusement, which the class shared, was in response to a passage from the ancient Chinese text, *The Analects of Confucius*, extracts from which had been read out on the same occasion as those from the Qur'an. Referring to proper gentlemanly behaviour the relevant aphorism says:

> '... On meeting anyone in deep mourning he must bow across the bar of his chariot; he also bows to people carrying planks. When confronted with a particularly choice dainty at a banquet, his countenance should change and he should rise to his feet. Upon hearing

a sudden clap of thunder or a violent gust of wind, he must change countenance.'[14]

A footnote explains that the term 'planks' is traditionally understood to mean 'census tablets.' As already indicated in Chapter 2, I also made clear to the class that my amusement did not stem from mockery but from wonder at the fact that being able to recite passages such as this formed the basis of the exam for the Chinese civil service, for nearly two millennia one of the most effective state bureaucracies in the entire pre-modern world. Not only did I make the source abundantly clear; I was visibly holding a copy of *The Analects* in my hand as I read from it. The complainants must, therefore, have either been acting with deliberate malice, or been both particularly inattentive in class and very ill-informed about the core text of their own faith. Once the true facts had been established, I heard nothing further officially about the matter. However, BRISOC's complaint-and-campaign later alleged that the University had ignored repeated complaints about Islamophobia in my teaching and other output over many years including that I had laughed at the Qur'an. This seemed to confirm that the 'Confucian confusion' was, and probably still is, doing the rounds.

Universities and historic wrongs

In May 2019 there was a vigorous debate at a Law School Meeting (the School's 'legislature') concerning what the University of Bristol should do about historic wrongs, including resources indirectly received from slavery. Based on my own contribution, I drafted a proposed Law School blog which I then circulated to the handful of other colleagues who had participated. The core thesis was that a number of tricky issues would remain even if the tainted benefit were formally recognised, awareness about it raised, a full public apology issued, and recompense offered. As I pointed out, the priorities of the descendants of the direct victims may not correspond with those which reverberate round ivory towers. And unless such parties are consulted, there is a risk that subtle forms of elite domination may simply be reconstituted.

---

[14] J. Pelikan (ed), *Sacred Writings – Confucianism: The Analects of Confucius* (Quality Paperback Book Club, 1992), p. 151.

A tiny minority of the recipients aggressively denounced the draft as, amongst other things, 'very stupid,' 'an affront,' 'poorly researched, one-sided, provocative for all the wrong reasons and offensive,' 'smacks of privilege,' based on 'very little thinking,' and reflecting 'extremely poorly upon' the School. Some demanded that its publication be stopped at all costs in order to avoid damaging our inclusivity policy. As a result, the blog's editor declined to publish, and instead referred the matter to the Law School Research and Impact Committee. However, within a few days, and long before the Committee made its decision, a revised version was published in the online current affairs journal *The Conversation*, which seeks to bring academic research and opinion to a wider audience.[15] No issue about its research credibility arose. It rapidly received over 10,000 hits plus over 90 comments, all but a handful positive. Eventually the Committee decided against publication as a Law School blog, but not on the basis of the critics' complaints. The purpose of Law School blogs, it held, is to showcase research being conducted in the School. And, in their view, the proposed contribution was not based on my research. The Committee thus, not only presumed to know more about the scope and remit of my research than I do myself; it also ignored the fact that it would have been impossible for the blog to have been written without the issues in question having been properly investigated.

A child born in an African village

Events accelerated further in 2020. In response to a student complaint that October, I was advised by senior Law School management to apologise for an observation I made in a lecture about rights theory in the HRLPS series. I said that, according to the best interpretation of the 'natural rights' tradition, a 'child born in an African village' has the same inherent entitlement to survive and to flourish as the children of the British royal family. I was told that the phrase – 'child born in an African village' – is a 'derogatory stereotype.' And this in spite of the fact that it was clearly used to express solidarity with, and in

---

[15] https://theconversation.com/what-should-british-universities-do-about-benefits-received-from-past-wrongs-116761.

support for, some of the poorest children on earth. Nevertheless, not wishing to contest the matter, I apologised. However, in a subsequent lecture on global poverty and development in the same series, I pointed out that, since Africa is the poorest continent in the world, children born there are statistically more likely to be poorer than those born anywhere else. This did not give rise to any complaint.

The Charlie Hebdo massacre

Not long after this episode, I was informed by senior Law School management that another student had complained about an issue that had arisen in a different part of the HRLPS unit. This time it was about the use, in the Islam, China and the Far East lecture, of the Charlie Hebdo massacre as an illustration of the traditional Islamic death penalty for blasphemy and insults to the faith. I undertook to use in future, the Ayatollah Khomeini's fatwa against Salman Rushdie in 1989 – to which I'd referred in the past – and the Pakistani and Iranian penal codes which prescribe capital punishment for such offences. I understand that this was conveyed to the complainant. I heard nothing more about it until, like the 'Confucian confusion,' it resurfaced in BRISOC's complaint-and-campaign. The issue is considered further in Chapter 4.

Named as an Islamophobe at a public rally

In early 2021 I also found out that one of the University's own anti-racism student advisers had named me as an Islamophobe at a public rally in Bristol in December 2020, after BRISOC's formal complaint had been lodged but before I found out about it. She proudly boasts on her Facebook page about having done so.

BRISOC's formal complaint

Formal student complaints at the University of Bristol are ostensibly governed by the *Student Complaints Procedure*.[16] The *Good Practice Framework for handling complaints and academic appeals* – drafted by

---

[16] https://www.bristol.ac.uk/media-library/sites/secretary/documents/student-rules-and-regs/student-complaints-procedure.pdf. According to this document it has not been amended since July 2019.

the Office of the Independent Adjudicator for Higher Education, an independent registered charity – also provides relevant, non-prescriptive, guidelines reflecting basic principles of fair play and procedural justice.[17]

BRISOC's complaint was admitted by the University in November 2020 even though it was manifestly malicious and vexatious, a feature considered more fully in the following chapter. It also suffered from the following procedural defects: failure to raise it through any of the Law School's many relevant channels; failure to comply with application deadlines; exclusive reliance upon anonymous sources; and an implacable refusal on the part of the formal complainant to participate in informal resolution, mediation or conciliation. Any one of these flaws, which I did not discover until long afterwards, should have rendered it inadmissible. But, ignoring them all, the University entertained it anyway. The failure officially to inform me of the fact or substance of the complaint for three and a half months also robbed me of an equal opportunity to present my case. The procedure the inquiry followed is also open to question and was far from expeditious. During the entire official investigation and thereafter, the University also declined to do anything to stop BRISOC's potentially life-threatening social media campaign which unquestionably constitutes egregious misconduct.

The Law School stage

The Student Complaints Procedure provides:

'Wherever possible, concerns raised by students should be resolved informally without recourse to formal procedures. If a student has a complaint about any aspect of University life, it should be raised with an appropriate person at the earliest opportunity. Faculties, schools and divisions that provide services to students should inform students who to contact in the first instance if they have a complaint.'[18]

The Law School expects any grievance about teaching materials, or a member of staff's alleged misconduct, to be brought, in the first instance, to the attention of the tutor concerned. If this is not appropriate, or leaves

---

[17] Office of the Independent Adjudicator for Higher Education, *Good Practice Framework for handling complaints and academic appeals*, https://www.oiahe.org.uk/resources-and-publications/good-practice-framework/
[18] *Student Complaints Procedure*, para. 1.2.

the matter unresolved, it should then be raised with the relevant personal tutor, unit coordinator, student representative, degree director, with designated staff in the Student Administration Team, and/or be referred to the staff-student consultative committee. These avenues are not mutually exclusive. Nor, apart from beginning with the tutor in question, should they be pursued in any particular order. To the best of my knowledge BRISOC's complaint against me was not raised through any of these channels.

Application deadlines

The *Student Complaints Procedure* also provides: 'Complaints must be brought promptly' and 'the University will not accept complaints that are made longer than 90 days after the matters complained about, unless there is good reason for the delay.'[19] In similar terms, para. 53 of the *Good Practice Framework* states that, 'upon receipt of a formal complaint, the provider should undertake an initial evaluation to check that the complaint is submitted ... within any deadline.' It adds that failure to comply 'might result in ... the complaint being rejected .....' Providers are also reminded of 'the need to exercise discretion where there is good reason, supported by evidence, for late submission .....'[20]

In common with most units, teaching in HRLPS in 2019-20, had finished by the end of March 2020. So, to be formally admissible, BRISOC's complaint should have been submitted by the beginning of July 2020 at the latest, not 30 October, as it was. Furthermore, as a result of the 'blended learning' regime, instituted in 2020-21 to address the challenges presented by the Covid pandemic, no lectures (now referred to as 'narrated PowerPoint presentations') were delivered in person that year. They were, instead, audio-video recorded and uploaded to the relevant website as teaching progressed. The one on Islam, China and the Far East, at the centre of BRISOC's complaint, preceded the relevant seminars and was not made available to students until 5 November 2020.

This means that BRISOC's complaint was lodged well after 90 days following the delivery of the 'offending' material in 2019-20, and before

---

[19] Ibid, para. 1.6.
[20] *Good Practice Framework*, para. 34.

it had been presented in 2020-21. To the best of my knowledge no reasons for any delay in the submission of the complaint with respect to 2019-20 have ever been given, let alone good ones. And there can certainly be no good reasons for it having been made before the relevant material had been delivered in 2020-21.

Anonymous complaints

The *Student Complaints Procedure* provides that: 'Anonymous complaints may only be accepted at the discretion of the University Secretary.'[21] This contrasts with the OIA document which states, that while 'it is good practice for the provider's regulations to permit students to be supported, advised or represented by third parties ...,' it should 'not be necessary to bring anonymous complaints.' [22] It adds that:

> 'exceptionally, however, a provider may decide to consider an anonymous complaint if *there is a compelling case – supported by evidence – for the matter to be investigated*. Providers should explain to students that raising a concern anonymously might impede the investigation and communication of the outcome.'[23]

As *Al Jazeera* later disclosed (see below), BRISOC's complaint was formally submitted by the Society's then President, Aamir Mohamed, a medical student, who had not taken HRLPS, had no direct knowledge of, and was in fact very badly informed about the issues in question. The complaint, therefore, depended entirely upon hearsay and rumour allegedly supplied by anonymous sources. I know of no reason why the University should have admitted BRISOC's complaint notwithstanding this defect, let alone a *compelling case supported by evidence*. It should, therefore, have been rejected on this ground alone without having been considered on the merits at all.

Mediation and conciliation

In addition to informal resolution, contemporary arrangements for complaints against any bureaucratic decision typically encourage

---

[21] *Student Complaints Procedure*, para 1.8.
[22] *Good Practice Framework*, para. 11.
[23] Ibid, para. 13. Italics added.

mediation and conciliation in an attempt to avoid the time, effort, and cost involved in initiating full-blown formal processes. Not surprisingly this is reflected in both the *Student Complaints Procedure* and the *Good Practice Framework*.[24] The key to success lies in the quest for a solution which may involve explanation and enhanced understanding – possibly including apology, forgiveness and forgetting – on both sides. Obviously, this can only happen if each party is fully involved. And it is even more important when, as in my case, the formal complainant has no direct knowledge of the issues raised, no expertise in the relevant academic fields, and purports to represent anonymous others who may or may not even exist. Yet the University accepted without apparent challenge, the express rejection of mediation and conciliation by the claimant who maintained that the seriousness of the complaint precluded both. I did not receive the formal complaint until mid-February 2021, three and a half months after it had been lodged. I would have been perfectly willing to have engaged in mediation at any point in the controversy, especially before BRISOC launched its vitriolic social media campaign. But the University's failure to inform me of the accusations, and BRISOC's refusal to contemplate even the possibility of any co-created solution, rendered this impossible.

An equal opportunity for parties to present their case

The delay of three and a half months from the date of the submission of the complaint (30 October 2020), to being informed of its substance (15 February 2021), also constitutes a clear breach of the OIA's requirement to allow 'each party an equal opportunity to present their case'[25]. This is because, by its very nature, BRISOC's social media campaign put me under considerable pressure to respond as quickly as possible. In fact, I submitted my formal response to the University's inquiry, including full replies to the Assessor's questions, on 25 February 2021, just ten days after having received a copy of the formal complaint. By contrast, BRISOC had months, if not years, in which to prepare their case.

---

[24] *Student Complaints Procedure*, para. 21; *Good Practice Framework*, para. 40-49.
[25] *Good Practice Framework*, p. 4.

An expeditious process

The Student Complaints Procedure provides:

> 'On receipt of the Complaint Form the Student Complaints and Mediation Manager will refer the complaint to an appropriate person for consideration at the Local Stage. In the case of complaints relating to academic matters, this will normally be the Faculty Education Manager or Faculty Education Director.'[26]

However, when I first received the formal complaint document, I was officially informed that an Assessor – a senior academic from a Department, School or Faculty to which neither I nor the official complainant belonged – had been appointed to investigate and adjudicate it. On 24 February 2021 I received an email from her informing me that, amongst other things, she would be:

> '... following a process akin to the Research Misconduct process – i.e. ... acting as the Assessor and gathering in relevant information to determine whether I should refer the whole complaint (or any part of it) to a Panel for investigation or .... to an expert ... This process is not, as you know, set out in writing ... The alternative is that in accordance with ... existing University Procedures ... the matter is referred to HR under the Conduct Procedure for Staff (Ordinance 28). I had hoped that we would both be able to address this complaint in the robust way that you have described using this pilot process and seek early resolution ... My ideal as with any complaint in the area of teaching would be to seek a co-created resolution. I should make it completely clear however that you are not compelled to join in this pilot.'

Both the complainant and I agreed to the proposed 'pilot procedure,' in my case expressly on the grounds that it would be expeditious. The *Student Complaints Procedure* also states: 'The University aims to complete the Local Stage within 30 days of the submission of the complaint,'[27] and that it 'aims to convene the Review Panel within 30 days of the student's request to the Student Complaints and Mediation Manager.'[28] And according to the OIA, 'it is good practice for providers to complete consideration of a formal complaint or academic appeal and

---

[26] *Student Complaints Procedure*, para. 3.3.
[27] Ibid, para. 3.5.
[28] Ibid, para. 4.3.

any associated review within 90 calendar days.'[29] However over five months elapsed between the establishment of the University's inquiry and the Assessor ruling decisively in my favour. Just under a year also passed between the formal submission of the complaint on 30 October 2020 and the rejection of BRISOC's appeal against the Assessor's decision on 18 October 2021. This is hardly 'swift action' by any standard. The OIA guidelines also note that 'some complaints may require the provider to take particularly swift action' especially where complaints involve 'a threat of serious harm ... (or) ... issues of a highly sensitive nature.'[30] Given the potentially life-threatening nature of BRISOC's social media campaign, discussed further below, my case clearly should have triggered compliance with this obligation.

BRISOC's social media campaign

On 15 February 2021, frustrated by the delay in the resolution of its complaint and in flagrant breach of the OIA's guidelines, BRISOC launched a hostile social media campaign against both me and the University which posed a potential risk to my life and physical safety. This rapidly garnered over 7,000 'likes' on various social media platforms. The petition to have me sacked also quickly acquired over 2,000 signatures, rising by the summer of 2022, to over 4,100. This includes over 30 organizations, 17 of which are University of Bristol student societies, and 14 student Islamic societies at other British universities.[31] Given the absurdity of BRISOC's accusations, it is

---

[29] *Good Practice Framework*, p. 4 and para. 35.
[30] Ibid, para. 52.
[31] Organizations that signed BRISOC's petition include: University of Bristol Students Union, University of Bristol Multifaith Network, University of Bristol BME Network, University of Bristol Black Student's Network, University of Bristol Women's Network, University of Bristol Widening Participation Network, University of Bristol Black Muslim Society, University of Bristol Muslim Medics Society, University of Bristol Ramadan Project, University of Bristol Unity and Diversity in Law, University of Bristol Women In Law Society, University of Bristol Arab Society, University of Bristol Pakistan Society, University of Bristol Khaleeji Society, University of Bristol Bangladesh Society, University of Bristol Hindu Society, University of Bristol Film Department Society, Federation of Student Islamic Societies, University of Plymouth Islamic Society, University of Kent Islamic Society, University of Exeter Islamic Society, University of the West of England Islamic Society, London School of Economics and Political Science

doubtful if anybody who signed the petition – including the University of Bristol Unity and Diversity in Law group and the University of Bristol Women in Law Society, each of which is supported by the University of Bristol Law School – bothered to check their veracity.

BRISOC's campaign – which though now having receded into the shadows has yet to be abandoned much less retracted – was clearly intended to ruin my reputation, end my career, deprive me of my livelihood, and ostracise me from my colleagues. It has also been, at best, reckless with respect to the possibility that it may have inspired somebody else, especially with mental health issues, to exact punishment for my alleged insults to the Muslim faith by ending my life, just as the murderer of Samuel Paty in France did in reprisal for the latter's presentation of the Charlie Hebdo cartoons in a class discussion.[32]

I'm also reminded of the attempted murder of a friend from my days as a PhD student in Northern Ireland. In 1991 I was shocked to hear that, asleep one night at his home in Belfast, Adrian Guelke, a South African political scientist at Queens University Belfast (QUB), had narrowly survived a loyalist assassination attempt when the would-be killer's gun jammed. Reports later confirmed that Adrian was known to the South African authorities as a liberal opponent of apartheid, and that a member of the intelligence branch of the South African Defence Force had inserted his name into a police report which claimed that a South African academic at QUB was a member of the IRA. This was then circulated to the loyalist Ulster Defence Association which authorised the attack.

Closer to home, on 15 October 2021, widely-respected Conservative MP David Amess was murdered by a jihadi terrorist, in spite of having had very little connection with, or interest in, Muslims or Islam. After having carried out the attack, his alleged assailant, Ali Harbi Ali, was said to have told witnesses at the scene that he wanted 'every parliament

---

Islamic Society, University of East London Islamic Society, University of Cardiff Islamic Society, University of Loughborough Islamic Society, University of Birmingham Ahlulbayt Society, University of Aston Islamic Society, University of Durham People of Colour Association, University of Westminster Middle Eastern and North African Society, Documenting Oppression Against Muslims, UK Ahlulbayt Society, CAGE Organisation.

[32] See Ch 4.

minister who signed up for the bombing of Syria, who agreed to the Iraq war, to die.'[33]

The campaign statement

BRISOC's full campaign statement reads:

'The city of Bristol has been a vital force of resistance against all forms of hatred. Now, we must take a stand against the vile societal ill that is, Islamophobia. We urge all the students at Bristol and the wider community to join us in standing for justice and calling for the university to take swift action against Islamophobia on our campus.

The University of Bristol Islamic Society is alarmed by multiple complaints against Professor Steven Greer of the Law School for his reported use of discriminatory remarks and Islamophobic rhetoric. We are disappointed by the apathy and the lack of action taken by the university when these concerns were brought to their attention. The university has not held Professor Greer accountable nor taken the concerns of Muslim students seriously, despite numerous complaints raised by students over the last few years. After having engaged the university over a number of years without any progress, we feel it is now necessary to make the public aware.

Law students have reported that Professor Greer frequently expresses views in his classes that can be deemed Islamophobic, bigoted and divisive. For example, students have reported that Professor Greer has brought the Quran into class, read a verse and laughed at it. Further, he expressed that "most difficulties stem from the Islamic influence upon it" concluding that Islam is not human rights compatible.

Many other examples accumulate into a pattern of what can only be perceived to be hostility and bigotry towards Muslims which Professor Greer freely disseminates under the pretext of 'academic freedom.' The latest complaint brought forward is related to a Human Rights module in which Professor Greer makes false claims about Islam and Muslims. His use of the horrific events of the Charlie Hebdo attack as evidence of Islam's stance on freedom of speech is an example of the kind of Islamophobic rhetoric that aims to posit the actions of killers as being representative of the entire Muslim community and of Islam. The theme of collective punishment is repeated in a video uploaded by the Law school, where he explains that the disproportionate and discriminatory targeting of Muslims by the Prevent duty is justified

---

[33] 'Knifeman helped passenger on his way to murder MP, trial told,' *The Times*, 23 March 2022.

because "jihadi terrorism is the principle terrorist threat the UK faces." The Prevent duty has been widely criticised by various human rights groups, the UN and former police officers and whilst there is no research to support its effectiveness, there are multiple reports that condemn it as Islamophobic and racist.

These examples along with the rest of the lecture notes shown, expose a clear lack of depth of knowledge about Islam. They also show an institutional failing to understand how this kind of rhetoric will cause harm; not only to the Muslim students in his classes but also in the way these ideas will deepen divisions between Muslims and the wider society and increase discrimination and hate crime towards Muslims.

The gross misconduct that has been underway at the University of Bristol for years, without any accountability, is extremely concerning. The University of Bristol is an educational institution that has committed to "decolonising the curriculum" and ensuring that their curricula is 'inclusive in scope and delivery', we hope that they will act on the 'speak-up' culture they want to push forward. Despite this, our concerns were silenced for years under the banner of academic freedom.

The recent adoption of the All Party Parliamentary Group (APPG) definition of Islamophobia' has had no effect in practice and we feel that it is now our representative responsibility to highlight how the APPG definition of Islamophobia seeks to protect no one and is wholly not fit for purpose in addressing our experiences of Islamophobia, coupled with the fact that according to the university implementation of policies to protect its students have to be 'balanced' with "academic freedom."

Our demands:

From Professor Steven Greer:

A statement of apology to all Muslim students, making it clear that his remarks are an opinion, rather than objective truth. Removal of this material from his teaching and the module. A firm commitment from him not to make such statements in future teaching.

Failing this:

A consideration of further disciplinary action, including suspension and/or dismissal from the University of Bristol. A written apology for funding, supporting, and promoting Professor Steven Greer's work and teaching, as well as damage caused. Continuous detailed updates on this case to all Muslim students. A review of the systems in tackling/reporting Islamophobia at Bristol, which also involves the Islamic Society as the representative body of Muslim students on campus.

With your support, we are closer to bringing justice. Please share this petition and urge others to sign as well. Your support is much appreciated.'[34]

There is much that could be said about this. The specific allegations are addressed in the following chapter. But for now, it should first be noted that BRISOC's social media campaign is flagrantly in breach of relevant OIA guidelines and the University of Bristol's published expectations. According to the former it is 'good practice' for the procedures of higher education providers 'to set out the circumstances in which the entire complaint or academic appeal – or elements of it – can be kept confidential.'[35] All parties are also expected 'to act reasonably and fairly towards each other, and to treat the processes themselves with respect.'[36] The OIA states that it is good practice for policies and procedures to be in place 'setting out … the expectation that students, their representatives and staff members should act reasonably and fairly towards each other … and that the provider has a responsibility to protect its staff against unacceptable behaviour.'[37] It adds that such policies and procedures should 'set out the type of behaviour which would be considered unacceptable and the circumstances in which a student's access to staff or procedures might be restricted.'[38]

The University of Bristol's *Student Disciplinary Regulations and Procedure*, which apply to all 'registered students,' list the following, amongst other things, as types of misconduct.

'a. Any conduct which constitutes a criminal offence; b. Any conduct which constitutes sexual misconduct; c. Disruption of, or improper interference with, the academic, administrative, sporting, social or other activities of the University; d. Obstruction of, or improper interference

---

[34] https://www.change.org/p/university-of-bristol-stop-islamophobia-at-bristol-university-scrapthemodule. See also https://islamophobia-at-bristol-uni.carrd.co/. See also https://www.youtube.com/watch?v=M8dwH9x7F90.
[35] *Good Practice Framework*, para. 33.
[36] Ibid, p. 4.
[37] Ibid, para. 118.
[38] Ibid, para. 118.

with, the functions, duties or activities of any student or member of staff of the University, or any visitor to the University; e. Violent, indecent, disorderly, threatening, intimidating or offensive behaviour or language, whether expressed verbally or in writing, including online behaviour in electronic form; f. Bullying, harassment or unacceptable behaviour of any student or member of staff of the University, or any visitor to the University, on the grounds of sex, race, religion or belief, disability, sexual orientation, gender reassignment, age or other grounds, including online bullying and harassment...'[39]

Quite properly, the University routinely disciplines students found guilty of cheating in assessments. By sharp contrast, it has taken no steps whatever, in my case, to punish those who have harmed, or have sought to harm, me in the ways prima facie covered by items a. and d.-f. above. The University should, therefore, find out who orchestrated and led, and who has failed publicly to retract and apologise for, BRISOC's campaign and, if they are still registered students, discipline them now without delay.

The *Good Practice Framework* also states that it is 'good practice for providers to develop their own policies for dealing with ... insistence on pursuing what may be meritorious complaints or academic appeals in an unreasonable manner.'[40] The University of Bristol does not appear to have any such policies or procedures, at least none specifically concerning official complaints. Indeed, the *Student Complaints Procedure* appears to make even confidentiality contingent upon the complainant's election. For example, the only relevant provision states:

'If information is to be kept confidential, the student should make this clear to the person to whom a complaint is made. Students should understand that in exceptional circumstances it may be difficult for confidentiality to be respected, for instance where a criminal offence has been disclosed. Students should also understand that in some circumstances the demand for confidentiality may make it difficult for the University to assist them with their complaint.'[41]

---

[39] University of Bristol's Student Disciplinary Regulations and Procedure 2021-2022, Annex A, *Types of Misconduct*, https://www.bristol.ac.uk/media-library/sites/secretary/documents/student-rules-and-regs/student-disciplinary-regulations.pdf. These are very similar to those applicable to previous years.
[40] *Good Practice Framework*, para. 119.
[41] *Student Complaints Procedure*, para. 6.

The campaign statement also suffers from the following additional defects. The claim that BRISOC speaks for 'all Muslim students' is disputed by other Muslims. For example, Arshad Alam states: 'The criticism and censure of Professor Greer is ... not from all Muslims but from Muslim groups which have a distinct political agenda.'[42] There is also some confusion about whether 'the module' refers to the Islam, China, and the Far East topic on the HRLPS unit/course, or to the entire unit/course itself. However, given that only one topic, and part of another, provoked BRISOC's ire, the former appears more likely. The claim that 'numerous complaints' against me have been 'raised by students over the last few years,' is simply false. In fact, the only other relevant ones of which I'm aware concerned the 'Confucian confusion' in 2019 and the Charlie Hebdo issue in 2020-21 to which reference has already been made.

As soon as I became aware of BRISOC's potentially life-threatening campaign I appealed to the University to put a stop to it. I also reminded relevant officers that, having had a stroke in 2013, it was particularly imperative that I avoid the stress the campaign was already causing. I was, however, merely assured that BRISOC would be reminded of the duty to respect the confidentiality of the inquiry, already irretrievably broken. I was also advised that, if I had any concerns about my safety, I should contact the University's police officer, which I did. She answered my emails promptly, offered encouraging and supportive advice, and in the autumn of 2021, facilitated the instigation of a formal police investigation into my complaint that BRISOC was guilty of ongoing criminal harassment and intimidation. More about this later. In mid-February 2021, the University also warned me that, in spite of BRISOC's misconduct – including breach of their putative duty of confidentiality – I was still bound by mine and that I should not say anything publicly about the controversy other than that I denied the allegations. Concerned that failure to abide by this stipulation might prejudice my official exoneration, I have honoured this at all times, an issue to which I also return later in this chapter.

---

[42] A. Alam, 'Controversy over Bristol University Professor Steven Greer's "Islamophobia": Why Critical Discussion of Islamic Tradition Should Not Be Snubbed,' *New Age Islam*, 26 February 2021.

BRISOC's motives

Given that the material to which BRISOC objected had been delivered on an annual basis in substantially the same form in each of the preceding 14 years, including to many Muslim students, a puzzling question arises: why did the complaint-and-campaign erupt with such venom when it did? One answer is that it was prompted by the wider, comparatively recent but rapidly developing, phenomenon of academic 'illiberal leftism' considered more fully in Chapter 5.

However, there has also been speculation that two more specific factors may have been involved. Reference has already been made to one of these – the fact that, over the past few years, some colleagues at the University of Bristol and elsewhere have been trying to discredit my defence of the Prevent counterterrorist programme by playing the man not the ball. An official independent review of Prevent was launched by the government in January 2021, just a month before BRISOC's social media campaign against me began. Indeed, BRISOC's online assault may have been influenced by awareness that, with my retirement approaching in the summer of 2022, the academic year 2020-21 was their last chance to get me sacked, ruin my reputation, deprive me of my livelihood, sour the end of my career, and rob me of the trust and respect of colleagues before I disappeared into obscurity.

Another possibility is that the complaint-and-campaign was intended to put the University under pressure not to dismiss Sociology Professor David Miller, a prominent anti-Zionist conspiracy theorist then under investigation for academic misconduct including antisemitism. There has been speculation that BRISOC may have calculated that, if an accusation of Islamophobia were made against me, the University would either have to sack us both, retain both, or sack one and retain the other, each of which would create public relations problems.[43] By sharp contrast with my own case, Miller not only received vocal public support from many of his own senior colleagues; he was also publicly defended by internationally prominent anti-Zionists including Noam Chomsky.

---

[43] T. Young, 'David Miller may be a loon, but sacking him would open a Pandora's Box,' *The Critic*, 25 February 2021.

However, unlike me, Miller was sacked by the University in the autumn of 2021. Nobody but the University, and possibly David Miller himself, knows precisely why. But we do know, because the University has announced it, that a QC (now KC) decided that neither he nor I had been guilty of unlawful conduct. The University, nevertheless, decided that Miller's behaviour otherwise fell below minimum professional standards. By sharp contrast, I was never suspended and was eventually officially, and unreservedly, exonerated. Some have claimed that the difference in outcomes in the two cases indicates that the University tolerates Islamophobia but not antisemitism. But my case and Miller's provide no support for that whatever. Following University inquiries, I was unequivocally cleared of Islamophobia but Miller was found guilty of professional misconduct. Relying only on information in the public domain, that is all anyone can reliably say about the matter.

Reaction to BRISOC's campaign

There were various reactions to BRISOC's campaign, including on the part of the University, the Law School, the media, internet bloggers and others.

The response of the University and Law School

On 18 February 2021 the University responded to BRISOC's statement with one of its own which reads:

> 'We are working with the University's Islamic Society to respond to concerns raised about an individual member of staff. That process is still ongoing and under review and as such we are unable to comment further. We are in regular contact with the Society and the member of staff during this time.
>
> We are committed to making our University an inclusive place for all students. As part of our focus on this, we have been working closely with students from minority groups to try and understand their specific concerns and worries. A key outcome from these discussions was the adoption of the All Parliamentary Party Group definition of Islamophobia and the International Holocaust Remembrance Alliance (IHRA) working definition of antisemitism.

We seek at all times to abide by both our Free Speech Policy and our Public Sector Equality Duties. Specifically, we are steadfast in our commitment to freedom of speech and to the rights of all our students and staff to discuss difficult and sensitive topics. Universities are places of research and learning, where debate and dissent are not only permitted but expected, and where controversial and even offensive ideas may be put forward, listened to and challenged. Intellectual freedom is fundamental to our mission and values.

We also affirm our equally strong commitment to making our University a place where all feel safe, welcomed and respected, regardless of gender, race, sexual orientation, disability or social background. We would urge anyone who feels that they have been discriminated against or subject to hate speech or harassment, to contact our support services so we can offer appropriate help and support.'[44]

While this statement pays lip service to academic freedom, it belies the University's failure to do anything effective to protect it in my case. Indeed, the statement implies that, far from being malicious and vexatious, BRISOC's allegations may be true. There is, for example, no mention of the fact that I deny the charges. The second paragraph, where the substantive issue is first addressed, also leads by expressing a desire to understand the 'specific concerns and worries' of 'students from minority groups.' However, the core issue is not the rights of any minority but my academic freedom. The statement also makes no reference to those, intimidated by BRISOC's campaign from exploring the relationship between Islam and human rights properly, who may themselves fear being denounced as Islamophobic – 'Islamophob-ophobia' in other words. It was not until August 2022 when, at the inaugural conference of the Oxford Institute for British Islam, that I learned from an authoritative source that the University's statement convinced many Muslims that BRISOC's allegations were true. Not only is this alarming in its own right; it indicates how the University's statement *compounded* the risk to my personal safety stemming from BRISOC's social media campaign rather than *protecting* me from it.

---

[44] https://thetab.com/uk/bristol/2021/02/19/bristol-law-lecturer-under-fire-from-bristol-islamic-society-over-islamophobic-remarks-44304. See also University of Bristol Freedom of Speech Code of Practice, https://www.bristol.ac.uk/media-library/sites/secretary/documents/student-rules-and-regs/freedom-of-speech-code-of-practice.pdf.

Quoting the University's statement in full, the Law School also sent the following email to students and staff on 18 February 2021:

> 'You may have become aware of concerns raised by the University of Bristol Islamic Society about an individual member of staff. The University is working with the Society to respond to the concerns. That University process is ongoing and as such we in the School are unable to comment further at this time. I append the University's statement on the process at the foot of this email.
>
> I would like to underline our own commitment - in line with the University's vision - to making the Law School an inclusive place for all students, a place where all feel safe, welcomed and respected, regardless of gender, race, sexual orientation, disability or social background.
>
> We are of course also committed to freedom of expression and academic freedom, but this certainly does not provide protection for hate speech, racism or any form of unlawful prejudice. Where concerns of this nature are raised with us, we investigate them promptly, while recognising the need for thorough and impartial review, in accordance with due process, and for us to take appropriate action in response.
>
> We have worked hard in the Law School over several years to promote our shared vision of a diverse and inclusive academic community. In the last ten years, the proportion of BAME students in our overall population has increased markedly - amongst incoming Home Undergraduate students, rising from 8% to 28% in that period. We've provided mentoring opportunities to more and more of you, taking care to include those of you whose aspirations are for careers outside the areas of corporate and commercial law - perhaps in human rights, mental health law, migration or international development. We've initiated 'diversity dialogues' to ensure we hear from students from as many backgrounds and perspectives as we can, so that we can provide the support that's valued the most. We've founded a BAME law alumni network to facilitate links between our current BAME students and those who've graduated and are already in legal practice or other work.
>
> None of these measures and initiatives - whether individually or even collectively - can wholly counteract the racism and prejudice that remain woefully far too present in modern society, or fully insulate the Law School from their perverse influence. But I hope that they demonstrate our commitment to tackling these issues seriously - and that they will in due course contribute to a better, more equal and inclusive future for us all.

If you feel you have been discriminated against or who have experienced discrimination in the university (sic), please do seek advice or report it using the University's online report and support tool. You can also speak with the Law School's Racial Equalities Champion ... if you need any advice or support during this process ... If you have other concerns or anxieties, and would like expert advice, please do contact the University's Student Wellbeing Service or the Nilaari Counselling Service for Black, Asian and Ethnic Minority persons. If you have academic concerns, please contact your personal tutor in the first instance. I am also always happy myself to hear from and respond to students who'd like to raise matters with' the School's senior management team.

Like the University's statement, by failing to mention that I strenuously denied the charges, the Law School's email also implies that BRISOC's allegations may be true. It also fails to make any reference to the experience of those interested in legitimate critical engagement with Islam who may be suffering from Islamophobia-phobia. There is only a fleeting reference to freedom of speech and academic freedom. And even this is immediately undermined by the implication that my conduct may amount to hate speech, racism, or a form of unlawful prejudice which these freedoms do not permit. The rest consists of self-congratulation about the School's anti-racism credentials, coupled with the same one-sided plea for anyone affected by discrimination, but not by having their education sabotaged by the lies of a militant minority, to get in touch with the relevant support services. The commitment in question should also emphatically be to provide the support that is *most appropriate* not that which is '*valued the most.*' Unlike the latter, the former suggests that not everything demanded will be delivered. Furthermore, if 28% of home law undergraduates are BAME, this amounts to *overrepresentation* since, according to the 2021 census only 18% of the population of the UK is from such backgrounds. This also contrasts sharply with the fact that, in 2022, the University of Bristol came 113th in, and fourth from the bottom of, the *Sunday Times Good University Guide 2023* diversity and inclusivity league table.[45]

A much better shared statement from the Law School and the University would have been along the following lines:

---

[45] The Sunday Times, *Good University Guide 2023*, p. 49.

The University of Bristol Islamic Society (BRISOC) has accused Steven Greer, Professor of Human Rights in the University of Bristol Law School, of Islamophobia in his teaching and other public output. Professor Greer strenuously denies all charges. Both the School and the University are committed, wholeheartedly and equally, to maintaining and defending academic freedom and to rooting out Islamophobia and all other toxic social prejudices wherever they are found. An independent inquiry has been instigated to investigate BRISOC's allegations. Anyone with relevant first-hand evidence, including that which relates to either side of this controversy, is urged to submit it in confidence to the following address .... Any member of the University of Bristol who makes a public disclosure or claim of any kind about this matter before the inquiry arrives at a verdict, may be guilty of a disciplinary offence. Those who have done so already must publicly withdraw such remarks immediately or face disciplinary consequences.

On 19 February 2021 BRISOC's campaign was carried by both University of Bristol student newspapers, *Epigram* and *The Bristol Tab*,[46] and later by several Muslim websites.[47] However by this stage I had persuaded the University that its subsequent statements should make clear that I denied the charges. On 21 February, in a YouTube item entitled *The Student Perspective*, two University of Bristol students, one of whom describes himself as Muslim, systematically exposed the self-contradiction and non-sequiturs in BRISOC's *Evidence Report* (See Appendix D), explored in the following chapter. They also firmly concluded that nothing in it justified the claim that I'd been guilty of Islamophobia or that the module should be scrapped. Wisely they also cautioned against the knee-jerk signing of petitions without checking the facts first.[48]

The crisis became international when, on 25 February 2021, the Qatar-based news and current affairs broadcaster, *Al Jazeera*, published an online report about it, identifying Aamir Mohamed, then President of

---

[46] The report has disappeared from *Epigram's* website but is still available on *The Bristol Tab's* at: https://thetab.com/uk/bristol/2021/02/19/bristol-law-lecturer-under-fire-from-bristol-islamic-society-over-islamophobic-remarks-44304.

[47] See, eg https://www.islam21c.com/news-views/university-of-bristol-professor-called-out-for-islamophobic-rhetoric/; https://5pillarsuk.com/2021/03/05/bristol-university-islamic-society-demands-swift-action-over-islamophobic-remarks/.

[48] The Student Perspective, *Is Bristol Uni 'Funding Islamophobia'? Our Response to the Steven Greer Scandal*, https://www.youtube.com/watch?v=A7o35_MwrPw.

BRISOC, as a key source, and printing the eleventh of twenty-five PowerPoint slides from the 'Islam, China and the Far East' lecture in 2019-20.[49] It reads as follows:

> 'A British university professor has come under mounting criticism over what students described as his "Islamophobic" remarks and taught content. In a statement last week, the University of Bristol's Islamic Society (BRISOC) said it was "alarmed by multiple complaints against Professor Steven Greer of the Law School for his reported use of discriminatory remarks and Islamophobic rhetoric." Law students have claimed Greer "frequently expressed views in class that can be deemed Islamophobic, bigoted and divisive," said the statement, which was signed by several other student societies. Although Greer's accusers have gone public, he has been barred by the university from making any comment on the allegations because they are subject to an ongoing investigation and he is bound by a duty of confidentiality. He did however tell Al Jazeera he rejects the allegations.
>
> BRISOC's president, Aamir Mohamed, told Al Jazeera the first complaints came last September and the society lodged a formal complaint with the university in November. A law student at the university told Al Jazeera he filed an independent complaint about Greer last year. BRISOC is demanding an official apology from Greer and the removal of content it considers to be problematic, in a human rights module. The society also seeks an apology from the university for "funding, supporting and promoting" Greer's work and for its "delayed updates" since the complaint was made, said the statement. The university told Al Jazeera it has launched a process to address the issue.
>
> The principal complaint against Greer relates to a human rights module he teaches, titled Human Rights in Law, Politics and Society. BRISOC highlighted several lines in lecture slides they provided to Al Jazeera from the module. One of Greer's students described them as painting an overall "misinformed and bigoted view of Islam." In a section discussing "Islam and human rights," Greer listed freedom of expression as a "key challenge," and highlighted "insult to Islam was punishable by death." The slide gave the deadly Charlie Hebdo attack as an example.
>
> A student who attended Greer's class said he was shocked by some of the content, which gave the impression that Islam was "essentially bad" and "incompatible with freedom." "The Charlie Hebdo killing was a

---

[49] See Appendix B.

terrorist attack. Muslim leaders not only condemned the killings, but the fact that the professor actually used it as proof of Islam's stance on freedom of expression was absolutely appalling," the law student, who wished to remain anonymous, told Al Jazeera. "The professor cherry-picked his examples to put Muslims in such a negative light when there are examples of the contrary – he just chose to not talk about them," he said. On the same slide, Greer listed several other human rights challenges related to Islam, including freedom of thought, conscience and religion, and the position of non-Muslims in Muslim countries. Another section related to the position of women in Islam, said students, referring to lines that said Muslim women experienced "physical chastisement by husbands" and "women who wear hijab [were] less likely to work outside home or be involved in higher education."

A law student who attended the same module during the previous academic year said she felt "extremely uncomfortable, othered and hurt" on several occasions during Greer's classes. "Initially, I was interested to share an academic discussion on Islam, but I was left shocked and antagonised," said the student, who also wished to remain anonymous. "He singled out Islam as a sort of threat. It was another Islamophobic, misinformed and bigoted understanding of Islam. Not something I expected in a university and especially, a human rights module," she added.

According to FOSIS, an umbrella body of Islamic societies in UK universities, the Bristol case is not unique. "Numerous cases are brought to our attention regularly where universities have failed to recognise and adequately address the concerns of Muslim students and their experiences with Islamophobia," Muna Ali, acting vice president of student affairs at FOSIS, told Al Jazeera. According to the National Union of Students, there are more than 300,000 Muslim university students in the UK. An NUS study in 2018 revealed that one in three Muslim students in the UK had experienced abuse or crime at their place of study, while one in four said they would not report an Islamophobic incident. "Islamophobia remains largely unacknowledged and by extension, accepted and normalised in higher education," Sofia Akel, from the Centre for Equity and Inclusion at London Metropolitan University, told Al Jazeera. "Wilful negligence is complicity."

Disappointed with the university's response, BRISOC went public with its concerns last week. The university's Student Union issued a statement of solidarity. The campaign comes amid complaints about another Bristol University professor accused of anti-Semitism. A University of Bristol spokesperson told Al Jazeera they were "in regular contact with the society and the member of staff," and that a process of responding to BRISOC's concerns was "still ongoing and under review" and as such, they were unable to comment further.

In a statement, the university said it upholds the 2018 All Parliamentary Party Group (APPG) definition on Islamophobia – which describes it as a distinct form of racism – and that it was keen to create an "inclusive place for all students." It added that the university was also committed "to freedom of speech and to the rights of all our students and staff to discuss difficult and sensitive topics ... universities are places of research and learning, where debate and dissent are not only permitted but expected, and where controversial and even offensive ideas may be put forward, listened to and challenged."' [50]

This account suffers from three serious related defects. One concerns a marked lack of professionalism in how the story has been researched. In 2019-20, and previous years, the undergraduate unit in HRLPS was only open to final year students, the vast majority, if not all of whom would have left the University by the autumn of 2020. This means that, in all probability, none who took HRLPS in 2019-20, the only year relevant to the formal complaint, would have been available for interview in February 2021 unless BRISOC had referred *Al Jazeera* to them. And, of course, this is unlikely to have included any who did not subscribe to its complaint-and-campaign. Furthermore, since the only named student source is Aamir Mohammad it is impossible to confirm that any of the anonymous alleged sources cited ever took the unit. The report also fails to include a single quotation from any student, and there are many, who contacted the University's inquiry vigorously disputing BRISOC's claims. This may be because *Al Jazeera* didn't bother to find them, or because those who would have told the truth rather than retailing BRISOC's lies and misrepresentations, were understandably too intimidated and frightened to do so. Yet, a simple search would have revealed the analysis conducted by *The Student Perspective*, broadcast on YouTube only a few days before *Al Jazeera*'s report was published.

The second problem is, not surprisingly, that the report uncritically retails the same false allegations made by BRISOC's campaign statement as if they were true. As already indicated, the details are addressed in the

---

[50] https://www.aljazeera.com/news/ 2021 / 2/ 25 /british-law-professor-under-fire-over-islamophobic -content.

following chapter. However, thirdly, it also glaringly contradicts BRISOC's own account about the background to their complaint-and-campaign. Relying upon what it was told by Aamir Mohammad, *Al Jazeera* claims that the first complaints were made to the University in September 2020. Yet, BRISOC's own public statement maintains that the University had ignored 'numerous complaints' about me 'raised by students over the last few years.'

The evening the *Al Jazeera* story appeared, a suspicious incident occurred outside my home. I was putting the bins out at dusk when a woman in traditional Muslim dress crossed the street, produced a picture of a cat on her mobile phone, said it had gone missing, and asked if I'd seen it. I told her I hadn't. She smiled, thanked me and left and I returned inside. This could, of course, have been an entirely innocent, but very unusual, coincidence. However, when a cat disappears in our neighbourhood its owners don't tour the streets presenting a photo of it on their mobile phones. Instead, they pin posters including contact details, to telegraph poles and sometimes also display them in shop windows. Moreover, apart from this incident, in my 48 years as an adult, no traditionally dressed Muslim woman, has ever approached me in the street for any reason. I imagine this is also likely to be true of most white, non-Muslim men in Britain. There are, therefore, two other possible explanations for what happened. It might have either been prompted by innocent curiosity, inspired by the *Al Jazeera* story, or a reconnoitre for something more sinister. Conscious of the fact that I had been compared to Samuel Paty in the social media storm generated by BRISOC's campaign, the next morning I joined my wife on her previously arranged visit to friends on a heavily-guarded military installation a long way away. Had it not been for the alleged stray cat episode, for me to have accompanied her would have been a violation of Covid lockdown regulations at the time. The police, to whom the suspicious incident was reported, took it very seriously and appeared to regard our joint trip as an emergency compatible with the exceptions to the pandemic restrictions.

Since our stay at the base was limited to a few days, I also considered moving to Northern Ireland to live with my brother and his wife for a while. However, this would not only have involved abandoning my family in Bristol and travelling on a possibly crowded plane at the height of the Covid pandemic; it would also have signalled a fearful retreat. So, I decided to stay put and tough it out whatever the consequences. However, to reduce the risk I grew a long, Taliban-style, beard. Wearing contact lenses at the time, I also donned an empty spectacle frame when in public. Together these constituted a less than wholly effective disguise. For several weeks, on the few occasions I left home, mostly to buy a daily newspaper, I also carried a screwdriver just in case.

The controversy deepens

From the launch of its campaign until the autumn of 2021 BRISOC continued to pump out defamatory material on social media. I also received a number of hostile and threatening emails from third parties, but no death threats, all of which were referred to the police. Some very encouraging private support also came from a few colleagues, former and current students, and total strangers, including several Muslims. But nobody from the University of Bristol, or the entire academic profession in the UK or elsewhere, offered me any public support whatever. None of the University's three Muslim chaplains/contacts made any visible or discernible contribution to the controversy either. Human rights and employment law are among the most prominent themes taught and researched in the University of Bristol Law School. Indeed, until I introduce it in the 1990s, there was no human rights unit on the law curriculum at all. Quite rightly those who specialise in human rights, employment law, and cognate fields, publicly criticise and denounce violations wherever they find them; except that is when they happen to one of their own colleagues right under their own noses.

Blistering critiques of BRISOC's case were also published online.[51]

---

[51] Young, 'David Miller may be a loon, but sacking him would open a Pandora's Box;' https://www.afaf.org.uk/the-banned-list/; Alam, 'Controversy over Bristol University Professor;' Student Perspective, *Is Bristol Uni 'Funding Islamophobia'?*; Concrete Milkshake, *Islamofauxbia – The Smearing of Steven Greer*, https://concretemilkshake.wordpress.com/2021/02/22/islamofauxbia-the-smearing-of-steven-greer/amp/?__twitter_impression=true.

Two of these, in particular, swiftly demonstrated that it rested on nothing but falsehood and misrepresentation.[52] For example, one concluded:

> 'It should be abundantly clear ... that this is a shambolic and malicious attempt by an Islamic society and its supporters to shamelessly destroy the reputation and career of a serious academic simply doing his job. Bristol University must reject this complaint in its entirety, defend its employee from the smears of these cynical grievance-mongers, and preferably issue the Islamic Society with some pretty stern demands of their own.'[53]

There were several developments in March 2021. I discovered that BRISOC's Facebook page and Instagram account were retailing further lies allegedly from 'anonymous students.' At my request, the University of Bristol police officer also forwarded concerns about my personal safety to the Avon and Somerset Constabulary.

In the middle of the month, pleading for assistance, I contacted one of the Law School's reps in the trade union to which I belong, the University and College Union (UCU). She replied to the effect that this would not be possible because of a 'conflict of interest' stemming from the fact that she fundamentally disagrees with my analysis of Prevent and other issues. Instead, she recommended that I seek assistance elsewhere in the union. Fearing that the UCU would be more likely to support BRISOC than me, I decided not to do so. The wisdom of this decision was confirmed when, later in the year, the union publicly sided with a militant trans mob at the University of Sussex which drove Professor Kathleen Stock from her Chair in Philosophy, effectively, in her words, 'ending her career.'[54] The details are considered in Chapter 5.

However, I was not suspended from my job. Relieved of the last round of online seminars in HRLPS – on Human Rights, Terrorism and Counterterrorism – ostensibly for my own protection, I otherwise continued working from home as normal in compliance with Covid restrictions. On 14 March 2021 the Law School also required me to

---

[52] Student Perspective, *Is Bristol Uni 'Funding Islamophobia'?*; Concrete Milkshake, *The Smearing of Steven Greer*.
[53] Concrete Milkshake, *The Smearing of Steven Greer*.
[54] https://www.theguardian.com/education/2021/oct/12/professor-says-career-effectively-ended-by-unions-transphobia-claims. See also Ch 5.

remove the following question from a 'virtual pub quiz' for HRLPS students – "All jihadi terrorists are Muslim but few Muslims are jihadis. True or false?." I was told that a student had drawn attention to it and that it could not be included because it 'relates to issues being addressed in an ongoing university process.' In drafting the HRLPS exam papers, I was also later required to replace all reference to 'Muslims' and 'Islam' with less specific alternatives such as 'minority.'

From February to July 2021 the investigation took its course. Needless to say, the huge strain of supplying it with information contributed to a steep decline in my mental health caused by the many dimensions of the crisis. It was my first thought in the morning, my last at the end of the day, and often plagued me in the middle of the night as well. Sometimes I rose at 5.00am to record on the computer something I'd remembered, or which had been bothering me, as I tossed and turned in bed. I also feared that forgetting to mention the smallest detail in my defence, or to put my case in anything other than the clearest manner, could fatally prejudice the outcome.

Police investigations

On 14 March 2021 I learned that the Avon and Somerset Constabulary had informed BRISOC and the University of Bristol Jewish Society that investigations had been launched into allegations of Islamophobia and antisemitism at the University of Bristol. I was interviewed, but not under caution. Not long afterwards the police informed me that their investigation into my alleged misconduct had been dropped due to lack of evidence and the unwillingness of BRISOC to pursue their complaint any further in this context. My own complaint to the police against BRISOC, on the grounds of intimidation and harassment, eventually got nowhere. BRISOC steadfastly refused to cooperate and the police did not take the matter further.

Formal exoneration

On 10 June 2021 I instructed a solicitor, primarily in an attempt to obtain a date for the University Assessor to arrive at her decision. On the same day, the latter informed me about three main things. First, the University had employed a QC/KC to find out if I'd been guilty of harassment under the Equality Act 2010. But the QC/KC does not appear to have been officially asked if I'd been harassed by the complainants. Nevertheless, I raised this in my submission to her. I was also told that I would receive a copy of the report if I asked. I did. Five times. I'm still waiting. Second, the Assessor confirmed that, unless my behaviour in the past constituted harassment, the entire complaint would be rejected because it fell outside the scope of the 90-day limitation period. Although this should have been clear from the outset, it was not officially acknowledged for seven and a half months. Third, I was assured that, although everything would be resolved by the end of June, various avenues of appeal would be open to whichever party was dissatisfied with the result.

Broadly speaking three verdicts on the merits were, in principle, open to the University's inquiry. It could have upheld all BRISOC's allegations with the likely consequence that I would have been disciplined and possibly dismissed. Alternatively, it could have concluded that there was right and wrong on both sides. Depending on how it assessed the balance I would probably have escaped with a reprimand. However, on 23 July 2021, after five months and the collection of 378 pages of documents, and before my solicitor's letter had been sent, it opted for the third – each and every one of BRISOC's allegations was firmly, comprehensively, and unequivocally rejected. Since the Assessor's report is confidential I'm not at liberty to quote from it, nor to say much about the detail. However, I can say that I was not only totally exonerated; I was not criticised in any way. On the contrary, my expertise, together with my prompt and full compliance with the inquiry were praised. There were no 'ifs or buts,' no borderline issues where I was given the benefit of the doubt, nor any reliance upon technicalities which might have left any lingering doubts about the fact that not a single element of the complaints could be sustained. But, as will become clear later in this chapter, the Assessor's verdict proved to be merely an episode in the scandal rather than conclusively ending it.

The Assessor recommended that I should refrain from publicizing my exoneration until the University drafted a joint statement between me, itself, and the complainant. I indicated my willingness to cooperate in its production and also to engage in mediation. But each was on condition that the complainants publicly retracted their false, misleading, and distorted allegations, and publicly apologised for the harm caused. There was no mediation and the joint statement never materialized.

On 2 August 2021 I reported the news of my exoneration to the Law School's senior management and asked when my Law School colleagues would be informed. I also pointed out that there was evidence that some of them had supported BRISOC's campaign and that these were matters of the utmost seriousness which required further investigation. Each request was simply ignored. The failure of the Law School to make any announcement regarding my resounding official vindication was not only disappointing; it also denied me protection against the ongoing risk of personal attack and deprived me of what could, and should, have been its official support.

The TikTok video

On 18 August 2021, mid-way through a week's holiday in south Wales, I discovered that BRISOC had uploaded, a scurrilous TikTok video to their Instagram account. The full text is as follows:

> 'Students from Bristol University have recently come together to highlight Islamophobic remarks made by Law Professor Steven Greer. Both Muslim and non-Muslim students have complained about the discomfort that this has brought them. Some of the allegations include bringing the Qur'an into lessons even when it had nothing to do with the syllabus and making sweeping statements like calling Islam oppressive despite having no academic credentials in Islamic law. It's also been said that he has made fun of the Qur'an in lessons, mocked it, and called it utter nonsense. And a lot more. He argues that this is simply academic debate and it's part of his freedom of speech. Now I think this sparks a very interesting conversation about how, for decades, academic institutions have weaponised the concept of freedom of speech. Freedom of speech? Yea. Freedom of consequence? No. There is something fundamentally wrong that white western academics who have no proximity to Islam, for example being Islamically illiterate, having the authority to teach it. More importantly it's funny that they think this makes them objective when the teachings from these institutions have aided the continuing discrimination against Muslims. He is a professor at a very good university. Those are the future law makers that we're talking about. And unfortunately the

University have found no misconduct and have sided with the professor.....'

I do not recognise the young woman who delivered these remarks. And the fact that she reports what others have allegedly said suggests she has never been one of my students. The only things that can be confirmed in the entire video are that I do indeed lack 'credentials in Islamic law' (but, as I discuss more fully in the following chapter, this is not a relevant consideration), I do claim that everything I've ever said on any relevant occasion is covered by academic freedom, I am a professor at a very good university, some of my students may well become future law makers (some already have), and the University's inquiry did, in fact, clear me of misconduct. The rest is a pack of lies based on nothing but hearsay and rumour. But, as already indicated, lies like these could easily have inspired murder. On account of its proven failure to do anything effective about BRISOC's campaign, I decided not to tell the University about the video. Instead, I referred the matter to the police on the grounds that it, prima facie, constituted life-threatening criminal harassment and victimization. An investigation was opened but fizzled out. I know that BRISOC refused to cooperate, an insufficient basis for it being discontinued. I was, however, never given any other reason.

The Islam, China and the Far East module is scrapped

The fact that I had been exonerated, but had not been permitted to announce it even to my own colleagues, made it all the more important that, to demonstrate my innocence, I returned to teach the Islam, China and the Far East module on HRLPS as soon as possible in 2021-22, not least because I had little confidence that the University would ever fully publicly acknowledge my vindication.

Aware that my retirement, planned for the summer of 2022, was looming on the horizon, in the early summer of 2020 I had begun to prepare for the succession in HRLPS in 2022-23. Since only one colleague wanted to be involved, I assumed he would become unit coordinator for both the undergraduate and postgraduate units. So, in order to ease him into this role, I proposed that we would share teaching on a module-by-module basis in 2021-22. But the precise allocation was left open for further discussion. Then Covid struck. As indicated in the previous chapter, major changes had to be made to the delivery of HRLPS including streamlining the programme, in a format known as 'blended learning,' to six topics on the LLB – origins and conceptual debate; internationalization and globalization; Islam and China; democracy and democratization; legal institutionalization; and counterterrorism. This meant online delivery of audio-video recorded narrated PowerPoint presentations, and seminars involving a mixture of face-to-face and online teaching. However, literally just before the academic year 2020-21 began, a new colleague was appointed to the School's academic staff and immediately joined the teaching team for HRLPS. The easiest way to accommodate her, and to lighten both her teaching load and that of my other colleague, was for me to deliver the presentations on all modules, and for us all to conduct the seminars on a module-by-module basis, which we did.

Having survived the challenges of Covid in 2020-21, the three of us then had to settle the distribution of responsibility for 2021-22, my last year in full-time employment. The School had agreed that, for me, this should be on 50% study leave to which I was entitled under the standard one-year-in-four arrangements, in my case spread over the two academic years 2020-22. Given the ongoing University inquiry into BRISOC's complaint, by the early summer of 2021 my contribution to teaching HRLPS in 2021-22 remained in doubt. Had the Assessor found in BRISOC's favour, it is unlikely that I would have been permitted to have been involved at all.

However, following my exoneration in July 2021 I began to negotiate with my two colleagues – now the coordinators for the undergraduate and postgraduate versions of HRLPS respectively – what my contribution might be. By late August this had stalled over who would teach the Islam, China and the Far East module. It is also worth pointing out that neither of these two colleagues showed the slightest concern about this material in 2020-21. In fact, the one who had been a colleague for longest was not only willing, but eager, to teach the relevant seminars.

Suspecting that, in spite of my vindication, BRISOC's complaint had made both colleagues afraid of the possible consequences of teaching the module in any shape or form, on 4 September 2021, I emailed them with the following proposal: 'Having given this a great deal of thought, the only compromise which I think is viable is that I deliver the lecture and conduct all the seminars on "Islam, China and the Far East" to all LLM and LLB seminar groups in person, on campus, whatever the risks to my personal safety.' On 6 September I received the following reply.

> Having discussed 'what to do with the materials for HRLPS this year … we have jointly decided that we will not be running a cycle on "Islam, China, and the Far East" either on the UG or PG units. We have come to this decision for a number of reasons, some of which I know X has already explained in his correspondence with you (around the likelihood of recurrence of complaints, etc). We also feel that for pedagogical and student well-being reasons, it is important that Muslim students in particular do not feel that their religion is being singled out or in any way "othered" by the class material. We know that this was a problem for some students last year and as guardians of their welfare as well as their learning, we do not wish to have the experience repeated …'

This was immediately and eagerly endorsed by the Law School's senior management on the grounds that it was democratic because it was two against one and that 'Steven will understand.' The personal importance to me of delivering this material was completely ignored. Since it anticipates further allegations of precisely the same kind as those the Assessor had already found to be utterly without merit, it is difficult to regard the decision to scrap the Islam, China and the Far East module as anything other than a defiant repudiation of the outcome of the University's own inquiry. And it also, of course, constitutes a form of 'othering' in the name of preventing 'othering'!

Exhausted by the stress caused by the twin prongs of this crisis – the potentially life-threatening hostility of BRISOC's social media campaign and the lack of protection or anything approaching adequate support from either the University or the Law School – I was signed off work by my doctor in mid-September 2021.

The Mail on Sunday article

On 12 September the *Mail on Sunday* published my story with the headline: 'University clears don of being anti-Islam ... but then cancels his course anyway.' I quote it in full.

> 'A professor has hit out at cancel culture after his lectures were axed following a "vicious, militant" campaign by students who branded him Islamophobic. University chiefs rejected complaints that human rights expert Steven Greer had expressed "bigoted views" after a five-month investigation – but have still pulled his module from their syllabus. He accused senior academics of "capitulating" to the threats of students who had called for the module at Bristol University's law school to be scrapped over his 'reported use of discriminatory remarks and Islamophobic comments.' An online petition which was launched by members of the university's Islamic Society, Brisoc, attracted 3,700 signatures.
>
> Meanwhile, Prof Greer said he had to flee the family home amid fears for his safety following the campaign against him. Critics claimed a lecture slide that mentioned the 2015 terror attack on the Paris offices of Charlie Hebdo, a magazine that had published cartoons of the Prophet Mohammed, was "Islamophobic rhetoric." Prof Greer also highlighted the inferior treatment of women and non-Muslims in Islamic nations, and the harsh penalties handed out under sharia law. But he believes he largely came under attack because he supports the Government's Prevent programme to stop radicalisation, which critics have branded anti-Islamic.
>
> Prof Greer, who has worked at the university since the 1980s, told The Mail on Sunday: "Brisoc's campaign has been vicious and punitive and has put me and my family under intolerable stress. It has been very threatening and frightening." He revealed that he "came across a stranger loitering outside our home" shortly after news of the controversy emerged, adding: "They gave an implausible excuse and left. Was it just a coincidence or a reconnoitre? We'll never know. My family and I were, of course, very rattled by this. Taking no chances, my wife and I fled our home to stay somewhere safer for several days. Going public in *The Mail on Sunday* may increase or decrease the risk to my personal safety. I just don't know. But the attack upon me is an attack upon a fundamental freedom and this is something worth standing up for, even if I'm harmed as a result."
>
> Although a formal investigation came down in favour of Prof Greer, he received an email from academic chiefs last week which said his

module on Islam, China and the Far East was being dropped so Muslim students would "not feel that their religion is being singled out or in any way 'othered' by the class material." Prof Greer said: "Militant minorities are increasingly intent on dictating the content and delivery of university education through vilification, intimidation and threats. Their purpose is to silence lawful and legitimate opinion simply because they disagree with it. The law school has capitulated in a manner which is at variance with the result of the university's inquiry into my case."

Prof Greer faced particular criticism over his defence of Prevent, but said the allegation that the programme was Islamophobic had been "resoundingly discredited by the best and most recent research... it simply doesn't stack up against the evidence." Of the 697 cases taken on by Prevent last year, 43 per cent were for far-Right extremism and 30 per cent were Islamist. Prof Greer, whose book, *Tackling Terrorism In Britain: Threats, Responses And Challenges Twenty Years After 9/11*, will be published next month, is due to retire at the end of this academic year, but has been signed off work by a doctor because of the impact of the saga on his health.

Students can appeal the ruling in favour of Prof Greer, and a Bristol University spokesman said: "Our student complaints procedure has two stages and remains ongoing until both stages are complete. Material from the unit in question is still being taught but in a new format. This change is quite independent of the complaint raised and conforms with normal practice in the school in allowing the development of new teaching material to match students' current interests." Avon and Somerset Police said it was investigating a complaint of harassment. Brisoc did not respond to a request for comment. Their online petition referred to "a pattern of what can only be perceived to be hostility and bigotry towards Muslims which Prof Greer freely disseminates under the pretext of 'academic freedom.'" Toby Young, of the Free Speech Union, said: "Bristol's treatment of Prof Greer is outrageous. By kowtowing to the Islamic Society, the university has issued a gold-embossed invitation to activists to submit vexatious complaints about its employees.'"[55]

On the same day it appeared, I circulated a copy of the article to all 160 of my Law School colleagues. The next day I received one private supportive reply and two public ones which were openly antagonistic. One said:

---

[55] https://www.dailymail.co.uk/news/article-9980927/University-clears-don-anti-Islam-cancels-course-anyway.html

'Toby Young (a frequent contributor to the Daily Mail on free speech issues) and our colleague need no help in defending their right to free speech. They have adequate resources and have made their views known in the press repeatedly. I hope that those among our collegiate body who feel afraid or silenced can take this message as one of support for their own right to free speech, to criticise and scrutinise the views and actions of others.'

According to the other one:

'the Law school should unwaveringly stand behind and support marginalised students who have been brave enough to raise this matter. It is unacceptable to try to erase and minimise the experience of these students. The power imbalance between a longstanding Professor and undergraduate students is very significant and I am outraged that, rather than writing a careful apology and reflecting on the harm that has been done, this email was circulated in the first place. Sharing articles from the Daily Mail is frankly offensive: they are systemically racist, Islamophobic and transphobic. Effectively sharing from their platform is further evidence of how seriously the claims made by these students need to be taken. The welfare and well-being of students should be the most important consideration for us all. Especially marginalised students in a climate rife with Islamophobia and racism. I encourage others to speak up. Matters of justice and freedom are more important than job security.'

The second of these colleagues appears to find it much more offensive to be referred to the *Mail on Sunday* than to consider the substance of the issue reported. And both seem to advocate a novel legal principle – 'guilt even after having been formally exonerated.' Neither, of course, has seen the Assessor's report or a single one of the 378 pages collected in the course of the inquiry. I was also rapped over the knuckles by senior Law School management for circulating the email to colleagues. A separate email address was then set up to which contributions to the debate could be sent, the contents of which I have not seen.

I also sent the *Mail on Sunday* piece to nearly all the organizations to which I belong – including the Society of Legal Scholars, the Academy of Social Sciences and the Royal Society of Arts, the latter two of which I am fellow – asking only that they circulate my story to the membership not that they offer me any public support. They all declined without giving any credible reason.

Appeal

On 8 October a panel of three senior Bristol academics from Schools other than Law and Medicine (respectively mine and that of the formal complainant) unequivocally rejected BRISOC's appeal against the inquiry's decision and the University finally issued the following statement about the resolution of my case:

> 'The process of investigating a formal complaint made by the University of Bristol Islamic Society (BRISOC) against one of our Law academics, Professor Steven Greer, has concluded. After rigorous examination of the facts and considering the views of both parties, we can confirm that the complaint has not been upheld and those involved have been informed of the outcome.
>
> Allegations made against Professor Greer centred around the content of an optional human rights module which he has taught for 15 years at the University. Complex legal, regulatory and policy questions were raised relating to equality, academic freedom and freedom of speech.
>
> A QC appointed to review and advise on the content of the module found no evidence of Islamophobic speech and concluded that the material did not amount to discrimination or harassment and was intended as the basis for academic debate by the students who elected to study it. In addition, the issues discussed in relation to Islam were within the scope of the curriculum and therefore exempt from constituting harassment or discrimination under the Equality Act 2010.
>
> Although the complaint has not been upheld, we recognise BRISOC's concerns and the importance of airing differing views constructively. We welcome further discussions with the society to explain our decision and reaffirm our commitment to providing a positive and inclusive university experience for all our students.
>
> It is disappointing that both parties chose to breach the confidentiality of the process before both stages had been completed. We acknowledge that this has had a regrettable impact on Professor Greer in particular, who has been the target of abuse after BRISOC released details of the complaint on social media.
>
> In response to claims that the human rights module taught by Professor Greer has been cancelled, we can confirm that this is not the case. The

fundamental structure and content of the module remains; the changes made are of emphasis and in part designed to future proof the course by allowing a level of flexibility in the development of new teaching material to match students' current interests, the specialisms of the course's new conveners and their wish to deliver the material in a context that is both broad-reaching and respectful of sensitivities of students on the course.

This university, like all universities, encourages all students to engage with, debate, analyse and critique ideas and theories of all kinds within its academic programmes. Ensuring that all members of our community can exercise their right to free speech has always been and remains at the heart of our mission.'[56]

This is deeply unsatisfactory for several reasons. First, the University doesn't seem to understand the difference between the unit, HRLPS – which remains on the curriculum – and the Islam, China and the Far East module which has been removed. BRISOC's views were certainly not aired 'constructively,' nor is it clear why the University recognises their concerns or would 'welcome further discussions with the society to explain our decision and reaffirm our commitment to providing a positive and inclusive university experience for all our students,' but not with me. And, of course, the statement ignores the express reasons I was given by the new unit coordinators explaining why the Islam, China and the Far East module had been cancelled.

On 9 October 2021 *The Bristol Tab* reported the University's decision and my reaction. BRISOC's furious response was also quoted as follows.

'In a wide ranging attack on the university, the society also claim Bristol Uni has failed in their duty of care to students, failed in their promise to "decolonise the curriculum" and are "celebrating bigoted menfolk and advancing colonial thought." Bristol Islamic Society told The Bristol Tab: "We have seen no comment from the University acknowledging its impact on students, rather the spotlight has been on Greer's wellbeing. The university should, at the very least, acknowledge and support those students who have spent months in distress, with low self-esteem and suicidal thoughts."'[57]

---

[56] https://www.bristol.ac.uk/news/2021/october/complaint-outcome.html.
[57] https://thetab.com/uk/bristol/2021/10/09/bristol-islamic-society-furious-after-uni-clears-professor-of-islamophobia-allegations-47016. See also: https://5pillarsuk.com/2021/10/12/bristol-university-exonerates-professor-accused-of-islamophobia/

On 14 October 2021, the student newspaper, *Epigram*, published the following statement from me in full:

> 'Following an almost eight-month University inquiry and review, it is a huge relief to have been completely and unreservedly exonerated with respect to the utterly groundless allegations of Islamophobia made against me by the University of Bristol Islamic Society (BRISOC). This decision, originally reached at the end of July, was unanimously confirmed by a University review panel on 8 October 2021.
>
> Nevertheless, BRISOC's life-threatening social media campaign, which began in February, not only continues unabated, but was re-energised in August with the sharing, on their Instagram page, of fresh and even more scurrilous falsehoods.
>
> While the University's statement of 8 October announces my complete and unequivocal exoneration, it simultaneously undermines it in the following ways. Recognising "BRISOC's concerns" is utterly incompatible with the result of the inquiry and review which found these to be totally without foundation. BRISOC has never sought to "air differing views constructively." On the contrary, they have consistently resisted constructive engagement in favour of the pursuit of a vicious social media campaign which both sought my dismissal and cynically put my life at risk.
>
> I did not breach confidentiality by leaking the result of the University's inquiry to the Mail on Sunday on 12 September 2021. There is no duty of confidentiality regarding information already in the public domain. BRISOC broke confidentiality in February (with respect to their original formal complaint) and in August (with respect to the outcome of the inquiry) ... a matter currently being investigated by the police. By contrast, I was perfectly legally entitled to override any duty of confidentiality with respect to the outcome of the inquiry in order to protect myself from harm. While acknowledging that I have been subject to "abuse," the University fails to point out that this has been, and continues to be, at the hands of BRISOC and that, in spite of repeated pleas, the University itself has still done nothing to stop it.
>
> To suggest that it was necessary to restructure the degree unit at the heart of BRISOC's baseless allegations, in order to be "respectful of the sensitivities of students on the course," is totally at variance with the result of the official inquiry and review. It is also grossly defamatory in so far as it implies that there was any disrespect hitherto. The modification of the syllabus in question... also calls the University's commitment to academic freedom into question.

The University of Bristol must immediately put a stop to BRISOC's ongoing social media campaign and explain why it has not done so sooner or face the legal consequences. BRISOC must also now remove all defamatory material relating to the complaint against me from all relevant sites and publicly issue a retraction plus an apology or face the legal consequences.'[58]

Sick leave

In spite of having been on sick leave from mid-September to the end of December 2021, there was no let-up in the time and effort required to manage the fall-out from the BRISOC crisis. Over this period and well into 2022 I spent a great deal of my time, typically after breakfast, enjoying the sun when it shone through the window, taking stock of the situation as it then stood, mind-mapping the issues and possible ways of dealing with it, and liaising with my supporters, friends and allies, of whom there were now many.

In an email, circulated to all Law School colleagues on 1 November 2021, I proposed that the School meeting on 10 November should endorse the following resolution, if possible to be released to the press via the University's Press Office: 'In the light of recent disturbing events, the University of Bristol Law School affirms its commitment to academic freedom and condemns campaigns of vilification, victimization, intimidation and harassment against anyone based upon opposition to their lawfully expressed contributions to legitimate academic and other public debates.' On 9 November I was informed by the Law School's senior management that, according to Human Resources, while on sick leave, I should not participate in the School meeting or any other University business. They added that, although there were 'reservations about putting your proposed item on the agenda anyway,' that was 'not something that now needs to be addressed.'

On 11 November 2021, with my doctor's approval, I participated in the online launch of my book, *Tackling Terrorism in Britain: Threats, Responses and Challenges Twenty Years After 9/11*, hosted by the think tank Policy Exchange and chaired by its Director, Dean Godson, who

---

[58] https://epigram.org.uk/2021/10/14/professor-steven-greer-speaks-out-on-his-exoneration-by-the-university-of-bristol/.

referred to the BRISOC scandal in his opening remarks. I was also joined by a panel of discussants including Nimco Ali OBE (CEO, The Five Foundation), Lord Carlile of Berriew QC/KC CBE (Former Independent Reviewer of Terrorism Legislation), Khalid Mahmood MP (Labour MP for Perry Barr and Senior Fellow, Policy Exchange) and Sir Mark Rowley (Former Assistant Commissioner for Specialist Operations, Metropolitan Police and Academic Advisor, Policy Exchange, since promoted to Commissioner of the Metropolitan Police). The event was well advertised in advance, nobody from the Law School raised any objection to my involvement, and, apart from Nimco Ali having to withdraw at the outset due to a faulty internet connection, it all went well.

In the autumn of 2021 the Bristol Free Speech Society, a student organisation at the University of Bristol, arranged an online interview with me about the BRISOC controversy, scheduled to be broadcast online on 1 December. Only a few hours before it was due to take place, the Law School's senior management emailed me to 'insist' that I did 'not attend … pending the outcome of an Occupational Health report.' The email added: 'depending on the OH report and future circumstances, it may be possible for you to attend such an event in the future.' This contradicted the conclusion of my GP that, for several reasons, my participation in this event was not remotely incompatible with being on sick leave. First, it was more likely to be beneficial than harmful to my mental health. Second, it was an extra-curricular activity and not part of my employment-related obligations. Third, it would not have been any different in principle from the webinar launch of my book on 11 November to which there had been no objection.

On 5 December 2021, I notified the Law School's senior management to the effect that I looked forward to cooperating with Occupational Health and Human Resources in facilitating my return to work on 3 January 2022. But I also identified several issues which, in my opinion, needed to be resolved first. The most important of these were that the University should require BRISOC to take down its ongoing potentially life-threatening social media campaign against me, publicly retract the false allegations upon which it was based, and publicly apologise for the harm they had caused. I also requested that those involved should be warned by the University that failure to do so would result in disciplinary consequences, that such an outcome must, in fact, lead to disciplining, and that, if it did, the University should issue a public statement, subject to my approval, that this had occurred.

I also made three other proposals. One was that the Law School should issue the following declaration to all its staff: 'Affirming its steadfast commitment to academic freedom, and condemning campaigns of vilification, victimization, intimidation and harassment against anyone based upon opposition to their lawfully expressed contributions to legitimate academic debates, the University of Bristol Law School warmly welcomes the return of Professor Steven Greer from sick leave following his unreserved official exoneration from false charges of Islamophobia, and wishes him well in the last few months of his full-time working life before retirement.' Another was to propose a series of mediation sessions – conducted on a one-to-one, face-to-face basis by a professional, independent mediator – between me and certain colleagues, whom I did not name, whose attitude to my case had made my return to work in the Law School problematic. A third was a request that the Law School should facilitate the publication of an article by me about Islamophobia and academic freedom on its blog site. Having been told that the mediation sessions would be voluntary I decided it was pointless to pursue them. And, in spite of an undertaking to publish the blog, none of these other requests was honoured. I was never told the reasons.

Return to work

Although the fit note from my GP expired on 3 January 2022, no attempt was made by my employers to facilitate my return to work until an Occupational Health consultation, conducted on the telephone on 24 January. The subsequent report focused almost entirely upon the need for the workplace issues, to which I'd drawn the attention of the University and the Law School, to be addressed. It made no reference to working from home which, in the consultation, I emphasised, had never raised any health-related issues. However, on 21 February, I received the following email from senior Law School management:

'... according to the Bristol Free Speech Society's Facebook page, you are now scheduled to participate in their event on Islamophobia and Academic Freedom on Thursday 24 February ... the OH advice states very clearly that you should not be undertaking any work activities at this time, in any place, because the work issues you have raised need to be resolved to prevent further exacerbation of stress ... I must therefore insist that you act in accordance with the advice and do not undertake any work activities until OH considers you fit to return to work. For the avoidance of doubt, that includes work activities conducted at home and externally, not just on University premises.'

The OH report says nothing of the sort. The only reference to working off campus is that: 'Steven feels he is fit to participate in external events as this is away from the main campus. In my opinion however, I do still feel that the outstanding work issues need to be resolved to prevent further exacerbation of stress in his role.'

Given the thrust of the rest of the report, and the conversation at the OH consultation, any reasonable interpretation of these two sentences is that, working from home including participating in external events, would not obviate the need to address the campus-related issues before I could physically return there. Not surprisingly the Law School's bizarre and twisted interpretation of the OH report – that I could not be permitted to work from home until campus-related issues which no attempt had been made to resolve were addressed – was merely a transparent, and indeed an express, attempt to prevent me from being interviewed online by the Bristol Free Speech Society. Nevertheless, on the advice of my lawyers, the latter was postponed for a second time. However, following another OH consultation, which unequivocally resolved any doubt, contrived or otherwise, about my immediate return to working from home, and a further attempt by the Law School to stop the event from taking place, the interview eventually went ahead on 30 March 2022.[59] All the issues it raised are covered elsewhere in this book.

---

[59] Bristol Free Speech Society's interview, *Islamophobia and academic freedom: a conversation with Professor Steven Greer*, available on YouTube at the following link: https://www.youtube.com/watch?v=-6q2o5058jA.

Appointed Research Director at the Oxford Institute for British Islam

Out of the blue, on 11 October 2021, I received the following email from the Muslim Education Centre of Oxford (MECO):

> 'The Muslim Educational Centre of Oxford (MECO) is a progressive and forward-looking Islamic organisation. We are dedicated to pristine Qur'anic principles, including unfettered free speech and uncensored individual expression (Q109:6). We strongly oppose the misguided BRISOC students who have called for your unwarranted dismissal. Their fundamentalist bigotry is a disgrace to the hallowed concept of academic freedom which must be defended at all cost. While we might not concur with all your opinions and perspectives, we publicly applaud your resolute determination to resist Islamic fanaticism and religious intolerance. These imported prejudices and foreign notions have no place whatsoever in 21st century UK.'

Aside from my formal exoneration, this was one of the most encouraging developments in the entire controversy. Having thanked MECO for their support, email correspondence and face-to-face contact ensued. It turned out that the Director, Dr Taj Hargey, was setting up the Oxford Institute for British Islam (OIBI), an independent, progressive, Muslim public policy think tank and research institute with strong academic credentials, dedicated to promoting fresh inquiry, bold rationalism, and creative solutions for contemporary British Muslims in a cosmopolitan and inter-faith environment.[60]

At the beginning of January 2022, I was, therefore, very pleased to be formally appointed OIBI's first Visiting Research Fellow, a part-time, non-stipendiary position held in conjunction with my post as Professor of Human Rights at the University of Bristol Law School. As Dr Hargey stated in the announcement: 'We are delighted … to host Professor Greer as OIBI's first Visiting Research Fellow and greatly look forward to working with him in devising and facilitating an exciting research programme relating to Islam in Britain.' I added that it was

> 'a tremendous honour and privilege to be the first Visiting Research Fellow at the Oxford Institute for British Islam' and that 'as a non-

---

[60] https://oibi.org.uk/news/; http://www.bristol.ac.uk/law/news/2022/steven-greer-oibi.html.

Muslim, I greatly look forward to the opportunity this presents to develop my research into Islamophobia and to enhance its impact far beyond the academy. I fervently hope this will include contributing to the formation of relevant public policy, and to improving understanding, and the relationship, between Muslims and others in the UK and beyond.'

Having assisted with OIBI's official launch in May 2022, and its inaugural conference at St John's College, Oxford that August, I was delighted to be appointed OIBI's first Research Director in September.

Negotiation

My personal situation improved further as a result of an invitation to attend, with about 20 others, a Distinguished Fellows Lunch hosted by the Vice Chancellor of the University of Bristol on 23 March 2022. Taking full advantage of the opportunity this presented I asked the VC if I could meet him privately to discuss my concerns about how the University had mishandled my case. He graciously agreed. At our meeting on 29 March he appeared sympathetic, though nevertheless non-committal, and undertook to discuss my case with the 'top team,' sadly the very officials responsible for mismanaging it in the first place. A few days later I email the Law School's senior management to inform them that, as a result of a signal failure to protect my best interests, I had lost confidence in them and proposed that the last few months of my full-time working life should be managed by somebody else.

Following each of these developments, a meeting with senior University officials was held on 28 April 2022. I began by stating that, in my view, this had two principal objectives: formally to convey to the University my acute sense of betrayal and injustice stemming from its failure to manage BRISOC's complaint with anything approaching the appropriate level of care, concern, and respect for me as an employee; and to explore what might be done to remedy it.

Having reviewed the principal facts about BRISOC's complaint-and-campaign, and the response of the University and the Law School documented elsewhere in this chapter, I asked the following questions. Why did the University entertain BRISOC's formal complaint in October 2020, in spite of multiple defects, any one of which should have resulted in it begin summarily rejected? Having nevertheless entertained it, why did the University not involve me in seeking to find a solution before BRISOC launched its social media campaign? Why did the University not warn BRISOC when, in December 2020, it threatened to 'go public,' that this would jeopardise its formal complaint and either expose those concerned to disciplinary proceedings or to a court injunction? Why has the University still not initiated disciplinary proceedings against those concerned in spite of manifest breaches of all relevant University codes of conduct, nor against one of its own student anti-racism advisers who denounced me by name as an Islamophobe at a public rally in Bristol in December 2020, thereby potentially putting my life at risk? Why has the University not investigated two societies which the Law School supports – University of Bristol Unity and Diversity in Law and the University of Bristol Women in Law Society – each of which signed BRISOC's petition to have me sacked without first checking its veracity? What does the University mean by 'recognising' BRISOC's 'concerns,' and that changes to the HRLPS unit were required in order to 'respect the sensitivities of students' taking it? Why was the Islam, China and the Far East module taken off the HRLPS syllabus, against my wishes, and expressly for the reasons the inquiry unequivocally rejected, and how does this square with its verdict?

I also outlined a series of proposals. Without delay, the University should discipline, for gross misconduct, those who had instigated BRISOC's campaign and the student anti-racism adviser who had named me as an Islamophobe at the Bristol rally. The University should also require BRISOC, upon pain of disciplinary consequences if they refused, publicly to retract all their allegations against me, to issue a public apology for the harm caused, and to remove all reference to their campaign, apart from the retraction and apology, from all their electronic and other platforms. Upon pain of disciplinary action if they refused, the University should require Unity and Diversity in Law and Bristol Women in Law to do likewise. The Law School should also email all its staff and students celebrating my formal exoneration, welcoming me back from sick leave, congratulating me on my appointment as Visiting Research Fellow at the Oxford Institute for British Islam, and reaffirming its commitment to academic freedom. I also asked that I be permitted, as is the custom, to say a proper formal, collective and public farewell to my colleagues at the annual Law School end-of-session summer party.

The officials concerned were attentive and receptive with respect to both the questions and the proposals and sought further information from me about the issues raised. But, understandably, as they said, they were not themselves in a position to provided definitive responses there and then. However, they undertook to seek further guidance from the University and to get back to me when this had been obtained. On 14 July 2022 I received a letter from a senior University official. Since it is marked 'Private and confidential' I am not at liberty to disclose its contents other than to say that it addressed the minor issues leaving all the major ones unanswered. In an unrelated development, in July, as a result of the close association I had formed with the Free Speech Union (FSU) early in the BRISOC scandal, I was appointed to the FSU's Legal Advisory Council. And on 26th of that month I did, in fact, say a formal farewell to colleagues, as requested, at the Law School's summer party. And on the day of my retirement, 30 September 2022, in keeping with a recently-established custom, I received a booklet of generous good wishes and fond memories from a few colleagues. But, from the end of my sick leave on 3 January 2022 to my retirement, I was never officially cleared to return to work either at home or on campus. Needless to say I simply ignored this and busied myself tidying up the loose ends of a sourly-ending career and laying the foundations for several future activities. In addition to my work with OIBI, these include volunteering at my local Buddhist centre and a food bank, and training to be a guide at Bristol Cathedral.

Litigation

Not long after the University's investigation began, friends advised me to obtain professional legal representation. However, in the event and as already indicated, this was not arranged until July 2021, just before I received news of the Assessor's decision in my favour. Correspondence then began between my solicitor and the University for a satisfactory settlement based primarily on the claim that, by not protecting me more effectively from BRISOC's potentially life-threatening social media campaign, the University had breached its duty of care as my employer. However, that autumn, correspondence with the University stalled without agreement.

I was very dissatisfied with the service my solicitor provided. It was a huge relief, therefore, when, out of the blue in January 2022, I received notice that she no longer worked for the firm and that another colleague was to take over her responsibilities. However, I decided, instead, to take advantage of this unexpected development to sever my connection with the firm entirely and to find alternative legal representation. The FSU not only found me a new team but also generously paid the first instalment of my costs from their fighting fund.

My primary objective in the post-exoneration phase of the BRISOC scandal has been to attempt, as far as possible, to hold accountable all those implicated in it in order to enhance the prospects of preventing anything similar from happening to anyone else. In principle, this might involve any combination of litigation, this book, and a media campaign linked to both. As far as litigation is concerned, the University of Bristol is, prima facie, exposed to a claim, not only for defamation, but also for breach of its duty of care as my employer, breach of a number of statutory obligations, and violation of my rights to academic freedom and to freedom of expression. Those who mobilized BRISOC's campaign also have a compelling case to answer with respect to a number of possible legal wrongs including: defamation; conspiracy to defame; harassment, intimidation and victimization; incitement of and conspiracy to harassment, intimidation and victimization; and conspiracy to induce the breach of my employment contract, the University's legal duty of care to me as my employer, and its legal duty to protect my academic freedom and freedom of expression. Possible remedies for all the legal wrongs are under active consideration by my lawyers. But deciding which to pursue will, as in any litigation, be a matter of strategic calculation.

Prima facie the University of Bristol is the most legally culpable of all relevant parties for having failed to take any steps whatever to prevent

BRISOC's potentially life-threatening social media campaign or to stop it once it began. The core argument here is that it breached its duty of care by failing to act as would any reasonable employer in its position. First, a reasonable employer would have rejected BRISOC's formal complaint in November 2020 on any one or more of the following grounds: it was manifestly vexatious and ill-founded; it was not raised through any of the Law School's many informal complaints channels; it was submitted long after the applicable deadline; the formal complainant was not party to any of the events or circumstances cited; the complaint was, therefore, effectively made by anonymous, unidentifiable, third parties; and the formal complainant refused to engage in mediation as required by relevant guidelines.

However, in spite of having failed to reject the application, any reasonable employer in the University's position would, nevertheless, have: immediately consulted an independent expert to ascertain whether or not a prima facie case had been established; notified me of both the fact and substance of the complaint in November 2020 as soon as it had been submitted; required BRISOC to submit to mediation involving me from the outset; warned BRISOC of the risk of disciplinary consequences if they 'went public' as they threatened to do in December 2020; warned BRISOC of disciplinary consequences if they failed to abandon their social media campaign, launched on 15 February 2021, and would have initiated such proceedings had they failed to do so.

Furthermore, no reasonable employer in the University's position would have: engaged in discussion with BRISOC from November 2020 until February 2021 without having officially notified me of the fact and substance of the complaint; taken nearly a year from October 2020 to October 2021 to settle it; forbidden me from making any public comment in my defence, apart from denying culpability, including by announcing my exoneration prior to the rejection of BRISOC's appeal in October 2021 on the spurious grounds that I was bound by a 'duty of confidentiality' (notwithstanding the fact that BRISOC had wantonly violated any they may have had); issued statements in February 2021 to the press and permitted the Law School to email colleagues implying that there was merit in BRISOC's accusations; having itself both failed to announce, and prohibited me from announcing, my exoneration from July to October 2021, withdrawn the Islam, China and the Far East module from HRLPS, exactly as BRISOC demanded and expressly for the reasons the Assessor rejected; publicly announced in October 2021 that, while I had been exonerated following an official inquiry, the University nevertheless recognized BRISOC's 'concerns,' and that the HRLPS unit had been altered in order 'to respect the sensitivities' of those taking it; declined officially to authorise my return to work, including from home up to and including the day of my retirement on 30 September 2022, in spite of clearance by OH not long after the expiry of my fit note on 3 January 2022.

Prima facie these multiple breaches resulted in a significant failure by the University to reduce the reasonably foreseeable risk of: physical harm by third parties stemming from BRISOC's social media campaign; irretrievable damage to my reputation as an internationally-renowned human rights scholar; loss of trust and respect on the part of my colleagues; serious and enduring harm to my mental and physical health, particularly since, having had a stroke in 2013 (of which the University was reminded), I was more vulnerable to the stress and anxiety of BRISOC's complaint-and-campaign than would otherwise have been the case.

As far as breach of its statutory duties are concerned, the University is obliged by legislation, including the Education (No 2) Act 1986 and the Human Rights Act 1998, to protect the academic freedom, and the lawful freedom of expression, of its staff. The 1986 Act also requires it to issue, and to take reasonably practicable steps to comply with, a code of practice setting out how it seeks to fulfil these obligations. By drafting and publishing a *Freedom of Speech Code of Practice 2021/2022*, it has met the first of these requirements. But, by removing the Islam, China and the Far East module in the context of BRISOC's ongoing social media campaign – without by this stage having permitted me to make, or itself made any public announcement regarding my official exoneration – the University stands accused of tacitly endorsing the allegations in the formal complaint, thereby further breaching its legal responsibilities to protect my rights to academic freedom and to freedom of expression.

The University is also exposed to a claim for libel particularly by publicly stating, on 8 October 2021, that it recognised BRISOC's 'concerns' and that the HRLPS unit had been altered to respect the sensitivities of those taking it, insinuating that I was not as innocent of the charge of Islamophobia as its own inquiry conclusively proved.

Confidentiality

One final law-related issue requires clarification. As already indicated, when BRISOC launched its vicious social media campaign the University insisted that, although this breached BRISOC's duty of confidentiality, I remained bound by mine. The statement of 8 October 2021, which accuses me of failing to honour it, can only refer to the *Mail on Sunday's* story about my case. There are, however, several powerful objections to the view that either party was subject to any genuine, legally-binding, duty of confidentiality at any point in the inquiry much less thereafter. And there are also grounds for believing that, even if we were, I had the stronger right to waive it.

First, no such requirement was an express condition of the complaint. It is not stipulated on the complaint form, for example, nor had either of us made any such formal, written commitment. It was at most, therefore, an assumed and merely implicit duty, the lack of clarity in the relevant scope and terms of which have been compounded by the confusion created by paragraph 6 of the *Student Complaints Procedure* cited above. As Mr Justice Ralton held in the recent case *of Rosario-Sanchez v University of Bristol*, where precisely the same issue arose:

> "There is no provision making the process confidential (the general law may well protect the data in any event) but I understand it is common ground that the process is treated as if confidential. However, there is no apparent sanction for breach of an understanding that the proceedings are to be confidential ..."[61]

Second, the University's conception of confidentiality does not tally with page 4 of the *Good Practice Framework* which states that there should be an 'appropriate level of confidentiality *without*

---

[61] *Raquel Maria Rosario Sanchez v University of Bristol*, Claim No.008LR988, in the County Court at Bristol, 21 April 2022, paras 25 & 132.

disadvantage.'[62] Yet by holding me strictly to my alleged duty of confidentiality, in spite of the fact that BRISOC had wantonly broken theirs, I suffered considerable disadvantage. As already noted, by July 2021, BRISOC had had five months in which publicly to trash my reputation and expose me to the risk of physical attack while I was instructed to remain silent. This predicament was deepened further, both by the requirement that I should not disclose the Assessor's verdict in my favour until the University permitted it, and by the removal of the Islam, China and the Far East module from the HRLPS syllabus.

Third, in August 2021, the TikTok video to which reference has already been made, revealed that I had been officially absolved. Since matters already in the public domain are no longer confidential, referring to my exoneration did not break any duty of confidentiality I may otherwise have had.

Fourth, duties of confidentiality are not absolute. For one thing they do not provide, as the University appears to think, cloaks of invisibility capable of being spread at will over bureaucratic processes and decisions to conceal their lack of justification. Clear exceptions to any legal duty of confidentiality include the need to expose serious misconduct – the 'whistleblower's defence' – and to avoid serious harm. By the autumn of 2021 the University had tried to silence me twice – first during the inquiry, then again with respect to the result. Its claim that my duty of confidentiality covered the entire complaints process, which they maintained was not complete until the appeal had been heard, lacks credibility. It is, after all, commonplace in legal proceedings for the first instance verdict of a court to be publicly announced and reported even though an appeal may subsequently be lodged. It appears, therefore, that officers of the University insisted upon a bogus duty of confidentiality in a vain attempt to control the release of information about the BRISOC controversy to protect what it perceived to be its institutional interests – sacrificing the academic freedom of one of its own senior staff in order not to jeopardise student recruitment by appearing to be hostile to minorities, an issue explored at greater length in Chapter 5.

---

[62] Italics added.

Conclusion

I have no reason to doubt that the two police investigations relating to my case, or the litigation launched by my second team of lawyers, have been professional and responsible. By sharp contrast, the other processes described above cast BRISOC, the University of Bristol, and the Law School in a very unfavourable light. As the following chapter will demonstrate in detail, BRISOC's complaint, and potentially life-threatening campaign, are nothing but a manifestly vexatious, malicious and toxic mixture of lies, distortion, misrepresentation, and wilful misunderstanding, derived from rumour and hearsay allegedly supplied by anonymous third parties. It has also been propelled by a malicious intention to harm underpinned by a shocking arrogance and lack of acquaintance with the relevant authoritative literature and informed debates. There are good grounds for believing it was motivated primarily by an attempt to discredit my public support for the Prevent counterterrorist programme, just as the official independent review began, and to rescue Professor David Miller from being sacked, just as the controversy in his case peaked. Neither worked.

Though bad enough in itself, this gross injustice has been compounded by smearing, marginalization, exclusion, ostracism, and 'othering' on the part of the University and the Law School. Although I am, of course, grateful not to have been suspended while the official inquiry was conducted, this aside, the University did several things which it should not have, and allowed others to happen which it could and should have prevented or stopped. First, BRISOC's formal complaint should have been rejected in November 2020 because it was manifestly vexatious and ill-founded and suffered from numerous fatal procedural flaws. Given that it was, nevertheless, wrongly admitted, the substance of BRISOC's complaint should, however, have been resolved swiftly, certainly within the specified 90 days. It should not have taken nearly a year between submission and the final decision on appeal. BRISOC's potentially life-threatening social media campaign, launched on 15 February 2021 – which has yet to be removed from their social media platforms in spite of the Assessor's verdict, the appeal, and my retirement – is also patently in breach of the OIA guidelines. Amongst other things, these explicitly require parties to act reasonably and fairly towards each other while a formal complaint is being processed. Providers are also responsible for protecting their staff from unacceptable behaviour.

Protest and disputes about ideas are not only perfectly legitimate in the academy; without them genuine academic inquiry is impossible. But seeking to silence an opponent, ruin their academic reputation, end their career, deprive them of their livelihood, prompt ostracism from their colleagues, and expose them to the risk of personal attack – merely because, as in my case, they summarise and report the relationship between Islam and human rights as discussed in the academic literature – are not.

My official exoneration by the inquiry should also have been an occasion for celebration by the University. Instead, it attempted to suppress news of this fact until it issued a public statement which both acknowledged my vindication while simultaneously undermined it. It also remains unclear why it had not been necessary to modify HRLPS at any point in the previous decade and a half in order to 'be respectful of the sensitivities' of students taking it as the University claimed was required from 2021 onwards.

The Law School has also behaved very discreditably. In the years before BRISOC's campaign, several unwarranted attempts were made to silence me from making lawful contributions to legitimate debates by playing the man not the ball. Fully aware of these, the School sided with my opponents on the Prevent-related 'racism and Islamophobia' twitter storm, the historic wrongs controversy, and the 'child born in an African village' complaint. It also promptly announced BRISOC's complaint-and-campaign in terms which clearly implied there was at least a case to answer. It was spineless with respect to the virtual pub quiz, the HRLPS exam, and the email to colleagues about the BRISOC scandal in February 2021. It then cancelled the Islam, China and the Far East module for precisely the reasons the University's inquiry rejected. In spite of the fact that my doctor regarded my participation as 'eminently sensible,' it also prohibited me from being interviewed by the Bristol Free Speech Society in both December 2021 and February 2022 on the grounds that I had not received approval from Occupational Health, the latter based on a bizarre interpretation of the OH report. Senior Law School management has also yet to do anything about the fact that two societies the School supports – Unity and Diversity and Women in Law – signed BRISOC's petition to have me sacked without having checked the veracity of the accusations upon which it was based, nor about other colleagues who have publicly endorsed the campaign. These, and other issues relating to the toxic environment at the Law School have also been drawn to the attention of the University, OH, HR and the School's senior management. Although taken seriously by OH, there is no sign they have yet been acknowledged by any of the other relevant parties, let alone been effectively resolved.

My appointment, in January 2022, as the first Visiting Research Fellow, and later Research Director, at the Oxford Institute for British Islam proves the falsity of BRISOC's accusations beyond any shadow of doubt. On the surface, this and my formal exoneration, may appear to indicate that the BRISOC controversy is over. But it has merely retreated to the shadows. While BRISOC failed to have me dismissed their complaint-and-campaign effectively removed me from the Law School for the last year of my full-time career, and the Islam, China and the Far East module from the HRLPS syllabus. With a bit of luck both this book and my law suit will bring it to a more satisfactory conclusion. I yearn for this, not least because the significance of what has happened to me far exceeds its personal impact, considerable though this has been. In the next two chapters I consider the bigger and wider issues. Chapter 4 examines the substance of BRISOC's complaint-and-campaign, while Chapter 5 considers its connection with the problems presented by illiberal leftism, of which it is a paradoxical manifestation.

Chapter 4

Allegations

Introduction

Some might regard BRISOC as a bunch of irresponsible students, accused by other Muslims of being 'fundamentalist,'[63] whose attempt to unseat and ruin me has patently failed. Since I've been publicly exonerated, it might also be argued that everyone concerned should regard the whole sorry mess as water under the bridge, forget it, and move on. I strongly disagree. I have, indeed, been resoundingly and unequivocally vindicated by the University's inquiry. But, as the previous chapter explained, both the University and the Law School have undermined it. The University has publicly 'recognised' both BRISOC's 'concerns' and the need to revise the Human Rights in Law, Politics and Society (HRLPS) unit in order to 'be respectful of the sensitivities of students' taking it.[64] For its part, the Law School has scrapped the Islam, China and the Far East module, precisely as BRISOC demanded, and expressly to avoid fresh complaints on the basis of the very accusations the inquiry unequivocally rejected.

However, even without the capitulation and obfuscation by the University and the Law School, there would still be a compelling public interest in a thorough rebuttal of the allegations at the core of BRISOC's complaint-and-campaign, not least because of its considerable educational merit. Indeed, at various points in the controversy, both the Assessor and senior Law School management encouraged me to do so once the inquiry was complete, an objective I intend to realise in this

---

[63] See, eg, email from the Muslim Education Centre of Oxford cited in the previous chapter and A. Alam, 'Controversy over Bristol University Professor Steven Greer's "Islamophobia": Why Critical Discussion of Islamic Tradition Should Not Be Snubbed,' *New Age Islam*, 26 February 2021.
[64] https://www.bristol.ac.uk/news/2021/october/complaint-outcome.html.

book as a whole, and in this chapter in particular. However, some preliminary observations are required before we proceed.

The substantive element in BRISOC's complaint-and-campaign has three distinctive characteristics. First, and of central importance, it is fatally flawed because it fails to distinguish between three things: Islamophobia – the visceral hatred of Muslims and Islam based on myth, prejudice, falsehood, caricature, stereotype, and half-truth; lawful and legitimate critical engagement with Islam, especially regarding its social, political, legal, moral, and economic implications; and innocent factual errors, emphases which could have been improved, or ambiguous points which could have been made clearer.[65] As the University's inquiry confirms, I have never been on the wrong side of the line between the first and second of these positions. Everything I know and have ever said about Islam in any context, derives from authoritative academic sources. Nor did the inquiry find that I had made any errors of fact or judgment. Indeed, in the past, I began my lecture on Islam, China and the Far East by announcing that if, as a non-Muslim, I had misunderstood any of the finer points of the faith, I welcomed being corrected. No one ever did. Nevertheless, as someone who believes we're all on a life-long learning journey, there may be scope for improvement in emphasis or clarification. But this is a long way short of Islamophobia.

The second characteristic of the complaint-and-campaign is that its substantive allegations exhibit each of the various ways in which anybody's statements and/or opinions might be misrepresented. These include outright lies, distortion through tendentious paraphrasing, changing the meaning of statements by taking them out of context, exceeding reasonable inference about supposed underlying attitudes, and reproducing true statements of fact claiming they are false. In fact, the complaint-and-campaign is nothing but a toxic mix of lies, distortion, and misrepresentation. In so far as it refers to written materials – produced by me for teaching or other purposes including publications – these are easily refuted. However, others concern the claims of anonymous putative third parties, including Muslim students who allegedly felt unsafe, othered, marginalized, victimized, intimidated,

---

[65] Alam, 'Controversy over Bristol University Professor.'

traumatized and even driven to suicidal thoughts by the course material and by how I presented it in lectures and seminars. But, since their identity is unknown, there is no way of ascertaining how many there were, who they are, or even if they exist at all. Many, then current and former students on HRLPS also emailed the Assessor strenuously contesting these accusations. And, in sharp contrast to those relied upon by BRISOC, the number and the identities of these sources are known to the inquiry. Some of BRISOC's most egregious allegations – particularly about the Uighurs, that I deny there are such things as racism and Islamophobia, and that there were numerous complaints about my alleged Islamophobia over many years – are demonstrable lies. This alone renders any claim, made in the complaint-and-campaign which cannot be independently verified, more suspect still. Rumours and hearsay of this kind will not, therefore, be considered any further here.

The third feature concerns the staggeringly chaotic, incoherent, 'shambolic and malicious,'[66] throw-enough-mud-at-the-wall-and-some-will stick character of the complaint-and-campaign. The 'mud' comes in many different forms and has been 'thrown' in various ways, including the formal complaint to the University, correspondence with the Assessor, statements to the press, and material presented on various social media platforms.[67] The allegations also grew in number and implausibility as the investigation proceeded. Notwithstanding the doubts about the existence and scope of the duty of confidentiality regarding the University's inquiry expressed in the previous chapter, there is no need to refer directly to any of the information BRISOC provided the investigation. They themselves very helpfully made all the key claims available in their seven-page published document, *Steven Greer: Evidence report*, reproduced in full in Appendix D. This is in seven parts – abstract, lectures, video/audio, articles, blogs, publications, and events. Even a cursory glance reveals that not a single element comes close to

---

[66] Concrete Milkshake, *Islamofauxbia – The Smearing of Steven Greer*, https://concretemilkshake.wordpress.com/2021/02/22/islamofauxbia-the-smearing-of-steven-greer/amp/?__twitter_impression=true.

[67] See Bristol Free Speech Society's interview, *Islamophobia and academic freedom: a conversation with Professor Steven Greer*, available on YouTube at the following link: https://www.youtube.com/watch?v=-6q2o5058jA.

'evidence' of any kind. It is rather a series of statements or arguments attributed to me, and links to websites, without the slightest attempt to make the case that any of it is Islamophobic. Some of the alleged quotes are patent fabrications. Others are garbled misquotations of what I did say. Yet others are true statements derived from the authoritative literature which have apparently prompted the response – 'OMG! How awful is this?! As Muslims we don't like it, therefore, it must be Islamophobic!'

Rescued from this primordial soup, the accusations fall into the following principal categories: the nature of the HRLPS unit and the Islam, China and the Far East module; my critique of the campaign to decolonize the University curriculum; the character of Islam, particularly regarding its history, the Qur'an, the sharia and its relationship with human rights, especially PowerPoint slides 11 and 12 in Lecture 3, 'Key human rights challenges' and 'The Arab Charter on Human Rights 2004,' reproduced in Appendix B; Islamophobia; the Uighur lie; jihadi terrorism; and the Prevent counterterrorist programme.

But before coming to this, let me address BRISOC's complaint about my lack of professional competence to teach anything to do with Islam, including the Islam, China and the Far East module, which, according to them, could only have been competently accomplished by a 'properly qualified' Islamic scholar.[68] Even if this were a valid criticism, not every 'Islamic scholar' is likely to be acceptable to BRISOC. For example, Dr Taj Hargey, Provost of the Oxford Institute for British Islam, to which reference was made in the previous chapter, is a Qur'anic scholar who thoroughly rejects what BRISOC take to be the implications of the faith for relevant debates. However, a further problem with this aspect of the complaint is that it conflicts with BRISOC's other gripe concerning my failure to limit the scope of the unit to law and not to trespass on other disciplines.

If BRISOC had bothered to find out they would have discovered that there is already a substantial literature on Islam by non-Muslims, just as there are substantial literatures on every other faith and ideology by

---

[68] For a refutation of this argument by a Muslim commentator see Alam, 'Controversy over Bristol University Professor.'

observers and commentators who are not themselves personally committed to the beliefs in question. This includes, for example, non-Marxist experts on Marxism and non-Nazi experts on Nazism. Besides, the focus of the Islam, China and the Far East module is much more upon the human rights implications of these ideologies than upon the relevant paradigms themselves. The primary qualification for teaching it is, therefore, expertise in human rights not Islam.

The nature of the HRLPS unit and the Islam, China and the Far East module

BRISOC makes several complaints about the scope and character of both the unit and the Islam, China and the Far East module, each of which is fully described in Chapter 2. But the most pervasive is that, afflicted by 'Eurocentrism,' 'orientalism,' and 'colonialism,' both the unit and the module conflict with the University's stated commitment to 'decolonize the curriculum' considered more fully in the following section.

Scope of the unit and module

As already indicated in Chapter 2, according to BRISOC, since HRLPS is part of the law curriculum, it should not have strayed into philosophy or religion. Yet, the obvious riposte is to be found in its title – Human Rights in Law, *Politics and Society* (italics added), where the term 'Society' embraces everything of relevance, eg, religion, morality, economics, etc, not covered by 'Law' or 'Politics.' As Chapter 2 pointed out, interdisciplinary studies are *de rigueur* these days. With degrees in both law and sociology I'm at least adequately qualified to rise to the challenges presented.

BRISOC also complains that Islam is the only religion 'singled out' for both inclusion in the unit and for criticism. This is simply untrue. Here again, the clue is in the title of the Islam, China and the Far East module, about half of which deals with Asian ideologies and faiths in addition to Islam. Indeed, the map used in the relevant lecture is a *Religious* Map of Asia. Much of the discussion about the geo-politico-ideological space further to the east of 'Muslim lands' concerns the influences of Confucianism, Buddhism, Daoism – as much spiritual traditions as secular philosophies – and the militant hostility of Maoism towards every aspect of traditional Chinese culture.

Christianity did not escape critical scrutiny either. After all, medieval Catholicism provided the ideological justification for feudalism. And it was opposition to feudalism that primed the liberal revolutions from which the modern human rights ideal arose. Nor is there any truth in BRISOC's allegation that the western human rights record is ignored. The first lecture in the HRLPS series reviewed, for example, the leading western intellectual critiques of rights and human rights. Communitarianism argues that individual responsibility to the community should take precedence over individual rights. Postmodernism is hostile towards all 'grand narratives' including 'universal human rights.' In its anti-liberal form feminism claims that the idea of human rights is just another masculinist concept contributing to the maintenance of patriarchy. And the more radical versions of cultural relativism regard the human rights ideal as merely a product of the western experience imposed upon the rest of the world by military, political and economic means. The last bullet point on slide 8 of the first HRLPS lecture, *History of debate about human rights: overview* simply says – 'Post-9/11: underpins entire unit.' In other words, everything that has happened in any part of the world, particularly in the past two decades, is relevant, including problems with western human rights compliance.

Eurocentrism, orientalism and colonialism

According to BRISOC, the course description for HRLPS is underpinned by the 'Eurocentric narrative' that Muslims are oppressed by their own religion and need a 'white saviour' to liberate them, and by problematic 'orientalist' and 'colonial' thought which marginalises minority ethnic peoples and religions and treats them as 'inferior.' These accusations are nothing more than clichéd, ill-founded, and lazy caricatures deriving from an academic discourse which is itself deeply problematic. But, since they connect with some of the issues raised in the following chapter, let me briefly demonstrate their absurdity here.

The unit is not remotely open to this malign interpretation nor are these accusations supported by any evidence.[69] Since my first foray into teaching human rights at the University of Sussex in 1985-86, two units in European Human Rights Law have been amongst the many I've taught. I've also published two books with Cambridge University Press about human rights in Europe.[70] Since the subject matter of these is appropriately focused entirely upon Europe, they are unapologetically 'Eurocentric.' But HRLPS was quite different. As indicated in Chapter 2, its scope extended well beyond law. It was also far from confined to the European geo-political-ideological sphere, as the description in the Unit Guide in Appendix A makes clear. It would, rather, have been 'Eurocentric' to have ignored the wider world, including Islam.

The accusation that the assumptions underpinning HRLPS are, nevertheless, 'orientalist' and 'colonialist' is beyond ridiculous. 'Colonialism' refers to the real-world imperialist conquest and subordination of foreign places, and 'colonialist' to the mentality that goes with it. 'Orientalism' is the view that the 'Orient,' ie north Africa, and everywhere east of Istanbul, is exotic, decadent, sensual, static, slothful and backward, and, therefore, ripe for western imperial intervention offering the allegedly superior attributes of development, dynamism, modernization, industry, secularism, and rationality.

For two reasons the evidence is overwhelmingly against BRISOC's allegation that the unit is either colonialist or Orientalist, let alone both. First, the topics collectively invite critical engagement with the west's understanding of human rights, that of non-western cultures, and with both western and non-western attitudes towards each other's conception of human rights and their respective track records. This is particularly true of five of the original nine topics – 'Origins and conceptual debate,' 'Internationalization and globalization,' 'Islam, China and the Far East,' 'Universalism, relativism and multiculturalism' and 'Poverty and development.' Second, the literature cited throughout the unit, and for

---

[69] See Ch 2.
[70] S. Greer, J. Gerards and R. Slowe, *Human Rights in the Council of Europe and the European Union: Achievements, Trends and Challenges* (Cambridge University Press, 2018); S. Greer, *The European Convention on Human Rights: Achievements, Problems and Prospects* (Cambridge University Press, 2006).

Islam, China and the Far East in particular, includes many contributions from authors whose names suggest non-western origins.[71] I make this observation fully aware that, although others may regard it as an important criterion for inclusion, I do not. For me, the utility of the contribution is what matters most.

Decolonizing the university curriculum

BRISOC also claims that I argue 'against those who advocate for "decolonising the curriculum."' True. But this was in an article in the *Times Higher Education* not in HRLPS.[72] They also maintain that the University's failure to discipline me for my multiple alleged offences of Islamophobia is hypocritically inconsistent with its declared commitment to decolonizing the curriculum. But they fail to explain why. The implication that HRLPS, or the Islam, China and the Far East module,

---

[71] See, eg, A. Saeed, *Human Rights and Islam: An Introduction to Key Debates between Islamic Law and International Human Rights Law* (Elgaronline, 2018); M. A. Baderin, *International Human Rights and Islamic Law* (Oxford University Press, 2nd edn., 2017); A. Ibrahim, 'A Not-So-Radical Approach to Human Rights in Islam' (2016) 96 *Journal of Religion* 346-77; M. Rishmawi, 'The Revised Arab Charter on Human Rights: A Step Forward?' (2005) 5 *Human Rights Law Review* 361-376; L. Jun, 'Human Rights Lawyers' Role in Rights NGOs in China: History and Future' (2018) 41 *Fordham International Law Journal* 1197-1214; Y. Zhengqing, L. Zhiyong, and Z. Xiaofei, 'China and the Remoulding of International Human Rights Norms' (2017) 38 *Social Sciences in China* 25-46; J. Na, 'China as an "International Citizen": Dialogue and Development of Human Rights in China' (2016) 14 *China: An International Journal* 157-77; ; T. Pogge & M. Sengupta, 'Assessing the sustainable development goals from a human rights perspective' (2016) 32 *Journal of International and Comparative Social Policy* 83-97; J. Zhao, 'China and the Uneasy Case for Universal Human Rights' (2015) 37 *Human Rights Quarterly* 29-52; A. Pillay, 'Revisiting the Indian Experience of Economic and Social Rights Adjudication: the Need for a Principled Approach to Judicial Activism and Restraint' (2014) 63 *International and Comparative Law Quarterly* 385-408; P. Chan, 'Human Rights and Democracy with Chinese Characteristics?' (2013) 13 *Human Rights Law Review* 645-89; B. Parekh, *Rethinking Multiculturalism: Cultural Diversity and Political Theory*, 2nd edn. (Macmillan, 2005); T. Modood, *Multiculturalism* (Polity, 2nd edn., 2013); I. al-Shatti, 'The state of democracy and human rights in the Arab ummah (nation)' (2016) 9 *Contemporary Arab Affairs* 523-35; A. Abdelali, 'Wave of change in the Arab world and chances of a transition to democracy' (2013) 6 *Contemporary Arab Affairs* 198-210; A. Bayat, 'The Arab Spring and its Surprises' (2013) 44 *Development and Change* 587-601; N. Hashemi, *Islam, Secularism and Liberal Democracy: Towards a Democratic Theory for Muslim Societies* (Oxford University Press, 2009).

[72] S. Greer, 'What does decolonising the curriculum actually mean?, *Times Higher Education*, 20 July 2020.

require decolonization, is also completely without merit. As Chapter 2 demonstrates, the unit fully acknowledges the role of colonialism and imperialism in achieving the global hegemony of the west, and the complex implications this has for the international status of human rights. And, as already indicated in Chapter 2, HRLPS notes that the core of the Islamic world in the middle east and north Africa is Muslim today as a result of conquest and the consolidation of the great Muslim empires from the 7th to the early 17th centuries, an observation BRISOC also believes is Islamophobic.

The allegation, though clearly risible, nevertheless provides a welcome opportunity for some critical reflection upon the case for 'decolonizing the university curriculum' which has been gathering momentum in the UK and elsewhere, particularly as a result of the Black Lives Matter protests in the spring of 2021. Beginning in South Africa a decade or so ago, the campaign was originally aimed at removing the lingering vestiges of racism and colonialism from what, and how, students are taught. It undoubtedly has resonance and relevance in those parts of the world which have been colonized and decolonized in the literal senses. But this is less obvious with respect to the west where it has, nevertheless, been uncritically embraced by the senior management of British universities including at the University of Bristol.[73] A draft 'inclusive curriculum' document, produced by the University of Sheffield in 2021 and aimed at 'decolonizing' the engineering curriculum, warned, for example, that Sir Isaac Newton may have

---

[73] F. Adebisi, 'Decolonisation Must Disrupt or it is Not Decolonial' (2020) *African Skies*; K. Pimblott, 'Decolonising the University: The Origins and Meaning of a Movement' (2020) 91 *The Political Quarterly* 210-16; F. Adebisi, 'Decolonising the University of Bristol' (2019) *African Skies*; E. Charles, 'Decolonizing the curriculum' (2019) 32 *Insights* 24; F. Nyamnjoh, 'Decolonizing the University in Africa' (2019) *Oxford Research Encyclopaedia* 1-36; M. Zembylas, 'The Entanglement of Decolonial and Posthuman Perspectives: Tensions and Implications for Curriculum and Pedagogy in Higher Education' (2018) 24 *Posthuman Pedagogies* 254–267; G. Dei, 'Decolonizing the University: The Challenges and Possibilities of Inclusive Education' (2016) 11 *Socialist Studies* 23-55; E. Tuck, and K. Wayne Yang, 'Decolonization is not a metaphor' (2012) 1 *Decolonization: Indigeneity, education & society* 1-40.

benefited from 'colonial-era activity.'[74] But didn't everyone in Europe at the time, particularly those who shared his class, status, gender etc, and others besides? According to the document, the purpose of drawing this to the attention of students, is to 'challenge long-standing conscious and unconscious biases' and to tackle 'Eurocentric' and 'white saviour' approaches to science and maths. However, surely the key issue is not Newton's racial identity and possible personal connection with slavery or colonialism, but whether this discredits his, or anyone else's seminal contributions to learning. In Newton's case such a suggestion is, of course, absurd. Gravity causes apples to fall from trees the world over no matter what the cultural or historical milieu of the orchard.

Another example is the recent announcement by University College London that, in order to improve their promotion prospects, members of the academic staff should 'engage' with the university's 'Liberating the Curriculum' initiative and limit the number of 'dead white men' cited in course materials.[75] This is not only in itself racist; but it would, of course, expose to potential exclusion, virtually the entire western intellectual tradition from the middle of the first millennium BCE until the present, including such heroes of many curriculum decolonizers as Marx and Engels who were, by the way, also notorious racists.[76]

Leaving aside the unexplained connection between the false accusation of Islamophobia, of which I was unreservedly exonerated, and the campaign to decolonize the university curriculum, there are four central problems with the latter. First, reflecting a conspicuous lack of serious critical engagement with what exactly 'decolonization' means in this context, the metaphor is wholly inappropriate and misleading. Secondly, the campaign puts the cart before the horse by assuming, rather than demonstrating, that a genuine systemic problem exists and that 'decolonization' is the solution. It also fails to indicate how such a

---

[74] 'Decolonization plan will tell Sheffield students of Isaac Newton's slavery links,' *The Times*, 26 April 2021. See also 'Maths at Durham University to be "decolonised": Guide urges staff to make subject "more inclusive,"' *Daily Mail Online*, 15 April 2022.
[75] 'Ditch white men of past says UCL,' *The Times*, 21 December 2021.
[76] C. Moore, 'Were Marx and Engels White Racists? The Prolet-Aryan Outlook of Marxism' (1974-75) 19 An *Berkeley Journal of Sociology*, 125-156; N. Weyl, *Karl Marx, Racist* (Arlington House, 1979).

programme would and should be implemented and what the detailed subject-specific implications would be. Third, delivering a 'decolonized curriculum' poses considerable challenges for academic freedom.

An inappropriate and misleading metaphor

According to one of the better definitions, the movement's objective is to create 'spaces and resources for a dialogue among all members of the university on how to imagine and envision all cultures and knowledge systems in the curriculum, and with respect to what is being taught and how it frames the world.'[77] While on the surface this seems worthy and uncontroversial, it is not clear in what sense it amounts to 'decolonization.'

Strictly speaking, 'decolonization' can only apply to that which has previously been 'colonized.' It means reversing and/or redressing the illegitimate appropriation and/or settlement of a territory by powerful outsiders. The term 'colonization' is also used by ecologists and others to refer to the process by which animals or plants establish themselves in places where they did not originally arise. But it is far from clear that the curricula of European universities, including in Britain, have ever been 'colonized' in any credible sense. Established in the early middle-ages to serve the interests of an indigenous church, aristocracies and states, they subsequently developed in a liberal, secular, and rational direction. It is difficult to see how any of this could credibly be regarded as any kind of 'colonization.' Of course, modern developments occurred in tandem with European, including British, imperialism, colonialism and the transatlantic slave trade. But it would not be true to say that, as the British acquired an empire covering a quarter of the world, every curriculum in each of the dozen or so universities in Britain and Ireland at the time celebrated, legitimized, downplayed or ignored the imperial project when they should have been doing the opposite. For one thing this would have been irrelevant to many courses of study, for example, maths, engineering, and physics. While it is certainly true that these academic disciplines were dominated by white, mostly privileged, nominally Christian men, it is difficult to see how the subject matter

---

[77] https://library.essex.ac.uk/edi/whatisdecolonisation.

itself was, and is, discredited by colonialism. After all, the fundamental truths of maths and the natural sciences are independent of the personal identities of whoever discovered them or the cultural or historical context in which this occurred. And although some of the hallmarks of the imperial past may persist in British and Irish universities to this day, their impact varies from subject to subject and institution to institution.

There are many other problems with the decolonization metaphor when applied to university curriculums. For a start, 'colonization' is not necessarily synonymous with 'racism' and 'racialization.' Nor is 'decolonization' the same as 'de-racialization.' Colonialism can, for example, occur within the same race. For instance, in the dark ages, the Uí Néil, a clan which shared the same Gaelic race/ethnicity/identity as everyone else in Ireland, conquered much of the north of the island in a vicious imperialist conquest which included 'tribal cleansing.' Similarly, in the middle ages, the Norman English colonized Wales and Ireland – same race but different ethnicities/cultures – long before the British set about colonizing and then decolonizing much of the rest of the planet.

Although often intimately connected with colonialism, racism need not have a colonial dimension at all. For example, the emperors of China regarded all non-Chinese as barbarians, including the 19th century Europeans they had no intention of conquering. Nor does de-racialization necessarily require 'decolonization.' A good example of the confusion which exists between the two agendas concerns the removal of racial bias from the curriculum in medicine by, for example, ensuring that dermatological textbooks include dark skin colours. According to the University of Bristol, this is an exercise in 'decolonization.'[78] But it would be more accurate to refer to it as 'de-racialization.'

Colonization is also an ancient and enduring global, and not just a relatively recent western, phenomenon. For example, some modern European empires, such as the Spanish in Latin America and the British in India, replaced and built upon pre-existing indigenous ones. And, as already noted, the middle east also bears the deep imprint of centuries of Islamic imperialism, overlain by more recent western interventions. In

---

[78] J. Hartland and E. Larkai, 'Decolonising medical education and exploring white fragility,' BJGPO, 25 November 2020.

the past few decades, China – though a victim of western and Japanese imperialism in the 19th and 20th centuries – has itself embarked upon a programme of historically unparalleled global neo-colonial expansion. Nor should we forget that, in 2022, Russia initiated a brutal attempt to revive its imperialist past with the unprovoked and illegitimate attempt to conquer, occupy, and subordinate Ukraine.

Furthermore, the post-Second World War decolonization of former European overseas empires rarely, if ever, inaugurated the kind of emancipation envisaged. Amongst other things, dictatorship, genocide, tribalism, famine, war, multiple human rights abuses, and national asset-stripping by corrupt elites in collusion with global capitalism, almost universally disfigured the process. Decolonization has also, simultaneously, been succeeded in the contemporary world by neo-liberalism, neo-colonialism and other forms of domination of the global south by the north. Multi-party democracy and particularly human rights, have also been denounced by some anti-colonialists as mere artifacts of western civilization, hypocritically foist upon the rest of the world by the military, economic and political hegemony of the west. It has also been argued that the human rights ideal is itself both a product and vehicle of western racist imperialism.[79] The place of human rights in a decolonized world is, therefore, deeply contested.

Third, curricular exclusions and marginalization have been, and are being, caused by processes other than colonization, racism or the legacies of empire – those stemming from gender, sexuality, and disability, for example. A genuinely decolonized curriculum would, therefore, inescapably be a form of, at best, limited inclusivity, precisely the defect of which existing arrangements stand accused. A campaign to increase diversity and inclusivity of all kinds would be much better instead.

Putting the cart before the horse

While racism and the legacies of empire could well be embedded in certain parts of the curricula of British universities, an official commitment to decolonize them also puts the cart before the horse. This

---

[79] C. Samson, *The Colonialism of Human Rights: Ongoing Hypocrisies of Western Liberalism* (Polity, 2020).

is because most, if not all institutions which have embraced this agenda, including the University of Bristol, have typically done so before the nature and dimensions of the alleged problem have been fully described and analysed. This is not only contrary to 'scientific management;' it sends a discouraging message to those members of staff who, like me, have long taught and researched in ways that do not require anything of the sort. Moreover, since the issue is not equally relevant across institutions, disciplines, courses, and modules, the campaign will, therefore, hold little or no interest for most scholars. For others it will be controversial, not least because opinions differ about what it means, why it is required, and how it should be implemented.

Several other potentially significant managerial challenges have not been thought through either. One option would be to set worthy, though vague general standards. Ignoring the difficulties with the metaphor, schools and departments would then be permitted to customize them according to their own requirements. But implementation would be difficult to monitor because senior University management would have to rely upon information supplied by schools, departments and students who may be wedded to one or other side of the debate. It will, therefore, be difficult to find out when, if ever, those parts of the curriculum deemed most in need of it, have been effectively 'decolonized.' The result is, therefore, more likely to be a vacuous exercise in virtue signalling than one which achieves palpable change.

Challenges for academic freedom

Some advocates of a decolonized curriculum have proposed the exclusion/inclusion of lawful texts or approaches to an academic issue according to whether they advance or retard the decolonization agenda. But to do so would be a gross breach of academic freedom and the values of open academic debate, reminiscent of battles over orthodoxy and heresy which scarred earlier phases of European history. A particular challenge concerns 'revisionist' accounts of empire which maintain that, in addition to suffering from modern European imperialism, colonized peoples also benefitted in some ways from it. This has, for example, frequently been the case when an imperial interloper has relied upon a policy of 'divide and rule,' recruiting and rewarding native allies and exploiting their typically long-standing grievances about domination, including by indigenous empires. This was true of the Moors in the Iberian peninsula in the 8th century, the Normans in Ireland in the 12th century, the Spanish in Latin America in the 16th century, and the British in India from the 18th century onwards. A commitment to academic freedom strongly suggests that accounts which include such perspectives should be included on any relevant curriculum, not for uncritical endorsement, but to invite debate about all relevant perspectives. However, some decolonize-the-curriculum activists seek to silence any equivocation about the evils of western imperialism on this ground alone.

The vetting of reading lists to ensure approved quotas from scholars allegedly marginalized by colonialism has also been proposed. Yet this is also fundamentally inconsistent with the most fundamental criterion for inclusion – the value of any given contribution rather than the identity of the contributor. An ideological test applied to reading lists might increase diversity and inclusivity, at least in a certain direction. But it would not, however, be a form of 'decolonization' because those whose inclusion is sought are only in a position to be considered *because of* British colonialism. In other words, had it not been for the British empire, the English language would be spoken only by a small nation on the periphery of Europe. With no more global significance than, for example, Danish or Icelandic, there would, therefore, be no campaign to include academics from other parts of the world writing in English because few, if any, would exist.

It has also been claimed that imperialists have been guilty of the 'crime of epistemicide,' the 'murder' of pre-existing indigenous belief systems. However, the encounter between indigenous and imperial beliefs has been much more complex than this misleading metaphor implies. Few, if any empires have ever sought rigid ideological uniformity not least because it is very difficult to achieve. Some, for example, that of the Mongols in the middle ages, were utterly indifferent to what subject peoples believed. Others, such as the Spanish and Portuguese in the Americas and elsewhere, were much more zealous in their attempt to impose the Catholic faith and to repress other alternatives. By contrast, the British empire exhibited a complex mix combining the assertion of ideological supremacy and the toleration of indigenous beliefs. For example, in the late 18th and early 19th centuries, despite the fact that Christianity was promoted particularly as the 19th century progressed, some high-ranking officials in the East India Company converted to Hinduism or Islam while remaining in post. In many places, complex hybrids between indigenous and imperial belief systems also emerged.

Although the west may have much to learn from the insights of non-western world views, it would be a mistake to regard all cultures as equally valid in every way, as some of the more extreme curriculum decolonizers appear to demand. In most cases, those non-western 'epistemes' which have declined in significance, or have entirely disappeared, have simply been discredited rather than having been 'murdered' or suppressed. Take female genital mutilation for example. Any proper appraisal of the practice will reveal that there are no credible grounds for believing that the failure to mutilate the genitals of young girls will bring disaster to the village, or result in promiscuity in adult life, as the traditional belief systems which practice it typically maintain. A commitment to academic freedom should involve the respectful study of traditional beliefs. But this should not include the attempt to restore to their former uncritically revered status, those that have simply been proven factually wrong.

The combined effect of the movement to decolonize the curriculum, and other illiberal-leftist trends discussed in the following chapter, is increasingly to limit academic debate only to those perspectives with which campaigners agree. Those with which they don't, are targeted for closure no matter how academically credible. This also tends to go hand-in-hand with the denunciation, as 'racist' or 'right wing,' of anyone who has concerns about the curriculum decolonizing campaign. Nor is it encouraging that, on the assumption that they are best placed to demand what should be done, the academic staff of some British universities have set themselves up at School and Departmental level as effectively 'decolonize the curriculum committees' on nobody's authority but their own. The legitimacy, expertise, and judgment of such self-appointed 'experts' is open to question and should certainly not be uncritically accepted by anyone, especially by the senior management of any university, without thorough scrutiny. Finally, the preoccupation with righting the undoubted wrongs of slavery in the past risks diverting attention from slavery in the present which, reliable sources maintain, is at least as substantial in scale as that of the historic transatlantic slave trade.[80]

The character of Islam and its relationship with human rights

BRISOC alleges that the Islam, China and the Far East module in HRLPS includes the following, allegedly Islamophobic, assertions about the character of the Muslim faith:

1. 'Islam spread rapidly through war, conquest, trade and conversion.'
2. 'Islam was a progressive faith insofar as it's open to all.'
3. 'An issue for Islam is the lack of an institution to interpret the faith.'
4. 'This is typical of non-western ideologies – non-narrative, non-systematic, and non-chronological. The style is elusive and elliptical, addressed to people already familiar with its message.'
5. 'Islamic law is uncompromisingly individualistic – big contrast to Western Society.'
6. 'Core normative concept here is obligation, not rights – Islam is fundamentally based on submission and the performance of obligations.'
7. 'Argues that "the source of political authority in Islam is revelation not reason" suggesting Islam is illogical and irrational.'
8. 'Islam is hostile to the modern conception of democracy.'

Leaving aside the question of whether I actually said all of these things in the manner alleged – I didn't – each is, in any case, debated in

---

[80] https://www.antislavery.org/slavery-today/modern-slavery/

the authoritative literature.[81] BRISOC could have made clearer that, in the lecture the statement cited in item 4 expressly referred to the Qur'an. And although 7 and 8 may be controversial, none of these statements is a personal opinion, nor is any 'Islamophobic.' In particular, observing that political authority in Islam has traditionally been based on 'revelation not reason,' certainly does not suggest that the entire Islamic faith is 'illogical and irrational.' This is also true, for example, of Christianity. And as the seminal mid-20th century sociologist Max Weber observes, systems of revealed truth may, nevertheless, employ sophisticated types of reasoning.

BRISOC also attributes to me, the following, allegedly Islamophobic, assertions about Islam and human rights, and about gender equality/inequality in particular:

1. 'Argues "Islam does not recognise human rights at all."
2. 'Argues HR and Islam are very different and thus largely incompatible.'
3. 'Argues that HR & Islam conflict.'
4. 'Pressure for Islam to address human rights caused by external forces of globalisation, westernisation & modernisation.'
5. 'Several other well-documented areas of friction in traditional political Islam with regard to human rights: position of women – divorce, custody of children, inequality in legal testimony (woman's testimony in Sharia court is worth half that of a man), position of

---

[81] For accounts of the early imperialist spread of Islam see, eg, P. Hitti, *History of the Arabs: From the Earliest Times to the Present* (Palgrave MacMillan, revised 10th edn., 2002), pp. 142-6. For a discussion of the structure and content of the Qur'an, including matters of style and presentation see, eg, M. Cook, *The Koran: A Very Short Introduction* (Oxford University Press, 2000). In common with all traditional societies, the key normative concept in traditional Islam was, and remains, 'obligation' rather than 'rights' see, eg, J. Schacht, 'Law and Justice,' in P. Holt, A. Lambton and B. Lewis (eds.), *The Cambridge History of Islam, Vol. 28B, Islamic Society and Civilization* (Cambridge University Press, 1970); X. De Planhol, 'The Geographical Setting' in Holt et al, *Islamic Society and Civilization*, p. 541. For discussions of the complex relationship between Islam and democracy see, eg, N.Hashemi, 'Islam and Democracy' in J. Esposito and E. El-Din Shahin (eds), *The Oxford Handbook of Islam and Politics* (Oxford University Press, 2013); K. Bokhari and F. Senzai, *Political Islam in the Age of Democratization* (Palgrave Macmillan, 2013); F. Volpi and F. Cavatorta (eds), *Democratization in the Muslim World: Changing Patterns of Power and Authority* (Routledge, 2008).

non-Muslims and other minorities in Islamic states – only Muslims are full citizens.'
6. 'Islam was a progressive faith insofar as it's open to all' (also relevant to previous section).
7. 'Argues that Islam promotes gender inequality.'
8. 'Women in Islam are not formally equal to men, all the ideologies benefit men.'
9. 'The Qur'an also permits the physical chastisement by a husband of his wife.'
10. 'Women who wear hijab less likely to work outside home or be involved in higher education.'
11. 'Most difficulties stem from Islamic influence upon it.'

Statements 1-3 and 7 are not direct quotes, and though some may be controversial, none is a personal opinion, nor is any Islamophobic. On the contrary, each is an issue discussed in the authoritative literature. This includes item 11 which, although the oblique quote makes no reference to it, relates to a standard critical observation about the Arab Charter of Human Rights 2004 discussed in Chapter 2.[82] Since item 6 is complimentary about Islam, it is a mystery how it could possibly be regarded as Islamophobic. Item 1 is taken from a PowerPoint slide presented at a panel discussion on 19 January 2010 entitled 'Human Rights and Islam: Muslim and Non-Muslim Perspectives,' hosted by the Muslim inter-faith organisation the Dialogue Society. It is also very misleading. As one of the critics of BRISOC's allegations notes, the presentation in fact distinguishes *three* positions found in the literature. These are that: the human rights ideal is western, un-Islamic, and does not fit a Muslim context at all well; Muslims discovered human rights long before the west and, because it is God-given, this conception is much to be preferred; Islamic and non-Islamic approaches to human rights, though different, are not fundamentally irreconcilable.[83]

A second objection BRISOC has to slide 11 concerns the relationship between Islam and women's rights. As can be seen from Appendix B, the text is highly schematic and requires a great deal of

---

[82] See Appendix B, slide 11; M. Rishmawi, 'The Revised Arab Charter on Human Rights: A Step Forward?' (2005) 5 *Human Rights Law Review* 361-376.
[83] Concrete Milkshake, *The Smearing of Steven Greer*.

further explanation and discussion which should have occurred in the relevant seminar. It simply states: 'Position of women – polygamy, divorce, custody of children on divorce, inequality of legal testimony, physical chastisement by husband, dress (women who wear hijab less likely to work outside home or be involved in higher education).' In my audio- video recorded narration I said that these were among the issues, discussed in the literature, concerning the roles of women in Islam, particularly their status with respect to men.[84]

A few quotations from the Qur'an give a flavour of some of the themes in this debate. 'Allah instructs you concerning your children: for the male, what is equal to the share of two females.'[85] Women's testimony in matters requiring witnesses is formally equal to that of half a man's: '... If the party liable is mentally deficient, or weak, or unable himself to dictate, let his guardian dictate faithfully, and get two witnesses, out of your own men, and if there are not two men, then a man and two women, such as ye choose, for witnesses, so that if one of them errs, the other can remind her....'[86] The subordination of women to men also appears to be required by the following text: 'Men are in charge of women by [right of] what Allah has given one over the other and what they spend [for maintenance] from their wealth. So righteous women are devoutly obedient, guarding in [the husband's] absence what Allah would have them guard. But those [wives] from whom you fear arrogance - [first] advise them; [then if they persist], forsake them in bed; and [finally], strike them. But if they obey you [once more], seek no means against them. Indeed, Allah is ever Exalted and Grand.'[87]

BRISOC has also maintained elsewhere, although strangely not in its *Evidence*, that it is Islamophobic to cite the Charlie Hebdo massacre as

---

[84] See, eg, I. Nicolau, 'Women's Rights in Islam' (2014) 6 *Contemporary Readings in Law and Social Justice* 711-20; K. Syed, 'Misconceptions About Human Rights and Women's Rights in Islam' (2008) 39 *Interchange* 245–257; A. Mayer, 'Cultural Particularism as a Bar to Women's Rights: Reflections on the Middle Eastern Experience' in J. Peters and A. Wolper (eds), *Women's Rights Human Rights: International Feminist Perspectives* (Routledge, 1995); J. Esposito, 'Women's Rights in Islam' (1975) 14 *Islamic Studies*, 99-114.
[85] *Holy Qur'an*, 4:11, https://corpus.quran.com/.
[86] Ibid, 2:282.
[87] Ibid, 4.34.

an illustration of the traditional Islamic death penalty for blasphemy.[88] As indicated in Chapter 3, in the autumn of 2021, even before I knew about BRISOC's formal complaint to the University, the Law School notified me that a student had complained about this. As also indicated, I replied to the effect that better examples might have been the penal codes of contemporary Pakistan and Iran, and the death sentence imposed in 1989 by the Supreme Leader of Iran, Ayatollah Khomeini, upon Muslim British-American, prize-winning author, Sir Salman Rushdie, for alleged blasphemy in his novel *The Satanic Verses*. I chose the Charlie Hebdo example largely because it was likely to be more familiar to students today than the Rushdie controversy which I've used in the past but which happened over 30 years ago.

But even if it may not be the best example, using the Charlie Hedo massacre as an illustration of the potentially fatal consequences of blasphemy in traditional Islam, cannot credibly be regarded as Islamophobic for two reasons. Accusations of blasphemy have long been, and still are, punishable by death in many parts of the Muslim world, including by mobs and free-lancers claiming no authority other than their own interpretation of the faith, exactly what happened in the Charlie Hebdo case. Second, how such conduct may be regarded by the various streams and schools of Islam is also precisely the kind of question a lecture should flag up for further exploration in a seminar, as was my purpose here. I did not intend or expect to provoke a formal, 'refusal-to-engage-in-dialogue' complaint instead.

Islamophobia

BRISOC makes two absurd claims about where I stand on Islamophobia. One is that, a few years ago, I chaired a 'banned Islamophobic talk led by Bristol's free speech society,' an unlikely promoter of 'anti-Muslim hate.' It is true that I chaired the event in question, a discussion about Extremism On Campus, featuring respected counter-extremism researcher Emma Fox. But it hadn't been banned.

---

[88] This was the murder, in January 2015, of a dozen French journalists, and the wounding of 11 others, by two French Muslim brothers in retaliation for the publication of several satirical cartoons about the Prophet Mohammad.

Nor was it Islamophobic. It was, rather, a responsible discussion about the vexed issue of political extremism in British universities. And far from being cancelled, it had merely been postponed on account of safety concerns stemming from BRISOC's threat to disrupt it by mobilizing, what it claimed would be a 200-strong protest against the speaker it accused of spreading 'anti-Muslim hate.' The rescheduled event went ahead against the almost inaudible chants of a handful of protesters.

BRISOC also claims that I deny there are such things as racism and Islamophobia. This is beyond preposterous. If they'd bothered to find out, they could easily have discovered that one of my many publications is a contribution to the University of Bristol Law School blog entitled – 'Know Your Enemy: Racism and Islamophobia.' As one Muslim commentator puts it: 'In the name of fighting *Islamophobia* and discrimination, … (BRISOC) …. basically want to stop any critical discussion of the Islamic tradition, both from within and without.'[89] What we take 'Islamophobia' to be is obviously crucial. Yet, regrettably there is no consensus even about what the term means or about where appropriate lines should be drawn.

A useful, though problematic, point of departure is provided by the *All Party Parliamentary Group on British Muslims Definition of Islamophobia*, published on 27 November 2018, which in their announcement of 16 February 2021, BRISOC cites only to repudiate.[90] The definition states:

> '*Islamophobia is rooted in racism and is a type of racism that targets expressions of Muslimness or perceived Muslimness.*
>
> Contemporary examples of Islamophobia in public life, the media, schools, the workplace, and in encounters between religions and non-religions in the public sphere could, taking into account the overall context, include, but are not limited to: calling for, aiding, instigating or justifying the killing or harming of Muslims in the name of a racist/ fascist ideology, or an extremist view of religion; making mendacious, dehumanizing, demonizing, or stereotypical allegations about Muslims

---

[89] Alam, 'Controversy over Bristol University Professor.'
[90] APPGs are informal, cross-party groups composed of Members of both Houses of Parliament, independent of government, with no official Parliamentary status and no powers granted by Parliament or any of its Committees.

as such, or of Muslims as a collective group, such as, especially but not exclusively, conspiracies about Muslim entryism in politics, government or other societal institutions; the myth of Muslim identity having a unique propensity for terrorism, and claims of a demographic 'threat' posed by Muslims or of a 'Muslim takeover;' accusing Muslims as a group of being responsible for real or imagined wrongdoing committed by a single Muslim person or group of Muslim individuals, or even for acts committed by non-Muslims; accusing Muslims as a group, or Muslim majority states, of inventing or exaggerating Islamophobia, ethnic cleansing or genocide perpetrated against Muslims; accusing Muslim citizens of being more loyal to the 'Ummah' (transnational Muslim community) or to their countries of origin, or to the alleged priorities of Muslims worldwide, than to the interests of their own nations; denying Muslim populations the right to self-determination e.g., by claiming that the existence of an independent Palestine or Kashmir is a terrorist endeavour; applying double standards by requiring of Muslims behaviours that are not expected or demanded of any other groups in society, eg loyalty tests; using the symbols and images associated with classic Islamophobia (e.g. Muhammed being a paedophile, claims of Muslims spreading Islam by the sword or subjugating minority groups under their rule) to characterize Muslims as being 'sex groomers,' inherently violent or incapable of living harmoniously in plural societies; holding Muslims collectively responsible for the actions of any Muslim majority state, whether secular or constitutionally Islamic.'[91]

This definition has, however, been rejected by the government and has been criticised by others on various grounds, particularly concerning problems with the alleged Islamophobia of many of the illustrations. Far from being Islamophobic, it is for example, an incontestable fact that, in its early history, Islam was indeed 'spread by the sword,' and that non-Muslim minorities were subordinate in Islamic states and, in some, this remains the case. Nor is it clear how accusing Muslims as a whole of being responsible for wrongs committed by a single Muslim or a group of Muslims, or holding Muslims collectively responsible for the actions of a given Muslim state, is necessarily Islamophobic, particularly if the activities in question were carried out in the name of the faith. In such circumstances, there may be scope for debate about the credibility of such claims. But it is not Islamophobic to engage in it.

---

[91] https://www.camden.gov.uk/documents/20142/4794543/APPG+Definition+of+ Islamophobia .pdf/f747d5e0-b4e2-5ba6-b4c7-499bd102d5aa.

Perhaps of greatest significance, however, is the assertion that 'Islamophobia is rooted in racism and is a type of racism that targets expressions of Muslimness or perceived Muslimness.' To begin with, it is not at all clear what 'Muslimness or perceived Muslimness' are, as opposed to 'being a Muslim' or 'adhering to Islam.' Although Islamophobia may coincide with racism in certain contexts, this is not always the case. Understanding the differences and similarities between various kinds of social prejudice, including Islamophobia and racism, is important not only for intellectual reasons, but also because a lack of clarity may militate against tackling them effectively.

In the popular sense, 'race'/'ethnicity' involves shared physical characteristics (particularly skin colour and facial features), plus assumptions about kinship and origins more often imagined than real. Standard components of 'racism,' typically based on myth, caricature and stereotype, generally include the belief that races possess distinct and inherent features including social practices, the sense that one's own race is superior to most if not all others, and express or implicit prejudice against people of races apart from one's own. 'Islamophobia' generally refers to irrational antagonism towards Islam and/or Muslims, also typically based on myth, caricature and misleading stereotype. Strictly speaking, a 'phobia' is a clinically observable anxiety disorder defined by recurrent and excessive fear of an object or situation. The term has, however, been extended to include individual and collective hostility towards minorities such as homosexuals (homophobia), foreigners (xenophobia), transexuals (transphobia), and Islam/Muslims (Islamophobia).

Racial and anti-Muslim discrimination can clearly overlap, particularly in England and Wales where over 90% of Muslims are non-white. According to UK law, and international human rights law, where this occurs, one element may constitute a form of indirect discrimination compounding the direct discrimination arising from the other. But religious prejudice is not simply a species of racism. For one thing, it can occur between people of the same race, as for example, it regrettably still does in Northern Ireland in spite of the Belfast/Good Friday Agreement 1998.

Adherents to global proselytizing religions, such as Islam and Christianity, also come from many races. And although it is generally impossible to change one's race or apparent race –take for example what happened to pop idol, Michael Jackson, when he tried – in principle changing religion is simply a matter of no longer believing in or practising it, and possibly converting to another. However, social and cultural pressures may make this a difficult or costly choice. A person's name may also continue to imply a religious identity long abandoned. Acts of racial prejudice are often triggered by visual cues. But religious affiliation is generally less visible without the distinctive names, clothing, or symbols – such as hijabs, crucifixes, or kippahs – which declare, or appear to declare it. Religions also invite reflection and debate, especially about their social, political and legal implications, in ways which race does not. The distinction between legitimate critique and prejudice is not, however, always easy to draw. It would, for example, be Islamophobic to declare that all Muslims are homophobes and are, therefore, stupid and/or wicked. But it is not Islamophobic to disagree with those who object, ostensibly on Islamic grounds, to school children being educated about LGBT+ issues.

What constitutes a 'race' or 'religion,' and how instances of each differ from one another, are not clear-cut either. It is, for example, a mistake to regard 'white'/'non-white' and 'Muslim'/'non-Muslim' as straightforward, mutually exclusive categories. For instance, some of the offspring of a white and non-white parent may look and feel white, while their siblings may look and feel non-white. The only formal test for being a Muslim is to endorse the shahada, the affirmation that there is only one true God and Mohammad is his Prophet. Yet, some Muslims, for example Salafis, regard other Muslims, for example Shia, as apostates or heretics, firmly outside the authentic community of the faithful. This, therefore, raises the paradoxical prospect of Muslims being capable of Islamophobic hate crime against other Muslims, including those of the same race.

And, in England and Wales, where Muslims constitute just under a third of the non-white population, there is plenty of scope for Islamophobia on the part of non-whites who are not Muslim. Each of the prejudices under consideration is also capable of supplanting the other. For example, antagonism towards immigrants in post-2nd World War

Britain initially manifested, and was debated, in racial rather than religious terms. Yet, the Satanic Verses controversy of the late 1980s and the events of 9/11, shifted the focus from colour-based racism against Asians in general and Pakistanis in particular, to hostility against largely the same minorities on religious, ie anti-Muslim grounds.

For these and other reasons it would, therefore, be more accurate to regard racial and religious prejudice as distinct types of social prejudice connected and disconnected in various complex ways. Ignoring this, the Parliamentarians' report misses a golden opportunity to provide the subtle illumination necessary to address the multi-dimensional social challenges Islamophobia and racism present.

The Uighur Lie

BRISOC maintains that I claim that 'if a particular piece of legislation impacts disproportionately against a group, it looks "superficially" like it is discrimination...this is the case with China – Muslims in re-education camps.'[92] Not only is this one of the most outrageous of all BRISOC's lies; it is one of the most dangerous. It also attracted the most hostile comments from those who signed the petition.

The Uighurs are a Muslim minority in Xinjian, a province in western China. Over the past few years, they have endured intolerable systematic repression by the Chinese party-state, including mass imprisonment without trial, forced 're-education,' plus many other human rights abuses. BRISOC alleges that I regard this horrendous experience as merely 'superficially discriminatory.' But they have declined to indicate where I said it. The reason is that I never did. Since this allegation combines a statement I made about counterterrorism in *Britain*, with the exact opposite of what I said in different places about the Uighurs, it is manifestly a deliberate lie rather than an innocent mistake. BRISOC has, therefore, either ignored or forgotten the fact that, in common with all credible ethical traditions, Islam forbids lying and the giving of false testimony in all but the most exceptional circumstances.[93] It certainly does not endorse telling potentially life-threatening lies in order to

---

[92] Appendix D, p. 2.
[93] See, eg, Qur'an 3:61 and 22:30.

bolster an otherwise thread-bare case aimed at harming innocent others. Well into BRISOC's social media campaign, the Uighur lie was quietly and unobtrusively withdrawn without apology or any acknowledgement that it had always, in fact, been a deliberate lie. But all mention of this has since disappeared. Yet, at the time of going to press, the original accusation remained on BRISOC's social media platforms, including the petition.[94]

The truth is as follows. In the HRLPS lecture on terrorism and counterterrorism I considered, amongst other things, the following key counterterrorism and human rights issues: killing by state officials; torture, inhuman or degrading treatment or punishment; asylum and immigration; detention without trial; terrorism-related offences; restrictions on movement, freedom of expression and association; freezing and seizure of assets; the British Prevent counterterrorist programme and the 'securitized Muslim community' thesis.[95] I pointed out that the last of these maintains that counterterrorism in Britain, particularly the Prevent programme, has turned Muslims in Britain into a 'securitized community' under systematic official suspicion. However, I also pointed out that, while this is a deeply flawed, though superficially plausible thesis for the UK, in other places such as China it is much more obviously true.[96]

I have also argued in several publications that, as far as Britain is concerned, the 'securitized Muslim community thesis' suffers from problems at every level including the conceptual, methodological, evidential, analytical, and logical, and that it has deeply problematic implications for public policy.[97] There are three central weaknesses. First, it is crude, binary, and one-dimensional, with the state and non-

---

[94] See Ch 3.
[95] See Appendix E, slides 24-27.
[96] Ibid, slide 26.
[97] See, eg, *Tackling Terrorism in Britain: Threats, Responses, and Challenges Twenty Years After 9/11* (Routledge, 2022) pp. 134-44; S. Greer, 'The myth of the "securitized Muslim community": the social impact of post-9/11 counterterrorist law and policy in the west' in G. Lennon & C. Walker (eds.), *Routledge Handbook of Law and Terrorism* (Routledge, 2015), 400-15; S. Greer, 'Anti-Terrorist Laws and the United Kingdom's "Suspect Muslim Community": A Reply to Pantazis and Pemberton' (2010) 50 *British Journal of Criminology* 1171-1190.

Muslims on one side, the Muslims on the other, and their relationship mediated by the suspicion of the latter by the former. The reality is, of course, much more complex and multidimensional. Second, there is no credible evidence that being a Muslim, in and of itself, systematically attracts the attention of policing and security agencies in the UK. But, with respect to jihadi terrorism it is, unquestionably and unavoidably, a necessary, though not a sufficient criterion. Third, it is very unclear what kind of counterterrorist law and policy directed against Islamist terrorism would not impact disproportionately upon Muslims since only they (albeit a tiny minority of Muslims anywhere) will be involved in it. By the same token, any counterterrorist intelligence-led initiative against right wing terrorism will also impact more upon relevant white, non-Muslim individuals, associations and networks than upon anyone else. Yet no one could credibly claim that this has unfairly 'securitized' the white non-Muslim community, or any part of it. I have also acknowledged that, in spite of the fact that these problems remain unanswered, the 'securitized Muslim community thesis' continues to dominate NGO and social science perspectives. The following two issues – jihadi terrorism and the Prevent counterterrorist programme – are interwoven with this debate.

Jihadi terrorism

BRISOC offers two main objections to my analysis of jihadi terrorism. One is that the 'Terrorism and Counterterrorism' lecture in HRLPS, the PowerPoint slides for which are reproduced in Appendix E, neglects or downplays other forms of terrorism, yet another falsehood. The fifth PowerPoint slide, 'Risks and harms: death and personal injury,' for example, summarizes the tallies for deaths caused by all kinds of terrorism, war, homicide, road traffic accidents, all accidents, and all deaths for, respectively, the US, western Europe and the world. The seventh slide, 'Terrorism in Europe: 1970s-2019,' expressly includes the bullet point, 'Jihadi and far right terrorism: 2001-19.' It is true that more was then said about jihadi than other forms of terrorism. But this was because, over the past two decades, the former caused significantly more casualties worldwide, including in Britain, than any other kind. As I said in the lecture, from 9/11-2019, an annual average of just under 8 people were killed in terrorist incidents in the UK.[98] In fact, more precisely, give or take a few incidents which could plausibly be regarded as either acts of terrorism or hate crimes, from the 7/7 London bombings to 2021, there were 108 fatalities due to terrorism in mainland Britain. The vast majority, 95 per cent, were perpetrated by jihadis, all but one of which, the Glasgow airport bombing of 2007, were in England.[99] Jihadi terrorists also accounted for just short of 100 per cent of the non-fatal casualties. BRISOC also alleges that the following statement is Islamophobic: "No typical jihadi terrorist, however, overwhelmingly young, male & Muslim." But this is simply a statement of fact deriving from official figures.[100]

BRISOC's second main complaint, which others have also made, is that it is Islamophobic to regard jihadi terrorism as 'Islamist.' Yet, this is undeniably one of its inherent characteristics. It is not a hostile Islamophobic attribution but merely reflects the fact that those involved in this kind of terrorism claim to be pursuing the Islamist objective of establishing a world-wide Islamic caliphate governed by a particularly uncompromising interpretation of the sharia. Coupled with many tribal, doctrinal, and other differences, both Islamism (which may or may not be violent) and jihadi terrorism (which is both Islamist and violent) have divided Muslims from each other as much, if not more than, they have united Muslims against everyone else.

There can, however, be no doubt that Islam itself is not the core problem. While the faith celebrates peace, it is not passivist. But it is not unique in that. Like the Bible, the Qur'an contains many verses justifying and extolling violence and warfare. But, since the earliest days, mainstream Islam has sought to regulate both the decision to take up arms, and how armed conflict is conducted, to conditions and limitations not so different from those found in the western 'just war' tradition. While this has produced some consensus with respect to abstract principles, several core issues, particularly what constitutes their

---

[98] See Appendix E, slide 10.
[99] Greer, *Tackling Terrorism in Britain*, Appendix A.
[100] Greer, *Tackling Terrorism in Britain*.

fulfilment, remain unresolved. Other religious and secular perspectives are similar. The relevant canonical texts in each context also require interpretation guided by factors both internal and external to the specific faith or ideology itself.

There are, however, two crucial differences between the Qur'an and the Bible in this respect. First, unlike the Islamic world, the west has undergone the Reformation, the Enlightenment, secularization and modernization. One important result is that the Bible has largely lost whatever official political status it once had. Most Christians now regard it as, at most, a divinely inspired source of insight, rather than a blueprint for public policy dictated, word-for-word, by God Himself. Second, unlike Christianity, the Islamic faith was born in armed self-defence which developed rapidly into territorial expansion and empire-building, initially propelled more by material than by ideological or spiritual motives.[101]

It is not surprising, therefore, that since the founding of their faith, Muslims have struggled with the question of what constitutes 'just' and 'holy' war, often disagreeing violently with each other about how, and against whom, it should be conducted. For them, as for adherents to most other religions and ideologies, the legitimacy of the resort to arms has been difficult to separate from the pursuit of worldly power. Nor has it been easy to find effective ways of ensuring that unnecessary savagery is avoided. But the fact that atrocities, including the deliberate killing of non-combatants, have been committed in the name of Islam – as they have also been in the name of every other faith and ideology the world has ever seen – does not mean they are sanctioned by any credible interpretation of Islam itself.

This is especially true of jihadi terrorism which can only be justified by a particularly warped version of the faith, radically out of step with mainstream and more reflective interpretations. However, because the current global jihadi threat stems principally from a particular post-Caliphate vision, it cannot be effectively addressed, either by state or society, unless this dimension is both acknowledged and tackled head-on by both Muslims and others. And, as already indicated, it should not be

---

[101] Ibid, Ch 2.

forgotten that the core of the Muslim world, the middle east and north Africa, are themselves 'Muslim lands' because of imperial Islamic conquest in the more distant past. Jihadi terrorism, both domestic and global, is, therefore, much less *anti*-imperialist than it is *alt*-imperialist. In other words, it venerates Islamic imperialism in what were, hitherto, non-Muslim lands, while condemning more recent western imperialism in what has since become the core of the Muslim world.

The threat from British domestic jihadi terrorism is, therefore, essentially a local manifestation of a global problem, from which no country in the world is immune, galvanized and focused by certain specific national social, political and religious factors. Although a sense of grievance, injustice and alienation is common to all jihadis, British domestic Islamist terrorism cannot adequately be explained simply in terms of a straightforward reaction by Muslims to material disadvantage, discrimination and/or anti-Muslim prejudice at the national level, real though this may be for some. At most, these experiences have provided the environment for the cultivation of the threat rather than having caused it.

The evidence also indicates that, while some of those attracted to British domestic jihad come from challenging backgrounds – including broken homes, poverty, and encounters with drugs, crime, and imprisonment – others have been well-educated, raised in prosperous, stable, and apparently well-integrated Muslim families with good material prospects. A key factor has often been the friction, experienced by second and subsequent post-migration generations, between, on the one hand, the dominant British culture characterized by liberalism, secularism, and pluralism, and on the other, the expectations and pressures of their family's 'folk Islam.' However, these variables at most provide only part of the explanation for domestic jihad. After all, other disadvantaged minorities in Britain have not responded to whatever injustice and social exclusion they have, or believe they have suffered, by resorting to indiscriminate violence on the streets of their own country.

The Prevent counterterrorist programme

BRISOC alleges that I have made the following claims about the Prevent counterterrorist programme:

1. 'Argues that counter-terrorism is not Islamophobic stating that PREVENT does not "inherently conflict with democracy, human rights" despite data from HR organisations arguing the contrary.'
2. 'Defends PREVENT and agrees Muslims must be targeted in order to be deradicalized.'
3. 'In favour of PREVENT and freedom of speech whilst ignoring the irreversible damaging effects it has upon the Muslim population.'
4. 'Defends PREVENT strategy and dismisses its negative effects rather than rationally addressing the implications of a political strategy that targets Muslims.'
5. 'Argues that "neither the Prevent duty nor the relevant legislation violates human rights nor do they have any of the other negative characteristics alleged by the anti-Prevent movement."'
6. 'Argues that the "UCU boycott is not only illegal, illegitimate and deeply flawed, but also potentially dangerous and irresponsible."[102] For context, the UCU boycott was "to boycott the requirements of the Act and the wider 'Prevent strategy' of which it is a part, on the grounds that they seriously threaten academic freedom, stifle campus activism, require staff to engage in racial profiling, legitimize Islamophobia, and jeopardize safe and supportive learning environments."'

Again, few of these are, or involve, direct quotations. The truth about the Prevent programme, and my analysis of it, is as follows. Prevent is one of the four Ps in the official counterterrorist framework known as CONTEST which has been supported and developed by every British government, Labour, Conservative and Conservative-Liberal Democrat Coalition, since shortly after 9/11. It aims to stop people from becoming or supporting terrorists by countering terrorist ideology and by challenging those who promote it ('counter-radicalization'), supporting

---

[102] The UCU, the University and College Union, is the principal trade union for university and college staff in the UK.

cooperative individuals who are particularly vulnerable to being drawn into terrorism ('de-radicalization'), and working with sectors and institutions where the risk of radicalization in this sense is considered high.[103] *Protect* is intended to reduce vulnerability primarily as far as national border security, transport systems, national infrastructure, crowded places both public and private, and British interests overseas are concerned. The distinctive contribution of *Prepare* is to mitigate the impact of terrorist attacks by bringing them to an end as swiftly and effectively as possible and by increasing capacity to recover in the aftermath ('resilience'). The purpose of *Pursue* is to detect, disrupt, prosecute, punish, and/or to control those who engage in terrorism both at home and abroad. The same generic challenges also arise with respect to each of the four Ps: risk assessment; effective and efficient bureaucratization, management, and use of resources; compliance with legality, constitutionality, and rights; accountability and review; and sensitivity to actual and perceived impact upon different sectors of society.

I do indeed defend the Prevent counterterrorist programme and I have also argued that it is not systematically discriminatory, racist, Islamophobic, or anti-democratic, nor does it systematically violate other human rights. Contrary to the claim in statement 2 above, I also maintain that anyone, and not just Muslims, should be targeted by Prevent if evidence-based concerns arise that they may be vulnerable to recruitment into terrorism.

As indicated in Chapter 3, in common with others, BRISOC maintains that to deny the Prevent counterterrorist programme is racist and Islamophobic is itself racist and Islamophobic. Such an absurd claim is no more credible than the obverse – denouncing those who oppose Prevent as terrorists or terrorist sympathizers. But, strangely, nobody including BRISOC, claims that any of the other three Ps is racist and Islamophobic. This suggests one of two equally implausible possibilities. Either, alone among the four Ps, Prevent suffers from racism and Islamophobia. Or, all or some of the other Ps are also afflicted by these

---

[103] HM Government, *Prevent* Strategy, Cm 8092, June 2011.

problems, but for some unknown reason this has not led to anything like the same condemnation.

For several reasons, the claim that the Prevent programme is racist and Islamophobic rests on very shaky ground. First, it is not clear how it can be inherently Islamophobic and racist, when it is based on a model pioneered against Islamists in Saudi Arabia and subsequently adopted and customized by many other, including predominantly non-white, Muslim countries, such as Australia, Denmark, Germany, India, Indonesia, Libya, Malaysia, the Maldives, Pakistan, the Philippines, Sri Lanka, Tajikistan, Uzbekistan and Yemen.[104] It is also difficult to credit the claim that the 'Muslim community' objects to its allegedly anti-Muslim character when, in fact, scientific polling shows that very few people, including Muslims, have even heard of it. And, when it is explained to them, the overwhelming majority, including of Muslims, immediately appreciate the justifications.[105]

Seeking to prevent jihadi and other forms of terrorism in Britain and elsewhere will and must inevitably involve both the 'securitization' of the population as a whole, and also the focusing of additional security attention upon, respectively, those predominantly non-white Muslim, and those non-Muslim white, networks, associations and communities, from which, according to reliable intelligence, different types of terrorism derive. But, providing this complies with an appropriate regulatory framework, and in particular is proportionate to risk, it will fall far short of systematically securitizing, criminalizing, stigmatizing, or victimizing the 'national communities' concerned.

Furthermore, a Prevent referral has nothing like the sinister implications BRISOC and its other more strident critics allege. The core objective is at least as much about protecting those referred to it from the risks they pose to themselves, as it is to protect others. Because the entire programme operates outside the criminal justice process it cannot

---

[104] C. Baker-Beall, C. Heath-Kelly and L. Jarvis (eds.), *Counter-Radicalization: Critical Perspectives* (Routledge, 2015), Chs 4, 5 & 13; R. Gunaratna, J. Jerard and L. Rubin (eds.), *Terrorist Rehabilitation and Counter-Radicalization: New approaches to counter-terrorism* (Routledge, 2011).

[105] J. Clements, M. Roberts and D. Foreman, *Listening to British Muslims: policing, extremism and Prevent* (Crest Advisory, 2020), p. 11.

'criminalize' anybody. And since any given subject's involvement is confidential, it is difficult to see how it can 'stigmatize' or 'victimize' anyone either, let alone entire communities, much less national ones. Most referrals go no further and only a tiny minority are forwarded to de-radicalization initiatives. Participation in whatever intervention is offered is voluntary and there are no formal sanctions for refusing to cooperate. A Prevent referral is, therefore, no more objectionable than a complaint to the police about a noisy late-night party, and less objectionable than being officially invited to attend road traffic safety training as an alternative to the addition of three points on a driving licence. The use of Prevent to spy and gather intelligence is formally prohibited and is also constrained by data protection laws which limit official information-sharing. The claim by some that these are, nevertheless, systemic features of the strategy has yet to be supported by any evidence.

It is also impossible to square BRISOC's perspective with the fact that the Prevent programme is also now being deployed more against white, non-Muslim, right-wing, and other forms of extremism, than against their Islamist counterparts. For example, in 2019/20, the last year before the figures were distorted by the Covid pandemic, only 24% of referrals concerned radical Islam, while 22% were for those relating to right-wing extremism. The remaining 51 per cent were for individuals with a 'mixed, unstable or unclear ideology,' of which, following initial assessment, no concerns persisted for almost half (47 per cent).[106] This continues to be the case as the more serious effects of the pandemic decline.[107]

I also stand by what I said about the UCU boycott of Prevent. In fact, the absurdity of the union's position is illustrated by the fact that the Bristol branch both supports it while simultaneously sitting on the committee which seeks to ensure the University of Bristol complies with the Prevent duty.

---

[106] Home Office Official Statistics, *Individuals referred to and supported through the Prevent Programme, April 2019 to March 2020 (England and Wales)*, 26 November 2020, Appendix A, Table 6.
[107] Home Office Official Statistics, *Individuals referred to and supported through the Prevent Programme, England and Wales, April 2020 to March 2021*.

In any case, there is next to no prospect of Prevent being scrapped or replaced by anything significantly different in the foreseeable future. No UK-wide party, likely to form or participate in government, is committed to such an objective. It is also particularly unlikely that the Conservatives will renounce it. Some on the Labour left are sympathetic to the campaign against Prevent. But the party's, now obsolete, manifesto for the 2019 general election merely called for an official independent review, since granted, rather than abolition. Any genuinely independent examination is likely to recommend improvements in accountability, transparency and legal clarity, and possibly various ways in which the programme might be strengthened. Finally, in his first speech as leader to the party's Covid-restricted virtual conference in September 2020, former Director of Public Prosecutions Sir Keir Starmer, signalled a major attempt to rebut the perception that Labour is soft on threats to national security, an adjustment difficult to reconcile with all but a modest reform of the Prevent strategy.

Conclusion

The relationship between Islam and human rights is controversial. Broadly speaking, three positions can be distinguished: the human rights ideal is western, un-Islamic, and does not fit a Muslim context at all well; Muslims discovered human rights long before the west and, because they are God-given, this conception is much to be preferred; Islamic and non-Islamic approaches to human rights, though different, are not fundamentally irreconcilable. The primary purpose of the relevant part of the Islam, China and the Far East module in HRLPS was merely to explore these perspectives and their implications. Nothing about this exercise, the discussion of jihadi terrorism or the Prevent counterterrorist programme, is remotely Islamophobic. On the contrary, such an inquiry is integral to any credible academic exploration, conceived and delivered as a sustained critical engagement with global current affairs through a human rights lens, or vice versa – the underlying rationale of the HRLPS unit. It would have been myopic and Eurocentric to have ignored it. The allegations that I deny there is such a thing as Islamophobia, and that I claim the persecution of the Uighurs by the Chinese party-state is merely superficially discriminatory, are simply demonstrable lies.

Prejudiced hostility towards Islam, or any faith or ideology, can and must be distinguished from responsible critical engagement with it. Islamophobia, like racism, misogyny, transphobia, xenophobia, antisemitism and many other social prejudices should be confronted and stamped out wherever encountered, including in universities. But, in a free society, critical scrutiny of all faiths and ideologies should be central to the mission of universities, especially in those parts of the curriculum where beliefs, ideas, and relevant legal, political and social issues arise. This should be characterized by reasoned debate, a measured and responsible tone, and content derived from authoritative sources, supported by reliance upon verifiable evidence distinguishing carefully between uncontested fact and competing interpretations; precisely what occurred in HRLPS before the Islam, China and Far East topic was taken off the syllabus. However, the fatal flaws in BRISOC's complaint-and-campaign do not end there. They are, in fact, particular manifestations of a deeper and more troubling malaise afflicting universities throughout the English-speaking world and beyond, considered more fully in the following chapter.

Chapter 5

Implications

Introduction

As already indicated, one of my objectives in writing this book is to document what happened to me in February 2021, and thereafter, in order to set the record straight. This chapter, however, pursues two of my other principal goals – to consider what light the bigger picture might shed upon this bitter experience and vice versa. The simple and undeniable fact is that my misfortune, and the issues it raises, are far from unique in universities throughout the English-speaking world and beyond. These venerable institutions are under assault from a rising tide of 'illiberal leftism' in unholy alliance with corporatized 21st century higher education,[108] characterised, amongst other things, by:

> 'the growing dominance of particular ideological perspectives on campus which, it is argued, are leading to a 'monoculture' that is hostile to alternative views, voices and beliefs; evidence that university academics and students who do not share these perspectives are experiencing a hostile environment on campus and, as a result, are 'self-censoring' their views; a growing tendency to prioritise student satisfaction over academic freedom; and, closely related, to prioritise

---

[108] See eg, L. Gutkin, 'What's the State of Free Expression on Campus,' *Chronical of Higher Education*, 27 January 2022; Chronicle of Higher Education, *Academic Freedom Now: Why Colleges Should Be Worried* (Chronicle of Higher Education Publications, 2021); Scholars at Risk Network, *Free to Think 2021* (SAR Network, 2021); A. Dershowitz, *Case Against the New Censorship: Protecting Free Speech from Big Tech, Progressives, and Universities* (Hot Books, 2021); A. Applebaum, 'The new puritans,' *The Atlantic*, 31 August 2021; E. Chemerinsky and H. Gillman, *Free Speech on Campus* (Yale University Press, 2017); J. Ronson, *So You've Been Publicly Shamed* (Macmillan, 2015); G. Lukianoff, *Unlearning Liberty: Campus Censorship and the End of American Debate* (Encounter Books, 2014); G. Lukianoff, *Freedom From Speech* (Encounter Books, 2014); N. Cohen, *You Can't Read This Book: Censorship in an Age of Freedom* (Fourth Estate, 2012).

the emotional or psychological safety of students over the pursuit of truth, reason and objective enquiry, which necessitate exposure to uncomfortable, challenging and/or controversial ideas.'[109]

This trend is also fuelling a backlash, particularly in the US, where those on the far right of the political spectrum have long been eager to ban or limit discussion of the issues to which all progressives, and not just illiberal leftists, are committed.[110] The current crisis in British higher education raises a key question considered in this chapter and the next: how should the deepening tension between academic freedom and the demands of militant minorities be managed? We begin here with the core issue – academic freedom – followed by a review of the challenge presented to it by the illiberal left, before presenting a critique of this ideology and considering responses to it.

Academic freedom

The strongest, most coherent and most convincing defence of academic freedom derives from classical liberalism – a commitment to liberty, equality, and fraternity as expressed by democracy, human rights, the rule of law, cosmopolitanism, and open, effectively regulated markets. At its core lies the right to freedom of expression.

Freedom of expression

Long the subject of discussion amongst jurists, philosophers and others, freedom of expression has, in particular, been extolled as vital to a free society by such diverse luminaries as Milton, Locke, Voltaire, Mill, and Orwell. The case rests on several powerful arguments.[111] First, as social creatures with language and many other forms of self-realization including art, music, dance and religious ritual, the freedom to express ourselves is vital for our communication, our relationships with each other, our individual wellbeing, and our collective and individual

---

[109] M. Goodwin, *Is Academic Freedom Under Threat?* (Legatum Institute, 2022), p. 1.
[110] P. Basken, 'How can US universities combat threat of teaching restrictions?,' *Times Higher Education*, 23 February 2022.
[111] See, eg, K. Whittington, *Speak Freely: Why Universities Must Defend Free Speech* (Princeton University Press, 2019), Chs 2-3; Chemerinsky and Gillman, *Free Speech on Campus*, Ch. 2; Lukianoff, *Unlearning Liberty*, pp. 18-35.

identity and self-governance. Second, the exchange of ideas, the discussion of the methods and evidence upon which they are based, and the giving of cogent reasons for conclusions reached, enables us better to understand ourselves, each other, and our place in the natural and human spheres. But none of this can be fully achieved unless marginal, unfashionable, and unpopular views are included. As George Orwell once famously observed – free speech is pointless if it doesn't permit telling people what they don't want to hear, especially it might be added, if they need to hear it. Third, free and frank debate is indispensable if, as a species, we are to have any hope of tackling effectively the problems facing us and life on the planet. Fourth, without adequately protected free expression, other basic freedoms become much less secure because their violation will be more difficult to expose and, therefore, to correct.

All credible contributions to debates about freedom of expression recognise, however, that it is not absolute and that it can, and must, be subject to limits. Philosophers and others have speculated about where relevant lines should be drawn. But the most consequential, real-world distinctions are provided by law. While some have argued for minimum legal restriction, including upon hate speech,[112] this is not the position in the UK. Since 2000 when the Human Rights Act 1998 (HRA) came into force, the gold standard has been the European Convention on Human Rights (ECHR). This is likely to remain central to British law whatever becomes of attempts, such as the recently shelved Bill of Rights Bill, to reform the HRA.

According to a summary provided by the Ministry of Justice, the principal objective of the draft legislation was to 'overhaul the Human Rights Act and replace it with a Bill of Rights' in order to 'reinforce our tradition of liberty whilst curtailing the abuses of human rights, restoring some common sense to our justice system, and ensuring that our human rights framework meets the needs of the society it serves.'[113] Since

---

[112] N. Strossen, *Hate: Why We Should Resist It with Free Speech, Not Censorship* (Oxford University Press, 2018); J. Rauch, *Kindly Inquisitors: The New Attacks on Free Thought* (University of Chicago Press, 2nd ed, 2013).
[113] https://www.gov.uk / government / publications/bill-of-rights-bill-documents#:~:text= Strengthens%20domestic%20institutions%20and%20the,Increases%20democratic%20oversight.

Brexit made no difference to the UK's membership of the Council of Europe, the substantive content of the ECHR – the Council of Europe's principal achievement – has remained the backbone of UK human rights law. The core goals of the bill included eleven items: recognising the right to jury trial; limiting the power of the courts with respect to certain rights; reducing burdens on public authorities; ensuring that public protection is given due regard in how rights are interpreted; limiting the territorial application of human rights law; implementing a permission stage to human rights litigation to eliminate less serious cases; recognising that responsibilities exist alongside rights; strengthening domestic institutions and the primacy of UK law especially affirming the UK Supreme Court as the final judicial arbiter of the scope of human rights; increasing democratic oversight of human rights law; and enhancing Parliament's role in responding to adverse Strasbourg rulings. Much of this is controversial and hotly contested. But, at the top of the list, and of particular significance for the issues discussed in this book, was the eleventh item: 'Strengthens the right to freedom of speech. We are attaching greater weight to freedom of speech, defined as the exchange of ideas, opinions, information and facts, as a matter of utmost public interest, and widening the responsibility for attaching this greater weight to all public authorities.' However, on 27 June 2023 the Justice Secretary announced that the government had decided not to proceed with the British Bill of Rights Bill. Nevertheless, rather than being scrapped, some of its provisions are likely to be revised for incorporation in several separate pieces of legislation including a bill to enhance protection for free speech..

In the meantime, and in all probability thereafter, Article 10 ECHR, will remain at the heart of UK human rights law. It provides:

1. Everyone has the right to freedom of expression. This right shall include freedom to hold opinions and to receive and impart information and ideas without interference by public authority and regardless of frontiers. This Article shall not prevent States from requiring the licensing of broadcasting, television or cinema enterprises.
2. The exercise of these freedoms, since it carries with it duties and responsibilities, may be subject to such formalities, conditions,

restrictions or penalties as are prescribed by law and are necessary in a democratic society, in the interests of national security, territorial integrity or public safety, for the prevention of disorder or crime, for the protection of health or morals, for the protection of the reputation or rights of others, for preventing the disclosure of information received in confidence, or for maintaining the authority and impartiality of the judiciary.

The European Court of Human Rights (ECtHR) has affirmed that the right to freedom of expression is vital for the kind of ideas, views, opinions and outlooks – including those that 'offend, shock and disturb' – upon which a pluralistic, tolerant, broadminded, progressive and democratic society depends.[114] And as UK judge, Lord Justice Sedley, observed in *Redmond-Bate v Director of Public Prosecutions*: 'Free speech includes not only the inoffensive but the irritating, the contentious, the eccentric, the heretical, the unwelcome and the provocative ... Freedom only to speak inoffensively is not worth having.'[115] Under the ECHR states have both the negative obligation not to violate Article 10 themselves, and the positive duty to ensure that its exercise is adequately protected between private parties. The majority of complaints in Strasbourg about breaches of this provision concern liability for alleged defamation, where fine balances typically have to be struck between the right itself and the protection of reputations.

Article 10 ECHR raises two core questions: What kinds of expression are included, and what types of restriction may legitimately be imposed under what circumstances?[116] 'Expression,' for the purpose of this provision, includes the spoken and written word, drama, art, graphics, dress, nudity, symbols and symbolic acts conveying opinions and ideas of a political, social, cultural/artistic or commercial kind, through, for example, publications, meetings, broadcasting, theatre, cinema, the Internet and advertising.

Certain forms of expression are, however, inherently beyond the scope of this provision. These embrace: those hostile towards core

---

[114] European Court of Human Rights, *Handyside v United Kingdom* (1976) 1 EHRR 737.
[115] (1999) 7 BHRC 375 at para 20.
[116] For a summary of the extensive jurisprudence see, eg, S. Greer, J. Gerards and R. Slowe, *Human Rights in the Council of Europe and the European Union: Achievements, Trends and Challenges* (Cambridge University Press, 2018), Ch 3.

Convention values, an invocation of Article 17 ECHR, which denies the protection of the Convention to anyone engaged in the destruction of any of its rights or their more extensive limitation than the ECHR itself permits; those seeking to deny, belittle or defend the Holocaust, and possibly in certain circumstances, other clearly established crimes against humanity; or, providing any formalities, conditions, restrictions or penalties imposed are proportionate, those that incite violence or hatred. Content, form, tone, context and consequences – including the applicant's status, the addressees, any relevant legitimate public interest and the likely public impact – will often be critical in determining whether any particular expression is permitted or not.

The ECtHR has generally sought to identify and to specify the 'duties and responsibilities' referred to in Article 10(2) according to the characteristics of the applicant. So, for example, journalists, NGOs and campaigning organizations have an obligation to act with due diligence in seeking to provide verifiably accurate and reliable information and grounded opinion in good faith, and according to their professional ethics. Judges and lawyers should maintain the authority and impartiality of the legal process by expressing *ex curia* opinions with discretion. Civil servants should refrain from joining extreme political parties and from expressing views that might compromise their neutrality. On the other hand, while politicians have considerable latitude with respect to the opinions they express, in doing so they should show appropriate respect for the democratic process. Employees should also avoid personal attacks when publicly criticizing colleagues or their employers, an issue highly pertinent to this book.

The Article 10(2) limitations, 'legitimate purposes,' are to be construed narrowly and are subject to the principle of proportionality and to a variable wriggle room, or 'margin of appreciation,' available to states. However, they are not always easy to distinguish from each other, and the Court does not always indicate clearly which one or more has been applied. For example, in cases involving terrorism, criminalizing the expression of certain views may be permitted in the interests of national security, public safety and/or the prevention of disorder or crime. In cases where an interference is admitted but justification pleaded, the severity of the official sanction will often be the deciding factor in determining whether or not there has been a violation. The ECtHR is, however, generally unsympathetic to blanket bans and is typically most concerned about the proportionality of restrictions and sanctions, and with the provision of adequate procedural safeguards against arbitrariness.

The 'protection of morals' is arguably the most controversial of the Article 10(2) limitations, largely because morality is so nebulous, variable over time and space, and there may be little or no European consensus on detailed content or upon what is necessary and legitimate to protect it. Although the Court has repeatedly affirmed that the right to freedom of expression encompasses views and representations that 'offend, shock and disturb,' it has, nevertheless, invoked both the 'protection of morals' and the 'rights of others' to endorse restrictions upon forms of expression precisely on this basis. The legitimate limits of the right to express critical, satirical or 'obscene' views about a given religion have also proven difficult to specify with precision. However, notwithstanding generous margins of appreciation, a shift can be detected in the development of the 'gratuitous insult/abusive attack' test in the case law, from concern for the sensitivities of religious believers, to more scope for the right to criticise and satirise religious faith. Determining whether or not this criterion has been satisfied can, however, be highly controversial.

The 'rights of others' also provide the axis around which conflicts revolve between the media's freedom of expression and the right to respect for the private and family life of celebrities, public figures and others in the media spotlight. Here, as in other areas, proportionality and context, including the extent to which the information is already in the public domain, are of particular importance. The scope of the right to respect for private life tends to be limited by freedom of expression according to how justifiable the alleged intrusion is. Examples include the disclosure of discreditable private conduct inconsistent with a positive public image or the honourable discharge of an important public responsibility. As far as advertising is concerned, in order to prevent unfair competition and to secure a level playing field, wide margins of appreciation have also been applied to the 'protection of the reputation or rights of others.' This is especially the case with respect to the circulation of ideological viewpoints in the broadcast media, particularly during election campaigns.

The case for academic freedom

Broadly speaking, academic freedom concerns the implications, in the academic context, of the general right to freedom of expression.[117] But before coming to that we first need to consider what universities are for and, in particular the relationship between their mission and the distinctive quest for 'social justice' which ostensibly underpins the current threat to academic freedom posed by the illiberal left.

The formal mission of the contemporary western university is fundamentally concerned with the preservation, development, refinement, pursuit, and restless correction of knowledge, insight and understanding. This has substantive, methodological and normative dimensions. It is 'substantive' insofar as it is organized around certain fields and sub-fields open to reorganization as scholarship develops. It also embodies a distinctive method of inquiry characterized by robust subject-independent generic tests – moulded according to given disciplines – regarding the comprehensive collection of relevant evidence including that which may confound preconceived hypotheses. This includes subjecting data to painstaking impartial analysis, and to expressing conclusions in carefully reasoned, cautious and measured terms which go no further than that which the evidence supports.

The mission of the contemporary western university is 'normative' insofar as it also embodies a cluster of other values characteristic of a liberal, cosmopolitan, and progressive democratic society. These include deliverable commitments to diversity and inclusivity in two key senses. One involves tackling effectively the under-representation of many kinds

---

[117] Whittington, *Speak Freely*; Chemerinsky and Gillman, *Free Speech on Campus*, Ch 3; J. Rauch, *The Constitution of Knowledge: A Defense of Truth* (Brookings Institution Press, 2021); J. Lackey (ed.), *Academic freedom* (Oxford University Press, 2018). See also the 2020 report by the UN Special Rapporteur on freedom of expression, www.ohchr.org/EN/Issues/FreedomOpinion/Pages/AcademicFreedom.aspx, and Art 13 of the EU's Charter of Fundamental Rights: 'The arts and scientific research shall be free of constraint. Academic freedom shall be respected.'

of excluded or marginalized groups among staff and students. The other entails a commitment to academic freedom which ensures that lawful contributions to legitimate academic debates are not excluded particularly by campaigns of intimidation, vilification, victimization, harassment, suppression, censorship, unwarranted reprimand, compelled apology, dismissal, or worse.[118] Indeed in several states, including Austria, Estonia, Finland, Germany, Spain and Sweden, academic freedom is expressly constitutionally protected.[119] Since there can be no genuine diversity or inclusivity if lawful contributions to legitimate academic debate are censored on ideological grounds, discovering and debating what 'social justice' is, and what its implications might be, are, therefore, integral to the mission of the contemporary university, with higher profiles in certain disciplines than in others. Realizing this objective must also be subject to the overriding goal of the western university – the pursuit of knowledge in the widest sense – not the other way around.

Like the right to freedom of expression generally, the right to academic freedom is not unlimited nor has there ever 'been a golden age of unfettered free speech on campus.'[120] Spats, fall-outs, and intellectual or personal feuds have long been commonplace amongst scholars. And, because critiques of ideas are also themselves exercises of the right to freedom of expression, they are also integral to the rough and tumble of academic life. A particularly notorious public academic insult was, for example, that of Arthur Schopenhauer, a 19th century German philosopher, who once described Hegel, another then contemporary German philosopher, as a 'flat-headed, insipid, nauseating, illiterate charlatan, who reached the pinnacle of audacity in scribbling together

---

[118] See, eg Whittington, *Speak Freely*, Ch. 1; The American Association of University Professors, *Declaration of Principles on Academic Freedom and Academic Tenure* 2015; B. Campbell and J. Manning, *The Rise of Victimhood Culture: Microaggressions, Safe Spaces, and the New Culture Wars* (Palgrave MacMillan, 2018), pp. 216-43; Lukianoff, *Unlearning Liberty*, pp. 67-70.
[119] T. Slater (ed), *Unsafe Space: The Crisis of Free Speech on Campus* (Palgrave Macmillan, 2016), p. 119.
[120] J. Williams, *How Woke Won: The Elitist Movement that Threatens Democracy, Tolerance and Reason* (Spiked, 2022), p. 99.

and dishing up the craziest mystifying nonsense.' [121] But a disrespectful put-down is one thing. It is quite another to seek to silence an intellectual opponent by having them shunned, disciplined or sacked on trumped up charges alleging discreditable views such as racism, sexism or Islamophobia, which they haven't expressed and don't in fact hold.

In the final analysis, the scope of academic freedom in the UK should closely follow the contours of freedom of expression generally. In other words, since it carries with it 'duties and responsibilities,' it may be subject to 'such formalities, conditions, restrictions or penalties as are prescribed by law and are necessary in a democratic society' for the range of interests found in the second paragraph of Article 10 ECHR. Like freedom of expression generally, content, form, tone, context, and likely consequences should also be critical in determining whether or not any given exercise can be allowed. If not, whatever sanction is applied should be proportionate. But there is, of course, a grey area between what is permissible and impermissible in academic, as in non-academic contexts. The views of reasonable people may also differ as to where appropriate lines should be drawn. However, the presumption, though capable of being rebutted, should always favour free expression with the burden of proof lying upon those seeking to restrict it.

Writing in the US context, Chemerinski and Gillman – respectively Dean of the University of California Berkeley School of Law and Chancellor of the University of California, Irvine – helpfully identify more precisely what universities can and cannot lawfully or legitimately do with respect to academic freedom.[122] Although the American and UK legal contexts are not identical – the main difference being that the First Amendment to the US Constitution permits hate speech which in the UK would be unlawful – the relevant principles are, otherwise, the same.

Universities cannot lawfully censor or punish speech merely because someone finds it offensive. Nor can they be expected to comment upon, or to condemn, every exercise of expression on campus merely because somebody might object to it. But they can punish unlawful speech,

---

[121] A. Schopenhauer, *On the Fourfold Root of the Principle of Sufficient Reason* (Open Court, 1974), p. 1.
[122] Chemerinski and Gillman, *Free Speech On Campus*, Ch 5.

including that presented on the internet and/or social media, if, for example, it causes or threatens harm, including psychological harm beyond mere hurt feelings. Universities cannot discriminate against their academic staff or students on a content-basis regarding anything they may lawfully say in a non-professional context. But they can, if necessary, censure them if it falls below acceptable professional standards or peer assessments regarding the quality of scholarship or teaching.

Content-based restrictions on lawful expression cannot be imposed in university accommodation. But limits on lawful speech may be justified in order to ensure a supportive living environment there. Protestors cannot lawfully be deprived of the opportunity to express their views effectively on campus. But time, place, and manner restrictions may be imposed to prevent disruption to normal educational and administrative activities. Universities cannot censor or punish speakers, on a content basis, for leafleting or posting lawful opinion. But, in the interests of good governance and the maintenance of a level playing field, they can issue and enforce relevant content-neutral regulations. Although members of the academic staff are at liberty to provide 'trigger warnings' in advance of the presentation of course materials, these cannot lawfully be required.

Universities can offer physical and virtual 'safe spaces,' including by supporting the efforts of students to self-organize in ways that reflect shared interests and experiences. But they cannot lawfully use the safe space concept to censor the lawful expression of ideas or points of view merely because some students might find them offensive. Students and academic staff cannot lawfully be prevented from using words considered by some to constitute 'microaggressions,' not least because these are inherently subjective and ill-defined. But, in an attempt to create a respectful working environment, universities may seek to make students and staff aware of the potential impact certain words could have in some contexts. As a condition for recognition, universities may require student organizations to be open to all students. They can also impose sanctions on such organizations, and/or their members, for unlawful speech or other unlawful conduct. But they cannot deny recognition to student organizations or impose sanctions for the lawful views or ideas expressed by the organization, its members or its speakers.

Academic freedom and illiberal leftism

As already indicated, challenges to academic, and other, freedoms may arise from both the 'illiberal left' and the 'illiberal right.' However, while illiberals at both ends of the political spectrum share the same commitment to silencing opponents, their reasons for doing so are fundamentally different. For the contemporary illiberal left it is, ostensibly in pursuit of the liberation of certain putatively disadvantaged social groups, a departure from the left's historic mission – *universal* human emancipation. The illiberal right, by contrast, wants quite the opposite. In Britain right-wing objections to academic and other forms of freedom, though not common, tend to be more prevalent outside universities. But in the academy itself they have a significantly lower profile not least because the dominant ideology, particularly in the arts, humanities and social sciences, is centre-to-far-left.[123]

Origins of the illiberal left

The 'illiberal left' is a loose movement which has emerged in universities across the English-speaking world and beyond, particularly in the past decade or so. It has two key characteristics. First, influenced indirectly by Marxism, it affirms that there can be no hope of 'social justice' unless liberal democracy is ditched in favour of an alternative, the characteristics of which and the manner of its replacement, are far from clear. Second, the movement's principal modus operandi takes the form of small, mostly online, mobs of militant students and academics who seek to silence, often successfully, lawful contributions to legitimate academic debates by others. Rather than engaging with the issues themselves, the militants instead prefer to vilify, victimize, harass and shame those with different views, and to recruit all-too-compliant university management in cancellation campaigns. Often the perspectives

---

[123] Williams, *How Woke Won*, pp. 97-98; Goodwin, *Academic Freedom*, pp. 1, 2, 8-10;, E. Kaufmann, 'Academic freedom in crisis: punishment, political discrimination, and self-censorship.' CSPI Report No. 2, 2021.

of those targeted, myself included, merely envisage different ways in which universal human emancipation might be conceived and achieved.[124] Like the 'wrong kind' of snow or leaves on the railway track, those in the cross hairs of the illiberal left are more likely to have the 'wrong kind' of aspiration for social justice rather than opposing it in principle. This is why the defence of academic freedom is so wrongly derided as a 'right wing issue' by many on the academic illiberal-left. In fact, given the almost complete absence of genuine right-wingers in British academia, especially in the humanities, law and social sciences, most of its victims are likely to be on the left of the political spectrum themselves.[125]

The emergence of 'illiberal leftism' is generally dated from the 2010s. But it has a much deeper history. In the 1970s and 1980s, invoking various forms of Marxism, student and academic militants argued that the most significant differentials in global power, wealth, privilege and status derive from the social classes created by capitalism. At the same time militant feminists maintained that the most fundamental form of domination is, and has always been, patriarchy, the subservience of women to men. In the 1990s postmodernists claimed that any faith, ideology or theory – including Marxism, liberalism and feminism – which seeks to explain the human experience in universal terms, is doomed to failure, because, in order to get its message across, each must inescapably rely upon infinitely indeterminate language open to competing interpretations. And, because there is no objectively correct standard facilitating their reconciliation, these are all locked in perpetual conflict. However, since it is itself both an explanatory 'grand narrative,' and also retains the classic leftist commitment to human liberation, postmodernism is doubly self-contradictory. From the 2000s onwards, critical race, multicultural, post-colonial, and identity theorists have also

---

[124] Campbell and Manning, *Victimhood Culture*, pp. 64-5; J. McWhorter, 'Academics are really, really worried about their freedom: Some fear for their career because they don't believe progressive orthodoxies,' *The Atlantic*, 1 September 2020; T. Slater (ed), *Unsafe Space: The Crisis of Free Speech on Campus* (Palgrave Macmillan, 2016); K. Powers, *The Silencing: How the Left is Killing Free Speech* (Regnery, 2015).

[125] See, eg, A. Romano, 'The second wave of "cancel culture": How the concept has evolved to mean different things to different people,' *Vox* 5 May 2021; B. Mullen & J. Rak, 'Academic freedom, academic lives: an introduction' (2019) 42 *Biography* 721-736.

come to greater prominence with their 'caste system of victimhood'[126] and a 'hierarchy based on "identity."'[127] In the driving seat of this movement, Critical Race Theory maintains that the institutions of liberal democracy are so thoroughly infused with racism they are incapable of being reformed and must be overthrown instead.[128] This perspective suffers from several problems not the least of which is that it assumes all the minorities allegedly oppressed by the dominant white, male, heterosexual, middle class, share common interests. They don't.[129] And, as already noted in the previous chapter, Marx and Engels, to whom this movement also owes a particular intellectual debt, were each notoriously racist.[130]

Characteristics of illiberal leftism

The academic illiberal left's case for seeking to achieve social justice by significantly restricting the liberty of the putative 'beneficiaries of oppression' rests on three main arguments.[131] First, the illiberal activities in question are themselves said to be a form of expression protected both by academic freedom and by the right to freedom of expression.[132] Second, 'privileged white males,' particularly those late in their careers as tenured academics, stand accused of dominating and distorting relevant academic debates in a manner which perpetuates the exclusion of those from marginalized backgrounds who, it is said, would otherwise bring a more truthful emancipatory perspective to bear. The former should, therefore, be required to keep quiet and allow the voices of the

---

[126] *The Economist*, 4-10 September 2021, p. 7; see also Campbell and Manning, *Victimhood Culture*.
[127] A. Dershowitz, *Cancel Culture – The Latest Attack on Free Speech and Due Process Cancel Culture* (Hot Books, 2020), p. 68; Williams, *How Woke Won*, p. 2.
[128] Williams, *How Woke Won*, 156-66; D. Murray, *The War on the West* (HarperCollins, 2022), pp. 16-31, 255-73.
[129] D. Murray, *The Madness of Crowds: Gender, Race and Identity* (Bloomsbury Continuum, 2020), Conclusion.
[130] Murray, *War on the West*, pp. 174-83; C. Moore, 'Were Marx and Engels White Racists? The Prolet-Aryan Outlook of Marxism' (1974-75) 19 *Berkeley Journal of Sociology*, 125-156; N. Weyl, *Karl Marx, Racist* (Arlington House, 1979).
[131] D. Rubin, *Don't Burn this Book: Thinking for Yourself in an Age of Unreason* (Penguin, 2020).
[132] Dershowitz, *Cancel Culture*, pp. 27-29.

oppressed to be heard.[133] Third, such domination also allegedly harms the excluded in ways additional to being silenced, by, for example, being discomforted and humiliated through having to engage with 'offensive' course material and classroom interactions, and by having their academic and social progress more generally, blocked.

Before offering a critique of these arguments, the following sections consider the chief characteristics of the campaign of the illiberal left in the academy. A distinction can be drawn between the values affirmed and relevant activities. The former include 'woke/wokeism,' 'anti-othering,' 'victimhood culture,' 'snowflakery' and a commitment to intellectually 'safe spaces,' while the latter embraces 'virtue signalling,' 'witch-hunting,' 'virtual heretic-burning,' 'cancel culture,' 'Islamofauxbia,' and 'Islamophobia-phobia.' BRISOC's complaint-and-campaign against me exhibits features of them all.

Woke/Wokeism

While, to the best of my knowledge, BRISOC's complaint-and-campaign never used the term 'woke' – an adjective originally meaning 'alert to racial prejudice and discrimination'[134] – their allegations, nevertheless, have this characteristic. The term is said to have been first coined by Black American folk singer-songwriter, Huddie Ledbetter, aka Lead Belly. Referring to his 1938 song, *Scottsboro Boys*, which tells the story of nine black teenagers accused of raping two white women, Lead Belly advised everybody, to 'best stay woke, keep their eyes open.'[135] It can also be traced to a *New York Times Magazine* article, published by African-American novelist William Melvin Kelley in 1962, entitled *If You're Woke You Dig It*, which describes the appropriation of African American slang by white beatniks. Entering the wider vernacular in the 2010s, 'woke' has been defined as referring to certain types of left-wing social and political campaigns, and their adherents, concerning putative inequalities and injustices such as those associated with sexism, minority

---

[133] Williams, *How Woke Won*, p. 226.
[134] Ibid, Ch 1.
[135] https://www.vox.com/culture/21437879/stay-woke-wokeness-history-origin-evolution-controversy.

identity, white privilege, and the legacies of slavery. If this was all it meant, I would have no hesitation in subscribing to it myself.

But, unfortunately, the laudable vision which it originally espoused has been debased. For example, in 2015 the online Urban Dictionary defined 'woke' as: 'being aware ... knowing what's going on in your community (related to racism and social injustice).' This was, however, changed in 2018 to: 'the act of being very pretentious about how much you care about a social issue.'[136] By 2020 the term was increasingly being used to disparage far left movements and ideologies for their over-zealous, performative, and/or insincere demands about the injustices with which they claim to be concerned. The woke phenomenon is also strongly associated with the systematic denigration of western history and culture on the strange and mistaken assumption that, of all the world's 'civilizations' past and present, it is somehow uniquely open to merciless denunciation – 'judging ourselves by our worst moments and everyone else by their best.'[137] As already observed, the only future it is said to deserve is destruction and replacement by something else, the route to, and characteristics of which remain very unclear.[138]

Noting that there is little consensus about what the term 'woke' means and that, in spite of not being centrally coordinated it has 'come to dominate our most important institutions,' Williams offers the following conception:

> 'Woke activists are obsessed with race and gender identity to the exclusion of almost all other issues. Woke describes a moral sensibility that insists on putting people into identity boxes and then arranging the boxes into hierarchies of privilege and oppression with some groups in need of "uplifting" while others must beg atonement. To be woke is to speak of the importance of inclusion, diversity and equity, even if you are fabulously wealthy and have a lifestyle few can ever imagine. Just like a previous era's "political correctness" woke privileges performative displays and linguistic correctness above material

---

[136] Williams, *How Woke Won*, p. 13.
[137] D. Murray, *The Strange Death of Europe: Immigration, Identity, Islam* (Bloomsbury Continuum, 2018), p. 177.
[138] Murray, *War on the West*, pp. 1-11.

change... Those who question woke values are considered "problematic." Those who transgress must be silenced.'[139]

Above all, Williams argues, being woke allows members of the professional-managerial class, in universities and elsewhere, to bolster their position by claiming to speak and act on behalf of 'the oppressed' whose prospects in the west, against mounting evidence to the contrary, are said to have deteriorated rather than to have improved over the past few decades.[140]

Anti-othering

The term 'othering' – the process of marginalizing people by reference to some normatively irrelevant minority characteristic – is a contemporary version of the more familiar distinction between 'us and them.' Several observations can be made about it. First, it is impossible to have an awareness of self without a sense of 'the other,' that is to say of being distinct from everyone else. This kind of 'othering' is, therefore, unavoidable. Second, all human associations are based on criteria of inclusion and exclusion, each a form of 'othering' which may, or may not, be antagonistic to relevant 'others,' and may or may not be justified. For example, friendship is one type of inclusion/exclusion and family another. But neither is unjustified nor impermeable. A stranger may become my friend and a friend may join your family if they become your wife/husband, or marry one of your children or grandchildren. And, as we all know, we don't necessarily regard everyone in our families as our friends.

Third, in all societies criteria of inclusion and exclusion are often conceived, on various levels, in terms of ingroups and outgroups, permeable and impermeable to varying degrees. Membership of each is typically expressed, for example, by adherence to, and defence of, specific identity, customs, mores, culture, language, religion, territory, and so on. As the early twentieth century French sociologist, Emile Durkheim, observed, one way in which this manifests itself is between the 'collective conscience' – the repository of received truth and values –

---

[139] Williams, *How Woke Won*, pp. 2-3.
[140] Ibid, Chs 3 & 5.

and deviance from it. Different societies also have different conceptions of what matters most, hinging, as Durkheim also noted, upon the distinction between the 'sacred and profane.' The affirmation of the 'sacredness' of personal, individual, identity – particularly when it is self-constructed – is one of the most revered totems of woke and anti-othering.

'Anti-othering' also tends to be invoked by those in the ingroup who want to include some, or all, of those in the outgroup because they believe their exclusion cannot be justified by reference to a proper interpretation of the ingroup's values. They may even be more 'anti othering' than those in the outgroup themselves.[141] In illiberal-leftism, this also tends to rest upon several crude and/or patronizing assumptions, such as the view that members of the outgroup are equally disadvantaged and in the same ways, that they are all outraged by it,[142] and that full and authentic membership of any given minority depends upon accepting the antagonistic world view offered by opinion formers in a given minority and their allies outside.[143] Closer inspection may, however, reveal that differences between those in the outgroup are at least as sharp as those between the outgroup, on the one hand, and the ingroup on the other.[144] It is also not uncommon for those in the ingroup who are militantly committed to anti-othering, to claim the insight and authority to speak for the outgroup as a whole, typically without having consulted its members about how they see their own identities, interests, and priorities.[145] A classic example is the assumption that everyone in the outgroup is fiercely proud of, and assertive about, their minority identity when the truth is that some may prefer to keep quiet about, or even abandon, it altogether.

The influence of anti-othering upon the controversy stirred by BRISOC's complaint-and-campaign against me has manifested in two principal ways. First BRISOC claims that my teaching and other public

---

[141] McWhorter, 'Academics are really, really worried.'
[142] Williams, *How Woke Won*, p. 216.
[143] Murray, *Madness of Crowds*, p. 154.
[144] Ibid, p. 239.
[145] Murray, *Strange Death of Europe*, pp. 101, 132-3.

output has 'increased 'hate crime towards Muslims.'[146] But, apart from rumour and hearsay from anonymous third parties, no evidence has been provided. Second, anti-othering is also the express reason why the Law School dropped the Islam, China and the Far East module from the HRLPS syllabus against the clear verdict of the University's own inquiry.

Victimhood culture

At the heart of the challenge posed by the illiberal left is a 'culture of victimhood,' characterised by hypersensitivity to perceived insult, denigration, and disrespect, however minor and unintentional,[147] an attitude BRISOC shares. Campbell and Manning argue that responses to such perceptions vary according to which of three particular cultures – 'honour,' 'dignity' or 'victimhood' – applies.[148] Honour cultures, typical for example of male members of the aristocracies of medieval and early-modern Europe, valorise violent retaliation against those deemed responsible for personal slight or humiliation. By contrast, dignity cultures, characteristic of modern liberal democracies, value self-restraint and the referral of such alleged grievances to impartial bureaucratic processes, particularly courts. Like honour cultures, victimhood cultures encourage prompt and aggressive retaliatory self-help to putative offences against (minority) identity. But, unlike honour cultures, this tends to take the form of self-pitying appeals on social media. Like dignity cultures they too seek to enlist the support of relevant bureaucracies (particularly universities) in campaigns of career-and-livelihood-ending character assassination, also likely to precipitate ostracism from valued social relationships.

Coinciding with the rise of the illiberal left, victimhood culture is a comparatively recent phenomenon. Its appearance and trajectory can be attributed to a complex combination of factors. First, the emergence of modern knowledge economies has led to a huge expansion in the number of universities and students, and has also resulted in the gradual erosion of formal identity-based exclusions such as those which previously

---

[146] See Ch 3.
[147] Williams, *How Woke Won*, Ch 11.
[148] Campbell and Manning, *Victimhood Culture*.

barred women and racial or religious minorities. As the liberal rights revolution slowly developed throughout the 19th and 20th centuries, leftists laboured to remove the remaining formal and informal obstructions. As already indicated, 'progressive' anti-liberal perspectives maintain that, since liberalism is incapable of delivering on its own core commitments, it should be replaced by some other alternative, ostensibly more able to embrace those excluded on account of their minority identity.

But one of the central conundrums of contemporary victimhood culture is that, for three main reasons, the sense of being a victim is difficult to assuage.[149] First, it confers status and attracts rewards for those who successfully claim it. Second, it provides the rationale for a massive and expanding therapeutic industry purporting to address it. And, third, for each of these reasons any attempt to claim that victims are no longer being victimized, is likely to be bitterly resisted and attributed to the problem being denied rather than having been resolved.

Snowflakery and intellectually safe spaces

Contemporary emotional and psychological pressures on young people have produced an epidemic of mental ill-health across the western world. Sweeping university campuses, this has tragically led to some taking their own lives. Social media play a double role here. On one hand they promote the flaunting of success and 'coolness.' However, for those seeking 'poor you' validation and support from others, they also encourage proclamations of vulnerability, victimhood, and an inability to meet onerous expectations. Bullies have also been provided with a powerful weapon with which to threaten, intimidate, ostracize, and crush their unfortunate victims.

Only recently, having finally owned up to the contribution they themselves might be making to the crisis of student mental ill health, British universities have begun to provide a range of designated services. But whether the academic and other demands upon students are being effectively managed is debatable. It is, for example, an open question if attempts to make the 'student experience' less demanding – including by

---

[149] Williams, *How Woke Won*, pp. 233-35.

dumbing down intellectual and other challenges, and avoiding, or downplaying, controversial issues and topics in order to avoid giving offence, causing discomfort, or prompting trauma – are likely to prove effective. Psychologists, for example, understand that negative memories or associations, sparked by certain everyday occurrences, are best tackled by confronting rather than avoiding the triggers. And the chances that such traumas will be sparked by debates about, for example, the relationship between human rights and Islam, seems unlikely in the extreme. But even if this were the case, banning or restricting relevant discussion would not be the right way forward. Addressing the crisis of mental ill-health amongst young people is one thing. But seeking to accommodate every demand from an excessively self-conscious sense of vulnerability is quite another.

In the literal sense, a 'snowflake' is a very fragile, single ice crystal with a unique pattern, which quickly dissolves unless finely balanced conditions obtain. In the 1970s the term was used metaphorically to describe both a self-conscious, precious white person and, in particular, a black person perceived as suffering from the same pathology. Since the 2010s it has become derogatory slang for those allegedly hypersensitive to offence, incapable of dealing with views opposing their own, suffering from a narcissistic sense of their own uniqueness, and harbouring an unjustified sense of entitlement to success, praise and admiration. There is abundant evidence that this 'sanctification of fragility'[150] is gaining traction at a remarkable rate in universities throughout the English-speaking world and beyond.

In particular, snowflakery manifests in demands to make tertiary level education intellectually 'safe' by protecting members of putatively marginalized groups, both in the classroom and in the course of study, from anything that might make them feel uneasy on account of their identity, background or experience.[151] One feature concerns 'trigger warnings,' to which reference has already been made – messages alerting an intended audience or readership that something they are about to hear,

---

[150] Slater, *Unsafe Spaces*, p. 5.
[151] Williams, *How Woke Won*, p. 107; Whittington, *Speak Freely*, pp. 57-77; Slater, *Unsafe Spaces*; K. Malik 'Free speech and unsafe spaces,' *Pandemonium*, 10 April 2017.

see and/or read contains potentially distressing content which may cause flash backs to traumatic events in their personal past. While the failure to provide these did not feature in BRISOC's complaint-and-campaign against me, the demand for intellectually 'safe' spaces certainly did.

Campaigns derived from snowflakery and the demand for 'safe spaces' suffer from three principal defects. First, only certain types of safety are valued. For example, as a result of the vicious social media campaigns waged by students and academic colleagues against me and others, our places of work have become hostile, toxic, and potentially dangerous. Our physical safety has, therefore, been compromised in pursuit of the putative intellectual and emotional 'safety' of our students. BRISOC alleges that the course material on HRLPS – and in particular on the Islam, China and Far East module and how I taught it – made Muslim students feel vulnerable and unsafe, and that both it, and I, damaged their mental health. But, strangely, there were no complaints to this effect for the first decade and a half the unit and module were on the curriculum. Nor, as Chapter 3 noted, did any of those anonymous students who allegedly drew it to the attention of BRISOC in 2020, bother to raise it first through any of the Law School's many relevant channels.

Needless to say, everyone has the right, as far as is reasonably possible, to be kept safe from harm on campus. But this does not include being protected from having cherished beliefs exposed to even the most relevant and respectful critical inquiry, especially where they have implications for how people should behave and how society should be governed. And, as recounted in Chapter 3, however offensive my course materials and behaviour may allegedly have been to some of my Muslim students, it never resulted in any of them having to flee their homes in fear of their lives as I felt obliged to do the day after *Al Jazeera* covered my story. Nor did they report me to the police for harassment, vilification and victimization as I have reported BRISOC. In fact, when the police asked them if they wanted to make such a complaint, they declined.

The second problem with snowflakery and intellectual safety is this. If protecting minorities from harm includes banning or restricting responsible critical engagement with their beliefs where relevant, the central rationale for the modern university – the fearless quest for knowledge and truth – will be fatally compromised because issues of considerable importance, both for knowledge and for the governance, regulation and functioning of society, will be neglected.

A third difficulty is that, although it has its defenders,[152] self-absorption of this kind is precisely the opposite character trait required of the well-educated leaders of tomorrow. In the quest for solutions to all contemporary and future challenges, Universities should be seeking to cultivate the robust, honest, and frank exchange of ideas rather than self-protective unwillingness to confront opposing views, unwelcome facts, or uncomfortable realities.

It is not entirely clear what has given rise to the current pandemic of extreme risk aversion and the urge to advertise it.[153] The emergence of a 'safety culture' in society more widely over the past few decades – evidenced, for example, by schools banning such harmless pursuits as 'conker fights,' a long-established school-boy tradition involving hitting a fallen chestnut attached to a string against an opponent's – probably has something to do with it. It may also be connected to 'helicopter parenting,' where educated middle class parents 'hover' over even their grown-up offspring in an attempt to keep them safe and improve their prospects.[154] So-called 'compensation culture' – where, when anything goes wrong, attempts are made to hold somebody else legally responsible – may also be implicated.

Virtue signalling

'Virtue signalling' is a pejorative term – used with increasing frequency since 2015 – to refer to the public expression, typically of a wokeish viewpoint on social media, where the primary purpose is to advertise the signaller's moral rectitude and good character, through horrified condemnation, rather than to offer anything concrete about the alleged injustice in question. BRISOC's campaign also shares this

---

[152] See, eg H. Jewel, *We Need Snowflakes: In Defence of the Sensitive, the Angry and the Offended* (Cornet, 2022).
[153] See G. Lukianoff and J. Haidt, *The Coddling of the American Mind: How Good Intentions and Bad Ideas are Setting up a Generation for Failure* (Penguin, 2018).
[154] Campbell and Manning, *Victimhood Culture*, p. 259.

characteristic in so far as it seeks to broadcast self-righteous indignation about an entirely imagined and confected 'injustice' – my alleged Islamophobia – at least partly in order to attract the notice, sympathy and support of fellow travellers.

And this brings us to one of the curious paradoxes of my case and that of others in a similar position – the well-documented phenomenon (particularly in France) of 'Islamo-leftism,' the alignment of the illiberal-left with conservative Muslim organizations, the latter of which have, at best, an ambiguous commitment to any credible conception of social progress apart from that which they think might advance their own cause. For example, while hitching their wagon to the illiberal left's social justice campaign, student Islamic societies in Britain have also insisted upon gender-segregated meetings and have hosted openly and unapologetically homophobic, misogynist and antisemitic speakers.[155] Yet this has been condoned by their illiberal-leftist allies, apparently because, in their binary world, repressed minorities share certain irreducible common interests against the 'system,' the 'establishment,' or the 'status quo' ('my enemy's enemy is my friend'). Therefore, since Muslims are deemed to be a repressed minority, discussion of possibly illiberal features of their culture are taboo on the assumption that this would, otherwise, play into the hands of the oppressors.

Witch-hunting, virtual heretic burning, and cancel culture

In the literal sense a witch-hunt is a search for those, typically women, suspected of witchcraft, and to put them on trial for their lives. However, in its contemporary metaphorical sense, the term has come to mean a highly visible official or unofficial campaign often involving elements of moral panic and mass hysteria. Ostensibly intended to uncover subversive activity or disloyalty, the purpose of the modern witch-hunt is to silence and intimidate opponents.

In the narrow sense, 'heresy' is an interpretation of any faith or ideology which those who subscribe to the traditional, orthodox perspective regard as a mortal threat to their power, identity and beliefs.

---

[155] S. Khan with T. McMahon, *The Battle for British Islam: Reclaiming Muslim Identity from Extremism* (Saqi Books, 2016), Ch 2, p. 127.

It, therefore, invites excommunication, banishment, execution, or other punishment. But, in the wider sense, it may also refer to the radical rejection of views generally held to be true, eg that the world is a sphere at a time when most believed it was flat. Key characteristics of literal and metaphorical heretic hunts not only include the levelling of accusations against genuine 'heretics,' but also false allegations against those entirely innocent of the relevant charge.[156] Anti-heretic hysteria also provides ample cover for ulterior motives including, for example, the participation in cancellation attacks by junior academics seeking to eliminate a more established rival in order to enhance their own job or promotion prospects.

Typically, contemporary illiberal-left witch-hunts and virtual heretic-burnings involve concerted, and usually collective, attempts on social media to block publications and/or other public output including by visiting speakers ('no-platforming') on the grounds that they are racist, fascist, or otherwise hold views hostile to minorities. Condemnation, denunciation, shaming, ostracism, boycotting, shunning, and 'cancelling' those targeted also tend to be involved.[157] Attempts may, for example, be made to have opponents disciplined or sacked by their employers, removed from some other office/position, ousted from social or professional circles, and/or in many other ways prevented or deterred from making their voices heard. As Dershowitz puts it:

> 'Cancel culture causes more problems than it solves. It falsely accuses; it applies a double standard of selectivity; it fails to balance or calibrate vices and virtues; it has no statute of limitations; it provides no process to challenge cancellations; it is standardless, unaccountable, not transparent and often anonymous; it hides personal, ideological and political agendas; it can be abused for revenge, extortion or other malign motives... It must be stopped...'[158]

BRISOC's complaint-and-campaign against me has all the hallmarks of the contemporary illiberal cancellation witch hunt and virtual heretic burning – arrogant and shockingly ill-informed self-righteousness, a

---

[156] Campbell and Manning, *Victimhood Culture*, Ch 4.
[157] P. Norris, 'Cancel culture: myth or reality?' *Political Studies*, 11 August 2021; Dershowitz, *Cancel Culture*.
[158] Dershowitz, *Cancel Culture*, p. 124. See also Williams, *How Woke Won*, pp. 37-42.

malicious intention to harm, the recruitment of gullible uncritical allies only too eager to jump on the bandwagon without bothering to check the veracity of the allegations, implacable demands for grovelling apologies or dismissal, and for offending contributions to scholarship and academic debates to be expunged.

And, as already indicated, I am, of course, far from alone. Over the past five years in the US, for example, the Foundation for Individual Rights and Expression (FIRE, hitherto the Foundation for Individual Rights in Education) recorded 426 incidents, arising more from the political left than right, in which ideological adversaries targeted scholars including by demanding an investigation, demotion, censorship, suspension, or dismissal. Typically, these were aimed at those who are tenured, white, and male, with the most common cause involving alleged views about race.[159]

Up to the end of 2021 the UK equivalent of FIRE, Academics for Academic Freedom, (AAF) listed 150 individuals associated with universities in the UK and Ireland who, *since 2005,* had been the subject of campaigns to silence or be sacked for the lawful expression of contributions to legitimate academic debates. This includes those 'no platformed,' including visiting speakers at universities from non-academic backgrounds. One hundred and seventeen of these, 78%, occurred between 2017 and 2021 inclusive, 30 of which were in 2021 alone. The list is not exhaustive, and several cases involved multiple cancellations as the campaigns in question developed. In May 2022, Toby Young, Director of the Free Speech Union (FSU) told a conference hosted by the centre-right think tank, Politiea, that the FSU now receives about a dozen requests a week for help from students and academics, castigated in various ways for exercising their lawful right to free speech.[160]

A particularly egregious case, like mine also involving the University of Bristol, came to prominence early in 2022. A PhD student at the University's Centre for Gender and Violence, Raquel Rosario

---

[159] https://www.thefire.org/research/publications/miscellaneous-publications/scholars-under-fire/scholars-under-fire-full-text/. For an international perspective see Norris, 'Cancel culture: myth or reality?.'

[160] https://www.dailymail.co.uk/news/article-10862647/Cambridge-don-claims-woke-critics-branded-white-supremacist-teaching-classics.html.

Sanchez from the Dominican Republic, took the University to court alleging indirect sex discrimination, victimization and harassment under the Equality Act 2010, and breach of the University's duty of care.[161] Shortly after her arrival in Bristol in 2017, Ms Rosario Sanchez had been targeted by militant trans activists for chairing a meeting of Women's Place UK, a gender-critical feminist group to which the militants object because of its concerns about the implications of gender self-identification for, amongst other things, women-only spaces.[162] This turned out to be the beginning of a systematic and relentless campaign led by another, transgender, PhD student, removed from the Centre following a complaint lodged with the University by Ms Rosario Sanchez. Disciplinary proceedings were initiated against the bully but terminated 18 months later because she claimed they were damaging her mental health.

On 21 April 2022 the county court at Bristol found in favour of the University. Mr Justice Ralton held that there was no evidence of a policy, criterion or practice of sex discrimination against the claimant, as required by the Equality Act. Nor was the University indirectly guilty of harassment or victimization under the same legislation. The judge also found that the University had discharged the duty of care it owed the claimant. He noted that Ms Rosario Sanchez had faced 'violent, threatening, intimidating behaviour or language' and that a 'lack of care' and 'incompetent' decisions had led to lengthy delays in hearing the disciplinary case against the ringleader of her critics. But Mr Justice Ralton, nevertheless, held that there was no evidence of malice or any strategy on the part of the University to shut the claimant down. However, the observation that, 'ultimately the proceedings came to nothing and ... (the bully) ... was left gloating,'[163] points to the Achilles

---

[161] R. Rosario Sanchez, 'Called "scum" for daring to stand up for women - yet "Britain's wokest university" did nothing to help,' https://www.dailymail.co.uk/news/article-10553553/RAQUEL-ROSARIO-SANCHEZ-got-no-protection-trans-rights-extremists-Bristol-University.html, 25 February 2022; 'Raquel Rosario Sánchez on Bristol's "hollow victory" in trans row: PhD student says her legal defeat raises important questions about duty of care owed to students who face harassment,' THE, 18 May 2022.
[162] See Williams, *How Woke Won*, Ch 9.
[163] *Raquel Maria Rosario Sanchez v University of Bristol*, Claim No.008LR988, in the County Court at Bristol, 21 April 2022, para. 132.

heel of the entire judgment. It indicates that a student can lead a campaign of bullying and harassment against another student at the same institution – merely for making lawful contributions to legitimate academic debates – and then thwart the disciplinary process by claiming it is damaging their own mental health; a get-out-of-jail-free card if ever there was one. The fitness-for-purpose of such proceedings is, therefore, seriously open to question. The failure to pass this test also fatally undermines the claim that the duty of care the University of Bristol owed Ms Rosario Sanchez had been properly discharged.

There were several other high-profile cases in the UK in 2021. In reverse chronological order, these include the following. Students at Durham University called for the disciplining of Professor Tim Luckhurst, a college principal, for having invited controversial journalist, Rod Liddle, to give an after Christmas-dinner speech, and for calling the student walkout and shouts of abuse which followed, 'pathetic.' Mr Liddle began by joking about the absence of sex workers at the event, a mocking reference to the fact that the University of Durham had recently issued guidance to its students about how to work safely in the sex industry. He also said: 'It is fairly easily proven that colonialism is not remotely the major cause of Africa's problems, just as it is very easy to prove that the educational underachievement of British people of Caribbean descent or African Americans is nothing to do with institutional or structural racism.' The Durham branch of the University and College Union (UCU), the lecturers' trade union, demanded that Professor Luckhurst be disciplined and over 1600 individuals signed a letter condemning Liddle's invitation. Some Durham students asked to be transferred to another of the University's colleges, called for a rent strike, and apparently oblivious of the risk to the status of their own degrees, threatened to give the University a low score in student satisfaction surveys.[164] Professor Luckhurst, who apologised for his reaction to the student walkout, was briefly suspended and investigated by the University, but resumed work after the Christmas vacation. In January 2022, the University announced that, although its inquiry was

---

[164] 'College principal is back at work after row over Rod Liddle speech,' *The Times*, 28 January 2022.

complete, the process was ongoing and the results remained confidential. And in September 2022 it was announced that Durham Union Society, a student-run debating society, had invited Mr Liddle to speak in a debate scheduled for 11 November.

Also in December 2021, Professor Jo Phoenix resigned from the Open University to take up a Chair at the University of Reading, alleging constructive dismissal on the part of her former employer for having failed adequately to protect her from bullying by trans activists opposed to her gender critical views. In common with other gender critical feminists, Professor Phoenix had expressed concerns about certain aspects of trans rights legislation, had argued that women may change their gender but not their sex, and that mere self-identification as a woman potentially threatens women-only 'safe spaces' such as refuges and prisons.

In November, Peter Huffam, suspended by the University of the Arts London in October 2019, went public about his case. Three anonymous postgraduates claimed that, in a language lesson, the class had been 'sexualised' and that the way in which Huffam expressed himself was inappropriate and made them feel uncomfortable. Students had been asked to complete an exercise which involved matching six descriptions about style from newspaper articles to six photos of fashion outfits. One newspaper's comment upon a photo of a woman said: 'Add a lick of purple lippy and some embellished heels and this look makes for one hot mama.' Having had his career thrown into chaos for over two years, Huffam received an apology from the University admitting his mistreatment. He is said to be seeking compensation.

Also in November 2021, the student president of the Cambridge Union, Keir Bradwell, informed members by email that a blacklist of speakers, who would never be invited to address the CU again, was being compiled. At the top was eminent art historian, Andrew Graham-Dixon who, a few days before, had offended some students during a lively debate. Theatrically mimicking Adolf Hitler, Mr Graham-Dixon later said his intention had been to illustrate how Nazism distorted views about everything including art. A number of prominent writers and actors, including Louis de Bernières and John Cleese, voluntarily 'blacklisted' themselves from the CU in solidarity. Fellow historian Guy Walters told *The Jewish Chronicle* that: 'The idea that Andrew Graham-Dixon has been blacklisted for performing what was clearly a satirical impression of Adolf Hitler is both disgraceful and deeply ironic.'[165] The CU responded to these criticisms by announcing that the proposed blacklist had been abandoned.

The case of Kathleen Stock, former Professor of Philosophy at the University of Sussex, is one of the most notorious and troubling of the British academic illiberal leftist cancellation cases so far. Following years of harassment from students and colleagues opposed to her gender critical views, Professor Stock received an OBE in the New Year's honours list 2021 for her academic work and defence of free speech. This prompted over 600 academics to sign an open letter condemning her 'transphobia' and to demand that she be stripped of the award. A hostile campus and Twitter campaign, led by a group of students calling themselves 'Anti Terf Sussex,'[166] was stepped up in October 2021 as the new academic year commenced. Activities included pasting 'STOCK OUT' signs, lit by burning flares, around campus and plastering buildings with posters calling for Professor Stock to be sacked on the grounds that she made trans students feel unsafe. Buckling under the intolerable stress of this ordeal, Professor Stock resigned from the University of Sussex shortly afterwards to (remotely) take up a position at the newly established University of Texas at Austin. Although the VC of the University of Sussex, Professor Adam Tickell, issued statements in Professor Stock's support, the University otherwise did nothing effective to protect her. She also accused the UCU, the union to which she belonged, of effectively having ended her career by issuing a statement which appeared to side more with her persecutors than with her.

In September 2021 the University of Nottingham finally accepted, subject to a year's probation, Fr Palmer's nomination by his bishop, as the University's non-stipendiary Catholic chaplain. The previous month Fr Palmer's appointment had been rejected because, although the

---

[165] 'Stars defend historian who mimicked Hitler,' *The Jewish Chronical*, 12 November 2021.
[166] TERF stands for 'Trans-Exclusionary Radical Feminist.'

University claimed to respect his right to hold anti-abortion and other conservative Catholic views, it did not like the 'tone' in which he expressed them. Fr. Palmer had tweeted that abortion is the 'slaughter of babies' and that the UK's proposed assisted dying bill would allow the NHS 'to kill the vulnerable.'

The same month several anonymous students used online forums to allege that Dr Neil Thin, a senior lecturer in social anthropology at the University of Edinburgh, was racist and sexist and made them feel unsafe. Dr Thin's offences had included criticising a Black Lives Matter meeting in which white members of the audience were not allowed to ask questions, and for opposing the renaming of the University's David Hume Tower, demanded by activists on the grounds that the eponymous enlightenment philosopher had used racist language and had been associated with slavery. One group, BlackED, also criticised Dr Thin for the statement on his Twitter biography that 'civilisation is for everyone.' Others called for him to be removed from the supervision of theses and for the slides of his presentations to be audited. The University defended Dr Thin's right to freedom of expression and said that any complaints would be dealt with internally. Unwilling to return to teaching on account of the unresolved toxic environment at his workplace, Dr Thin took study leave in 2021-22 prior to early retirement thereafter.

Several observations can be made about these and many other cases. Since over 223,000 academics are employed in higher education in the UK, 115 or so 'cancel culture' incidents in five years may seem to indicate that the problem is of negligible proportions.[167] However, for several reasons, numbers are not the only, or the most important, consideration. First, those teaching and researching certain subjects in arts, humanities and social sciences are vastly more exposed to cancellation than those in virtually every other field. Second, just a single attempted silencing of an academic for making a lawful contribution to a legitimate academic debate, by vilifying, victimizing and intimidating, would be one too many. And even if the direct victim is not silenced, they are likely to suffer considerable psychological, emotional, and other

---

[167] Figures for 2019/20, https://www.hesa.ac.uk/news/19-01-2021/sb259-higher-education - staff-statistics.

damage. Third, like the ripples from the proverbial stone thrown into the pond, the impact of any well-publicised cancellation case is also likely to spread far and wide. An incalculable number of others, particular those at the early stages of their careers, will almost certainly self-censor.[168] As a result, it is likely that few if any young academics at any UK university will be tempted even to explore the perspectives of the vilified, let alone publicly agree with them.

'Islamofauxbia' and 'Islamophobia-phobia'

At the heart of my ordeal lies a 'toxic trio.' One limb, already the subject of a substantial and expanding literature to which reference was made in Chapter 4, is Islamophobia – the visceral prejudice against Muslims and Islam based on myth, caricature and misrepresentation. But the other two are much less well documented or debated. One, 'Islamofauxbia' – the false accusation of anti-Muslim prejudice – typically intended to silence the kind of searching reflections upon Islam to which every religion and ideology should be exposed – derives from a failure to acknowledge that responsible evidence-based critical engagement with Islam is not Islamophobic. The regrettable irony is that Islamofauxbia is more likely to increase, rather than reduce, genuine Islamophobia. The third element, 'Islamophobia-phobia' – the excessive fear of being denounced as anti-Muslim – also often manifests as excessively uncritical 'Islamophilia.'[169] Sadly, this is where many non-Muslims in Britain and elsewhere find themselves; both very ill-informed about Islam and easily cowed into accepting that any criticism of it is Islamophobic.

There can be no doubt that BRISOC's campaign against me – derived as it is from lies, distortion and misrepresentation, stemming from rumour and hearsay supplied by anonymous third parties – is a

---

[168] Kaufmann, 'Academic freedom in crisis;' E. Chamlee-Wright, 'Self-censorship and associational life in the liberal academy' (2019) 56 *Society* 538–549; E. Noll, 'The ripple effect of censorship: silencing in the classroom' (1994) 83 *English Journal* 59-64; M. Kearns, 'The problems of campus culture: presumption and self-censorship,' *Heterodox Academy*, 12 March 2018.

[169] See, D. Murray, *Islamophilia: A Very Metropolitan Malady* (Self-published, 2020).

particularly savage example of 'Islamofauxbia.'[170] Nor can there be much doubt that it has prompted 'Islamophobia-phobia' on the part of the University of Bristol, the Law School, and many of my colleagues. My recruitment as the first Visiting Research Fellow, and later appointment as Research Director, at the Oxford Institute for British Islam, is, however, a very welcome example of Muslim 'counter-Islamofauxbia.'[171] It both constitutes a courageous attempt to bolster my exoneration from BRISOC's false charges, and powerfully discredits the less-than-subtle message the University and Law School have sent to the outside world that, in spite of my unreserved vindication, I may not have been totally innocent after all.[172]

Each element of this toxic trio is a prejudice or fear with negative social, political, intellectual and educational implications and none can be effectively tackled without each being addressed. The key lies in robust conceptualization, drawing distinctions as sharply as possible, honest acknowledgement that grey areas cannot be fully eliminated, genuine social scientific inquiry, plus tolerance, open-mindedness, and a commitment to the core values of liberal cosmopolitanism, particularly equality of concern and respect for the life-affirming and humane interpretations of all faiths and ideologies.

A flawed agenda

No convincing attempt has ever been made to present a sustained, coherent, and thoroughly-argued case against academic freedom. This is not least because, by itself relying upon academic freedom, or at least the right to freedom of expression, it would be self-contradictory.[173] Indeed, some of the 'progressive' scepticism about academic freedom regards

---

[170] A full account of the controversy is provided by the Bristol Free Speech Society's interview, *Islamophobia and academic freedom: a conversation with Professor Steven Greer*, available on YouTube at the following link: https://www.youtube.com/watch?v=-6q2o5058jA.
[171] https://www.youtube.com/watch?v=HE94eWYG6Pw; https://oibi.org.uk/news/; http://www.bristol.ac.uk/law/news/2022/steven-greer-oibi.html. See Ch 3.
[172] See Ch 3.
[173] See, eg, S. Korn, 'The Doctrine of Academic Freedom: Let's give up on Academic Freedom in Favour of Justice,' *The Crimson*, 18 February 2014; H. Marcuse, 'Repressive Tolerance' in R. Wolff, B. Moore Jr and H. Marcuse, *A Critique of Pure Tolerance* (Beacon Press, 1965).

coherence, the exercise of reason, the giving of reasons, the presentation of a thoroughly-considered and rationally-argued case, and engaging in debate, as themselves manifestations of the very academic culture to which they are opposed. As one commentator states: "'diversity of thought" is just a euphemism for "white supremacy."'[174] It is also said that at education colleges in the US, trainee teachers are being taught that the term 'diversity of opinion' is 'white supremacist bullshit.'[175] Closer to home, in 2020, Sunny Singh, Professor of Creative Writing and Inclusion in the Arts at London Metropolitan University, neatly captured these sentiments in the following pithy tweet: '…debate is an imperialist capitalist white supremacist cis heteropatriarchal technique that transforms a potential exchange of knowledge into a tool of exclusion and oppression.' The response this invites is – so we should prefer dogmatic assertion instead? In fact, the illiberal left's challenge to academic freedom comes, as all such challenges always have and always will, from those who want to assert their own freedom of expression and that of their allies, while denying the same to their opponents and enemies.

We know what illiberal-leftism is against – the exclusion and marginalization of certain minorities from and in the academy – and that it favours the opposite. We also know that, in an attempt to secure their own narrow conception of 'progressive objectives,' some illiberal leftists have no hesitation in resorting to vilification, victimization and intimidation against those whose vision differs even slightly from theirs. But there are several further problems with this paradigm and movement.

First, it is a mistake to regard the manifestations of illiberal leftism as themselves legitimate exercises of the right to freedom of expression. The same could, for example, be said of most, in not all, other forms of harmful conduct. Murder, rape, assault, indecent exposure and so on are undeniably forms of 'self-expression.' But they are not lawful or legitimate precisely because of the harm they inflict. In his otherwise excellent book, *Cancel Culture – The Latest Attack on Free Speech and*

---

[174] M Harriot, "'Diversity of thought" is just a euphemism for "white supremacy,"' *The Root*, 12 April 2018.
[175] L. Asher, 'How Ed Schools Became a Menace to Higher Education,' *Quillette*, 6 March 2019.

Due Process, Alan Dershowitz argues that cancel culture is both an attack upon free speech yet also itself a type of speech which is, and should be, legally protected. Expressing opposition to free speech should certainly not be unlawful. But, as Chemerinski and Gillman point out, forms of expression which cause, or attempt to cause, harms beyond mere hurt feelings – for example, severe damage to reputation and to mental health, the destruction of a career and livelihood, and threats to physical safety – are not, nor should they be. As a result, they should be unlawful for precisely the same reason that other forms of 'self expression' resulting in personal injury are.[176]

A second problem concerns how illiberal leftists propose to resolve conflicts between competing illiberal-leftist goals[177] Consider, for example, the following. An appointments committee arrives at the conclusion that the two best candidates for an academic post are a privately educated cis black female from a wealthy family, and a white trans male from a poor background who received free school meals at his inner city comprehensive. Who, according to illiberal-leftist wisdom should get the job? Either way a member of a minority will be rejected.

A third difficulty concerns knowing when illiberal-left utopia has arrived. Will it simply be when the proportions of hitherto excluded minorities amongst staff and students in the academy are the same as they are in the national population, in the UK about 18% non-whites, for example? Or should the sky be the limit? Or maybe the point of reference should be the ethnic etc characteristics of the global rather than the UK population, in which case whites would constitute only about 10% of academics in British universities.

Fourth, although illiberal-left allegations about the exclusion of certain minorities from the academy, and from academic debate in the UK, are not false in every respect, they are at most only partly true. The simple fact is that the academic landscape is much more multidimensional and complex than that presented by the crude binary picture invoked. Some disciplines, some institutions, and some individuals are, for example, more culpable than others. Many are not

---

[176] Chemerinski and Gillman, *Free Speech On Campus*, pp. 116-123.
[177] Murray, *Madness of Crowds*, pp. 231-56.

culpable at all. And while, in the past, various minorities have had little or no voice anywhere, contemporary information technology has transformed the terrain everywhere. An average elderly, white, male academic with no Twitter account, would, for example, be lucky if their serious scholarly book, which has taken a decade to write, were read by a few hundred students and scholars over, say, a five-year period. Yet someone like Rhianna, a young woman of colour, can instantly connect with, and influence, her 104 million followers with a single-sentence tweet expressing an 'off the top of the head' opinion, capable of being confirmed or changed an instant later with another.

Fifth, allegations levelled by illiberal-leftists may be, as in my case, simply false.[178] As already indicated, few of those targeted are opposed to social justice as such. Indeed, this is probably, and ironically, one of the principal reasons for illiberal left cancellation. Those who demand that everyone admires the emperor's new clothes, which they themselves have designed and fashioned, are unlikely to welcome those willing and able to demonstrate how naked he is.

A sixth problem is that, as the term itself suggests, 'illiberal-leftism' embodies a logical and normative contradiction. According to illiberal-leftists, the right of excluded minorities to genuine, non-discriminatory incorporation in the academy requires the suppression of the same right on the part of those who allegedly stand in their way – the subordination of liberty to fraternity and equality in other words. And yet, by invoking expressly or implicitly, the language of rights, illiberal-leftism logically implies the universal applicability of the full range of entitlements to everyone with relevant characteristics, in this case access to and participation in academic life to those with relevant skills.

But the final problem is probably the most serious of all. It is not surprising that, in the whole of human history, the coerced restriction of freedom has never led to a fairer, more equal, more inclusive and more just society. In all cases, without exception, the result has been either tyranny or anarchy. Sometimes, as in the case of the Chinese cultural revolution from the mid-1960s to the mid-1970s, it has been both together. Not surprisingly unjustified attacks upon any given freedom

---

[178] McWhorter, 'Academics are really, really worried.'

tend to beget such attacks on others. And, in the final analysis, the beneficiaries have always been, and are always likely to be, those in established or emergent elites who can best exploit the ensuing chaos to their advantage. The poor, the disadvantaged, the dispossessed, the marginalized, and the oppressed have always been, and are always likely to be, on the losing side whenever the tally is reckoned.[179]

Profile of illiberal leftism

Although there is evidence that the general public is not well-disposed to illiberal leftism,[180] they tend to be neither particularly well informed about it nor particularly exercised about the challenges it presents. Since the national media also tend to concentrate upon those issues which conform to the orientation of the outlet concerned, the centre-right press generally takes cancel culture stories more seriously than its counterparts on the centre-left. The profile of illiberal leftism also varies according to context in academia itself. As already indicated, it is, for example, more prominent in the humanities, arts and social sciences than in other disciplines. It also tends to be less critically received by students and administrators than by academics themselves.

Academics

According to a recent survey-based report spanning the leading academic institutions in Australia, Canada, the UK and the US...

> 'The good news is that most academics voice support for academic freedom, viewpoint diversity and oppose the idea of discriminating against those who hold nonconformist or contrarian views, even if academics who self-identify as left-wing are more likely to voice their dislike of right-wing voters than vice versa. The bad news is that we also identify a sizeable and radical minority of 'activist academics' who hold the opposite view: who support restricting academic freedom, who back the removal of speakers who risk offending the emotional safety of students, who prioritise the ideological goals of 'social justice' over academic freedom, who are openly intolerant of those who hold

---

[179] Chemerinski and Gillman, *Free Speech on Campus*, pp. 27, 40, 43.
[180] Williams, *How Woke Won*, pp. 242-47.

alternative ideological views and who say they have no problem with university administrators making political statements.'[181]

As already indicated, evidence of the division amongst academics include 'petition battles' generated by recent controversies with scores, or even hundreds, lining up on either side. Petitions have also been circulated condemning illiberal leftism itself on the grounds that it constitutes intolerance of lawful and legitimate opinion, indicates a vogue for unmerited public shaming, reduces complex normative and policy issues to crude and misleading binary moral certainties, has a chilling effect upon public discourse, especially by prompting self-censorship, and that there is, in any case, little or no good reason to believe that it contributes to the realization of the 'progressive agendas' to which those who practice it claim to be committed.

Denying that academic cancel culture exists, other academics appear to assume that any failure to support and defend excluded minorities would be a betrayal of the cause, even if the behaviour of some minority activists might be difficult to justify by any credible normative standard. There may also be a concern about the negative impact of any apparent equivocation regarding a given institution's commitment to an official wokeish profile. Some may fear that any support expressed publicly or privately for colleagues targeted by illiberal-leftist online mobs could result in their own exposure to victimization, and/or that it could jeopardise their chances of promotion, the next salary increment or, given increased reliance upon short-term rolling contracts, the prospect of being re-hired.

However, the dominant reaction of the most immediate academic colleagues of those threatened, bullied, vilified and/or cancelled for the expression of lawful contributions to legitimate debates, has typically been to maintain a strict, and possibly embarrassed silence. Rarely have any of those cancelled been robustly and publicly defended by their own colleagues at their own institutions.[182] This also occurred during the

---

[181] Goodwin, *Academic Freedom*, p. 13; See also E. Kaufmann, 'Few academics support cancel culture,' *Heterodox Academy Blog*, 17 March 2021; R. Lownie, 'Students must stand up for their professors' freedom of expression' *Areo Magazine* 24 May 2021.
[182] Applebaum, 'The new Puritans;' Hermanowicz, *Challenges to Academic Freedom*, pp. 15, 17, 29.

McCarthyite witch hunts in the US in the 1950s. Schrecker, for example, claims that the academic victims of McCarthyism reserved their ...

> 'bitterest condemnation for those of their colleagues who failed to support them ... especially the self-professed liberals among them ... In most cases it was not so much what these people did that upset the blacklisted professors as it was what they did not do. They did not organize; they did not protest; they did not do anything that reversed the tide of dismissals.'[183]

A sense of having been abandoned by my own colleagues has been a key feature of my own case as well. As indicated in Chapter 3, about two dozen of the academic staff at the University of Bristol Law School specialise in either human rights or employment law or both. Quite properly they study and criticise injustices in these fields in the UK and abroad. Yet, when it came to the violation of my human and employment rights by BRISOC, the University, and the Law School not one was prepared to breathe a whisper of public support. And very few offered any private support either. In a handful of post-exoneration encounters, several excused themselves by claiming they hadn't been fully aware of the scandal as it unfolded. Yet, in September 2021, I had emailed them all a copy of the *Mail on Sunday* article cited in Chapter 3 which sets out all the salient facts.

Students

Although arguably less critical of it than their teachers, the attitude of students towards illiberal leftism is also complex. For example, a survey of just over 1,000 UK undergraduates, conducted by the Higher Education Policy Institute, published on 23 June 2022,[184] found, amongst other things, that 79% of students believe: 'Students that feel threatened should always have their demands for safety respected' (up from 68% in 2016). Only 4% disagreed (down from 10% in 2016). Sixty-one per cent of those surveyed also believe that 'when in doubt' their own university 'should ensure all students are protected from

---

[183] E. Schrecker, *No Ivory Tower: McCarthyism and the Universities* (Oxford University Press, 1986), p. 308.
[184] N. Hillman, '*You can't say that!' What students really think of free speech on campus*, Higher Education Policy Institute, Policy Note 35, 22 June 2022.

discrimination rather than allow unlimited free speech' (up from 37% in 2016). The proportion who believe 'universities are becoming less tolerant of a wide range of viewpoints' has risen to 38% (up from 24% in 2016), a view significantly more prevalent among males (51%) than females (28%). Thirty-five per cent agree that 'if you debate an issue like sexism or racism, you make it acceptable' (twice the result, 17%, in 2016).

Thirty six per cent of respondents, over twice as many (15%) as six years previously, thought academics should be fired if they taught 'material that heavily offends some students.' A significant majority (77%) also wanted all university staff to be trained in 'understanding other cultures,' up from 55% in 2016. Only one-third of those polled (34%) agreed that 'all resources should be included for the purpose of academic study, regardless of content' (down from almost one-half of students, 47%, in 2016). Sixty-two per cent agree with safe-space policies (up from 48% in 2016), while 86% support trigger warnings (68% in 2016). Sixty-one per cent want universities, when in doubt, to subordinate unlimited freedom of expression to protection from discrimination, a significant increase from 37% in 2016. Only 17% advocated unlimited free speech, a fall from the previous figure of 27%. Just under half of those polled (48%) support the Government's proposal to establish a higher education 'free speech champion' in England, discussed in the following chapter. Not quite a quarter (23%) disagreed and the rest (29%) were uncertain.

However, 80% of students surveyed in another study, published in September 2022, claimed they were free to express their views, 65% said free speech and robust debate are well protected at their own institution, and 59% said that freedom of expression was not under threat.[185] Yet, 49% also felt that universities are becoming less tolerant of a wide range of viewpoints. Forty-three per cent (up from 25% in 2019) maintain that the risk of disagreeing with peers makes them feel unable to express their opinion. Broadly consistent with the earlier survey, 35% of the public

---

[185] This was based on two representative surveys of a total of almost 2,500 UK university students plus a number of representative surveys of the general public and referenced to similar surveys conducted in 2019, P. Duffy, *The state of free speech in UK universities: what students and the public think* (The Policy Institute, King's College London, 2022).

believe that debating issues such as sexism or racism makes such prejudices more acceptable, the figure is higher (46%) for students. Similarly, 41% of students (25% of the general public) believe that academics who teach material that offends some students should be fired.

Compliant institutions

It has been widely observed that wokeism has triumphed among senior management in universities across the English-speaking world and beyond. As a result, time-honoured academic values have been replaced by alternatives.[186] As Williams puts it:

> 'Rather than intellectual risk-taking, we have a culture of conformity. Rather than dissent we have consensus. Rather than challenging the status quo, we have adherence to predetermined values – and so often nowadays those values are woke.'[187]

University administrations have, for example, become much more willing to investigate staff for alleged minority-related 'misconduct,' even where the charges are patently fabricated, and to discipline them, including by dismissal for the most trivial professional shortcomings.[188] Several features of my own case are consistent with these trends. There was, for example, the Kafkaesque sense of having been made aware that I was under suspicion but for months not being told of the precise charges, being subjected to an official investigation governed by a procedure made up on the hoof, and having the offending module cancelled when I had been relying upon delivering it to demonstrate the fact that I had been unequivocally officially exonerated. And this is not to mention being defamed by the University's public statement in October 2021 – which announced my vindication while recognising BRISOC's 'concerns' and claimed that the HRLPS unit needed to be altered to protect the sensitivities of students – and the Law School's failure to deal with the hostile working environment which endured after

---

[186] See Williams, *How Woke Won*, pp. 91-108; 'Out of the academy,' *The Economist*, 4 September 2021, p. 14; Murray, *Madness of Crowds*, pp. 257-8; Hermanowicz, *Challenges to Academic Freedom*, pp. 12-13, 17-18, 37-42, 159-204; Campbell and Manning, *Victimhood Culture*, pp. 260-3; Lukianoff, *Unlearning Liberty*, pp. 69-75.
[187] Williams, *How Woke Won*, p. 106.
[188] See particularly Hermanowicz, *Challenges to Academic Freedom*, pp. 25-45.

months on sick leave and up to the day of my retirement on 30 September 2022.

Various institution-specific factors have produced this state of affairs. One concerns the introduction of market mechanisms to higher education, a development to which, paradoxically, the militants themselves stridently profess opposition. Of the 164 higher education institutions in the UK only about half a dozen are private. The others are public bodies which have, nevertheless, traditionally enjoyed considerable autonomy from the state. But this has changed significantly over the past few decades. Although remaining tax-funded institutions, most British universities have also increasingly had to compete with each other for contributions from the public purse for teaching and research, for fees from students, and for research grants from non-state sources.

A second factor, facilitated in the UK by the replacement of student loans for grants, has been the massive expansion in the number of university students, and in changing attitudes to their studies. In my experience, not so long ago, students were young learners, willingly guided by teachers who were generally respected for their experience and expertise. Now they are much more likely to be belligerent customers demanding a particular kind of product providing what they think they most need to succeed in their degrees and careers. They also expect to receive a particular kind of experience conforming with many of the wokeish attributes considered in previous sections. The result has been to turn university administrators into compliant service providers rather than, as they should be, fearless and independent guardians of the core university mission. Honest and open consultation with students is, of course, desirable. But this can never be on an entirely equal basis. Although technically adults, most students are typically young, inexperienced, and easily attracted by whatever appears to be the coolest fashionable fad. A few are vulnerable to seduction into dangerous, illegal activities, including by unscrupulous movements. And it is highly unlikely that any have a significantly better idea about the kind of education they need than those employed to provide it. Many appear simply to want the kind of spoon-feeding they received at school.

A third, related, factor has been a massive expansion in those parts of university administrations dedicated to satisfying an ever-expanding range of specialist services with their numerous codes, guidelines, and 'experts.'[189] It is a moot point whether those who staff them are as personally committed to illiberal leftism as the card-carrying militants themselves. But they certainly display little reluctance to accede even to the most jaw-dropping demands. On the contrary. Excessively risk-averse, brand-conscious, determined to make the curriculum as 'feel good' and undemanding as possible – and apparently fearful of the impact upon student satisfaction scores, the position of their institution in league tables, and the potentially adverse effect of being thought 'anti-woke' might have upon student recruitment – they tend to fall over themselves in their haste to capitulate to the online illiberal leftist mobs. Some of the customized services which have been created, for example those catering for disabled students, are worthy and necessary. Others manifestly are not. A prime example of the latter is the University of Bristol's widely ridiculed recent policy of allowing students to choose the Japanese feline pronoun by which they wish to be addressed.[190]

Conclusion

The outlook of the more militant and outspoken students at the University of Bristol, and other British universities – including their student unions which, of course, dominate most debates – is deeply infected with all the illiberal-leftist issues discussed in this chapter. BRISOC's complaint-and-campaign against me has also been peppered with wokeish, anti-othering, snowflakey, safe space demanding slogans and catch phrases. It also stems from an exaggerated sense of vulnerability and victimhood. Neither the unit nor the Islam, China and the Far East module victimized anybody. They each simply reprised, for reflection and discussion, arguments, issues and information widely debated in the authoritative literature. BRISOC's complaint-and-

---

[189] Slater, *Unsafe Spaces*, pp. 15, 17, 53, 120-21; Campbell and Manning, *Victimhood Culture*, p. 63.
[190] See, eg, https://www.independent.co.uk/life-style/catgender-bristol-university-pronoun-guide-b2010087.html.

campaign is also a palpable exercise in virtue signalling. Amongst its other objectives, it seeks to convey to Muslims that those involved are vigorously defending the faith while the message to non-Muslim student militants is that 'the Muslims' are on the same wokeish wave-length. And the latter is in spite of the fact that some of the more conservative implications of BRISOC's conception of Islam are glaring incompatible with any credible interpretation of 'progressive' left-wing ideology.

All the characteristics of contemporary witch-hunting and virtual heretic burning are also visible in abundance in BRISOC's complaint-and-campaign – the demand, in the absence of an abject apology, for my suspension and disciplining (including sacking) – and the scrapping of the Islam, China and the Far East module in any case. The complaint-and-campaign is also, clearly, a vicious exercise in cancel culture, motivated on the part of BRISOC by an Islamofauxbic attempt to silence me and others in order to eliminate any critical debate about Islam, including that which is reasoned, measured and evidence-based. In its turn it has produced a ripple of Islamophobia-phobia, not least on the part of the University and the Law School, one of the many other regrettable effects of which is that students interested in responsible critical engagement with Islam, including Muslims themselves, are now likely to be much more fearful of doing so than before. Nor would it be surprising if campaigns such as BRISOC's increased, rather than reduced, genuine Islamophobia in society at large.

Though exaggerated, some of the injustices allegedly suffered by the putatively marginalized and disadvantaged groups with which the illiberal left is concerned are, regrettably, palpable and real. But this does not mean that its strategy for dealing with them is either justified or effective. Constructive ways out of the current divisive and censorious climate need to be found instead. Some possible ways forward are suggested in the following chapter.

Chapter 6

Reflections

Introduction

This chapter seeks to summarize the issues discussed in the rest of the book and to consider how the challenges they present might be tackled. The take home message is very clear. I have done nothing wrong. I am not an Islamophobe and there isn't a scrap of reliable evidence that even suggests the contrary. Yet, I have been vilified, harassed and victimized by an angry online mob of intolerant and malicious Muslim students. While I have not been disciplined or sacked as they demanded, due to the problems they've caused, I was signed off work by my doctor from September 2021 to the beginning of January 2022. And, sadly, apparently suffering from a serious case of Islamophobia-phobia, my physical return to campus has been made difficult by my employers. The result is that, in addition to the cancellation of the Islam, China and the Far East module, BRISOC has succeeded in securing my physical removal from the University of Bristol Law School for most of the last year of my full-time working life, each for precisely the reasons the University's inquiry rejected. But, there are, nevertheless, a number of silver linings in these otherwise lowering clouds.

Context

For over a decade, without incident or complaint, I designed, single-handedly developed and taught the Human Rights in Law, Politics and Society (HRLPS) unit. Its introduction to the Law curriculum was, of course, approved by the Law School and the University of Bristol. Relying amongst other things, on student evaluations and peer review, it has also been audited every year since. Far from finding anything to criticise about either the unit or module, numerous colleagues and external examiners extolled it. Every year it attracted some of the brightest and more reflective law students, including a significant proportion of Muslims. The exam results were consistently amongst the best in any law subject. The Law School provides many avenues through which students can make complaints or suggest improvements, including about the curriculum, particular syllabuses, and the alleged misconduct of staff. For the first 13 years HRLPS was in operation nobody used any of these to raise any concerns whatever about it, or about me. Over this period, I also published a number of articles, blogs and other pieces addressing a range of related issues, especially counterterrorism.

BRISOC's complaint-and-campaign

Then everything went pear-shaped. But this was not entirely without warning. Over the preceding few years there had been several precursors, documented in Chapter 3, which the Law School had failed to address appropriately. In mid-February 2021 BRISOC publicly accused me of Islamophobia in my teaching and other public output. They tried to ruin my reputation, deprive me of my livelihood, end my career, and prompt ostracism from my immediate and other colleagues. They were also, at best, reckless about the risks their groundless and irresponsible allegations had for my personal safety, the harm to my mental health, and the impact upon my family.

The fact that BRISOC's formal complaint relied upon so many manifest and demonstrable lies indicates that it was not made in good faith. The most egregious of these are that I mocked the Qur'an in class, claimed the repression of the Uighurs by the Chinese party-state is only superficially discriminatory, that I deny there is such a thing as Islamophobia, and that the University ignored numerous complaints over many years about my allegedly Islamophobic views and conduct. There is also more than a lurking suspicion that BRISOC's social media campaign was timed to offer oblique support to Professor David Miller, accused of antisemitism and later sacked by the University for conduct unbefitting a university professor. It was also much more clearly and expressly intended to discredit my support for the Prevent counterterrorism strategy just as the official independent inquiry into it began.

In addition to the fact that it was manifestly vexatious and ill-founded, the University chose to entertain BRISOC's complaint in spite of the fact that it suffered from multiple procedural flaws. It was submitted long past the deadline for the 2019-20 session and before the relevant course material was delivered in 2020-21. The Office of the Independent Adjudicator's advice that anonymous complaints should only rarely be admitted, that complaints should be resolved within 90 days – and not almost a year as in my case – that they should be subject to mediation, and that those involved should be protected from misconduct from either party during the process, was also ignored.

Nevertheless, I have not yet been physically attacked by a militant Muslim seeking to exact the traditional death penalty for a perceived, though in my case entirely imaginary, insult to the faith. I assume, but cannot guarantee, that this risk has now diminished to negligible proportions. However, Sir Salman Rushdie, albeit an alleged Islamophobe with a much higher public profile than me, also thought that, by 2022, the threat to his physical safety stemming from the *Satanic Verses* controversy of the late 1980s, had all but vanished. Yet that August, at the age of 75, he was subjected to a vicious attack at a public event in the US which, though narrowly failing to end his life, nevertheless cost him an eye and the use of a hand. Although BRISOC has caused considerable damage to my mental and emotional health, they have failed to destroy it. Having been signed off work for four months, I have made a full recovery. And I have, of course, been unequivocally and unreservedly exonerated by the University's inquiry, unanimously endorsed upon appeal. In spite of deliberately misleading attempts by the University to undermine this, my appointment as Research Director at the Oxford Institute for British Islam (OIBI) has removed any lingering doubts that there might have been any substance to BRISOC's complaint-and-campaign. I now work closely with Muslims and others associated with the OIBI in pursuit of its mission to promote progressive Islam and to develop, under its auspices, my own research and other output, including this book.

Had BRISOC's formal complaint been made in good faith, most of the scandalous things documented between these covers are unlikely to have occurred. For example, if either BRISOC or the University had bothered to find out, they would quickly have discovered that I do not hate anyone, certainly not whole classes of people defined by their race, ethnicity, gender, nationality, or beliefs. As a student of ideas, I've also long been interested in all faiths and ideologies. And had BRISOC been willing to submit to confidential mediation, their complaint could, in principle, have been quickly and quietly resolved. Instead, brandishing their lies, distortions and misrepresentations, derived from hearsay and rumour, they jumped instead on the accelerating band wagon of illiberal-leftism, with its wokeism, hostility to (certain kinds of) 'othering,' exaggerated sense of victimhood, snowflakery, demands for intellectually safe spaces, virtue signalling, witch hunts, virtual heretic burnings, and cancel culture.

At the heart of BRISOC's complaint-and-campaign lies a chronic failure to acknowledge the difference between Islamophobia and critical engagement with Islam. Visceral hatred is the hallmark of prejudice. By contrast, critical appreciation is characterised by responsible scholarship and the discussion of insights derived from authoritative sources which rely upon verifiable evidence, distinguish carefully between uncontested fact and competing interpretations, and which are delivered in a measured tone.

The relationship between Islam and human rights is a case in point. Broadly speaking three positions can be distinguished: Muslims discovered human rights long before the west and, having been commanded by Allah, the Islamic conception is by far superior, a view held, naturally, only by some Muslims. A second position is that the modern human rights ideal is western and un-Islamic and does not fit well into a Muslim environment. A third is that Islamic and non-Islamic approaches to human rights, though different, are not fundamentally irreconcilable. The second and third of these positions have been articulated by both Muslim and non-Muslim commentators. The primary purpose of relevant elements of the Islam, China and the Far East module in HRLPS was simply to explore such perspectives and their implications. Nothing about this, any of the issues raised or discussed, or the manner in which any of it was conducted, was remotely

Islamophobic. On the contrary, the exercise was simply an integral component of a sustained critical engagement with national and international current affairs through a human rights lens. Indeed, given its undeniable global profile, to have ignored the debate about Islam and human rights would have been myopic and Eurocentric.

It would also have been absurd if an endeavour such as this did not include, as the Islam, China and the Far East module did, the exploration of attitudes in the Islamic tradition and 'Muslim lands' towards blasphemy, apostasy, non-Muslim minorities, women, and a range of other issues debated in the now-extensive literature. Prejudice against Islam and Muslims, like racism, misogyny, transphobia, xenophobia, antisemitism and others, should be confronted and stamped out wherever encountered, including in universities. But, in a free society, critical engagement with every faith and ideology, including Islam, should be central to those parts of the university curriculum where issues relating to beliefs, ideas, law, politics and society arise. It is highly regrettable that, as already indicated, in order to placate BRISOC, the University of Bristol and Law School capitulated to their demand to scrap the Islam, China and the Far East module in HRLPS for precisely the reasons the University's own inquiry thoroughly considered and conclusively rejected.

Together with many other cases, my experience clearly demonstrates that wokeism, snowflakery, selective hostility to othering, demands for intellectually safe spaces, and the attempt to 'decolonize the curriculum' are flourishing at the University of Bristol and other British universities. Underpinned by illiberal-leftism this has inspired witch hunts, virtual heretic burning, and cancellations derived from an intolerant, self-righteous militancy, coupled with shocking ignorance, arrogance and a malevolent intention to harm. Those who engage in such tribal atavism typically acknowledge accountability to nobody but themselves. And, as in my case, they are often prepared to cause significant and lasting damage to their victims on the basis of nothing more reliable than prejudice, hearsay and rumour.

Yet I have not been silenced. On the contrary, BRISOC has given me several public platforms I would not otherwise have had. These include the *Mail on Sunday* article, my book, *Tackling Terrorism in Britain* – at the launch of which the controversy was drawn by the host to the attention of an audience of diplomats, academics, senior civil servants and others – my online interview with the Bristol Free Speech Society available on YouTube,[191] my appointment as Research Director at the Oxford Institute for British Islam, and the publication of this book. But BRISOC's misconduct has almost certainly silenced others. Responsible critical engagement with Islam at the University of Bristol is now fraught with risk if not entirely off-limits. And the ripples are likely to spread far and wide.

In playing the man rather than the ball, BRISOC has also scored a series of spectacular own goals both against themselves and their faith. Their reputation is now in tatters. It is also a matter of considerable regret to everyone who, like me, opposes Islamophobia that their conduct is more likely to have stimulated than effectively challenged it in society at large, a consequence recognised by other Muslims.[192] They have also struck a hefty blow to the wedge which already divides tolerant and intolerant Muslims in the UK and elsewhere.

Those who mobilized BRISOC's campaign have a compelling case to answer with respect to a number of possible legal wrongs. These include: defamation; conspiracy to defame; harassment, intimidation and victimization; incitement of and conspiracy to harassment, intimidation and victimization; and conspiracy to induce the breach of my employment contract, the University's legal duty of care to me as my employer, and its legal duty to protect my freedom of expression and academic freedom. Legal remedies are under active consideration by my lawyers.

The University of Bristol and Law School in the dock

Instead of defending me from the injustice inflicted by BRISOC, the University of Bristol and Law School compounded it by smearing,

---

[191] Bristol Free Speech Society's interview, *Islamophobia and academic freedom: a conversation with Professor Steven Greer*, available on YouTube at the following link: https://www.youtube.com/watch?v=-6q2o5058jA.

[192] See, eg, A. Alam, 'Controversy over Bristol University Professor Steven Greer's "Islamophobia": Why Critical Discussion of Islamic Tradition Should Not Be Snubbed,' *New Age Islam*, 26 February 2021.

marginalizing, excluding, ostracizing, and 'othering' me. Each could and should have publicly affirmed their equal commitment to diversity/ inclusivity and academic freedom with much less equivocation about the latter. The sad irony is that there can be no genuine diversity if intolerant online militants, self-appointed to determine what advances progressive causes and what does not, are granted a licence to suppress the lawful expression of contributions to legitimate academic debates merely because they disagree with them.

Although declining to suspend me from my professional responsibilities, the University of Bristol was, nevertheless, initially reluctant to declare that I denied the charges. And when it did, I was prohibited both from publicly commenting upon the accusations, and later from announcing my exoneration when it occurred. Following the rejection of BRISOC's appeal against the Assessor's decision in my favour, the University publicly acknowledged my vindication. But, in doing so, it defiantly undermined its own inquiry by stating that it 'recognised' BRISOC's 'concerns' and that HRLPS needed to be revised in order to respect the sensitivities of students taking it. The University has also signally failed to explain how and why these 'sensitivities' became more acute in 2020-21 and thereafter than at any other point in the previous decade and a half, particularly since nothing of substance had changed over the relevant period.

As far as its duty of care to me as an employee is concerned, a number of other questions remain unanswered. Why was BRISOC's complaint admitted in spite of being manifestly vexatious and suffering from multiple procedural flaws any one of which should have resulted in it being rejected? Why was I not informed about the fact and substance of the complaint when it was officially submitted on 30 October 2020, nor invited to contribute to its informal resolution? Why was BRISOC not warned about disciplinary consequences when they threatened, in December 2020, to go public if their complaint was not swiftly settled, and presumably in their favour? Why was no attempt made, in spite of my pleas, to stop their vicious, potentially life-threatening social media campaign when it started in February 2021? Why have those involved, including one of the University's own student anti-racism advisers, not been required to discontinue it, publicly retract the false accusations upon which it is based, and to apologise for the harm caused? Why have they still not been disciplined for victimization, intimidation and harassment nearly two years later? Quite properly, the University routinely punishes students found guilty of cheating in assessments. By sharp contrast, it has taken no steps whatever to sanction those who have done me a much greater wrong. Why did it also take almost twelve months to acquit me, completely and resoundingly, of all BRISOC's allegations? Why have I also been silenced four times – once during the inquiry, again while awaiting a draft joint public statement between me, the complainant and the University itself about the result which the University never produced, and twice by the Law School with respect to the Bristol Free Speech Society interview which nevertheless eventually went ahead in spite of a third attempt to stop it?

And the culpability of my employers does not end there. For several years, the Law School refused to challenge a number of underhand attempts by a tiny cabal of hostile colleagues intent upon smearing me as a racist and Islamophobe, principally because, in common with many others, I maintain that the Prevent counterterrorist programme is neither. There are also subtle indications that BRISOC may have received their guidance and advice. Although the Law School knew about all these incidents, it chose to side with my opponents on nearly all relevant occasions. It was also spineless with respect to the HRLPS virtual pub quiz and exam, and the email to colleagues about BRISOC's complaint-and-campaign in February 2021. Even more consistently than the University, it has repeatedly failed to acknowledge that I strenuously denied all BRISOC's charges. In its email to students and staff in February 2021 it also subordinated academic freedom to self-congratulation concerning its own professed commitment to inclusivity and diversity. The Law School has also done nothing about the fact that two societies it supports – University of Bristol Unity and Diversity in Law, and the University of Bristol Women in Law Society – signed BRISOC's potentially life-threatening petition without checking its veracity, nor about other colleagues who have publicly supported their campaign even after my formal exoneration. A few of my Law School colleagues privately expressed their sympathy and solidarity. But not one breathed a whisper of public support. The rest maintained a stony silence both publicly and privately.

The Law School was fully informed that I had been officially exonerated in July 2021. Yet, it declined to notify colleagues that this had occurred. As lawyers, those concerned should have been very familiar with the distinction between the results of 'trials at first instance,' which are routinely reported, and the outcome of any appeal which happens sometime later. Early in the controversy senior Law School management encouraged me, when the dust had finally settled, to use the BRISOC controversy as a didactic opportunity. Yet, not long after my exoneration, the same people made my position untenable by cancelling the Islam, China and the Far East module, prima facie breaching the statutory obligation to protect academic freedom in the process. While this was, ostensibly, initiated by two very junior colleagues whose age and inexperience may provide some mitigation, its approval by those in senior managerial positions, is nothing short of a cowardly betrayal, heralding a disillusioning despatch at the end of a long and productive career spanning nearly 40 years.

In the autumn of 2021, following my unequivocal official exoneration, a resolution I proposed about academic freedom and cancel culture campaigns was not even put to the School Meeting for discussion as I had requested. And, in spite of the fact that my doctor regarded my involvement as 'eminently sensible,' I was also prohibited from participating in the Bristol Free Speech Society's online interview in December 2021 on the implausible grounds that I had not then received approval to do so from Occupational Health. Inexplicably, without objection on this or any other ground, I had been involved in the online launch of *Tackling Terrorism in Britain* a few weeks earlier. Furthermore, I have more than once drawn precisely what needs to be done about the toxic environment in the Law School to the attention of the School's senior management. Ignoring this, they have, nevertheless, persistently sought to thwart my return to working both from home and on campus in defiance of two Occupational Health reports.

Instead of defending diversity/inclusivity and academic freedom equally, in my case the University and the School have opted to sacrifice the latter to the former. The most plausible explanation is that, having nailed their colours so firmly to the wokeish mast, it would have been a huge loss of face – which they feared might also damage student recruitment – to have to admit that those purporting to represent a particular minority (Muslim students in this case) had behaved in a way that warranted condemnation rather than capitulation to their core demands.

Lessons to be learned

Several lessons should be learned from my experience and that of others in similar circumstances. First, it would be a grave mistake to dismiss the current witch hunts as mere spats in ivory towers or esoteric battles in the culture wars between fanatics on the political right and left. On the contrary, they are matters of fundamental right and wrong and as such should concern us all. They can, and have, destroyed reputations, ended careers, deprived those targeted of their livelihoods, and led to breakdowns in health and in relationships. In extreme cases, they may lead to suicide or even murder. And they almost invariably prompt widespread self-censorship, chilling freedom of speech, academic and public debate. Manifestly false accusations are also likely to be counterproductive, undermining rather than advancing whatever cause those concerned claim to represent. British universities also need to shake themselves out of the prevailing head-in-the-sand culture of denial about the problems posed to academic freedom, particularly by tiny cabals of militant illiberal-leftists.

But one of the most salutary lessons to be learned from my experience – which I'm sure would be echoed by others – is that its victims find it very difficult to enforce compliance with the many legal obligations British universities already have to protect academic freedom. These include section 43(1) and (2) of the Education (No 2) Act 1986 which requires higher education institutions in England and Wales to 'take such steps as are reasonably practicable to ensure that freedom of speech within the law is secured for members, students and employees ... and for visiting speakers.' This also provides that the use of university premises is not denied to any individual or group on the basis of his, her, or its beliefs, views, policy or objectives. Under section 202(2) of the Education Reform Act 1988 university commissioners in England and Wales are also under a duty 'to have regard to the need (a) to ensure that academic staff have freedom within the law to question and test received wisdom, and to put forward new ideas and controversial or unpopular opinions, without placing themselves in jeopardy of losing their jobs or privileges ....; (b) to enable qualifying institutions to provide education, promote learning and engage in research efficiently and economically; and (c) to apply the principles of justice and fairness.' The Equality Act 2010 also requires higher education providers not to discriminate unlawfully against, to harass or to victimize,[193] on the basis of, amongst other things, religion or belief.[194] In the exercise of their functions, public authorities – such as universities, schools and the NHS – also share the wider Public Sector Equality Duty (PSED) 'to have due regard to the need to … eliminate discrimination, harassment, victimization and any other conduct that is prohibited by or under this Act,' to 'advance equality of opportunity,' and to 'foster good relations' between persons who share a relevant protected characteristic and those who do not.[195]

Section 26 of the Counter Terrorism and Security Act 2015 (CTSA) imposes a statutory duty on specified public authorities, including universities, to have 'due regard to the need to prevent people from being drawn into terrorism' (the 'Prevent duty').[196] According to the Prevent Duty Guidance, the term 'due regard' means that specified authorities 'should place an appropriate amount of weight on the need to prevent people being drawn into terrorism when they consider all the other factors relevant to how they carry out their usual functions.'[197] Introduced as amendments to the Bill in the House of Lords, section 31(2) CTSA complements the Prevent duty in further and higher education with two other statutory obligations already provided by other

---

[193] Equality Act 2010, ss. 1, 13, 14, 19-27, 90-4.
[194] Ibid, ss. 4-12.
[195] Ibid, s. 149(1).
[196] The Prevent duty does not apply to Northern Ireland.
[197] Home Office Statutory Guidance, Revised Prevent Duty Guidance: for England and Wales, updated 10 April 2019, para. 4. 13 CTSA s. 29(2). 14 CTSA s. 33.

legislation – to have 'particular regard' to ensuring freedom of speech and for 'the importance of academic freedom.' The CTSA also provides statutory authority for the Secretary of State to issue both Guidance, to which relevant authorities 'must have regard' when carrying out their Prevent duty, and directions enforceable by court order.

However, in spite of these and other provisions, in 2017, a report commissioned by the University and College Union (UCU), Britain's principal academic trade union, found that, with one exception, legal and constitutional protections are less effective in the UK than those in any other state in the EU, to which the UK then belonged. According to the authors:

> 'in the overwhelming majority of instances, UCU members report statistically significantly higher levels of systematic abuse of their academic freedom, across a wide array of measures, than their European counterparts ... (T)he very low level of legal protection in the UK is mirrored by a low level of awareness of the rights of academic freedom, and a high level of abuse.'[198]

Compared to an average of 14% for the EU, 23% of UK respondents also reported being bullied on account of their academic views, while 36% admitted to self-censorship, by contrast with the EU average of 19%. And yet, in 2021, the UCU offered more support to the mob which drove Kathleen Stock from her chair in Philosophy at the University of Sussex than to her. Needless to say, universities should never capitulate to campaigns like BRISOC's. Vexatious and ill-founded complaints, such as theirs, should always be summarily dismissed. And even where they are wrongly admitted for consideration of the merits, common decency and common sense should remind us of the importance of harnessing the power of open and honest conversation in order to identify common ground. This should nearly always precede any resort to campaigns, investigations, disciplinary action, compelled early retirement deals, and so on. In the final analysis, we should all be content to live with irresolvable differences between lawfully expressed points of

---

[198] T. Karran and L. Kallinson, *Academic Freedom in the UK: Legal and Normative Protection in a Comparative Context*, Report for the University and College Union, 7 May 2017, p. 1.

view. Responsible academic leaders also need to learn how to use such disputes as pedagogical opportunities, helping students and staff better to appreciate the importance of debating complex issues in mature and considerate ways, and never resorting to defamatory attacks on individuals to win arguments.

Regrettably, this is not what currently tends to happen. Instead, University administrators generally acknowledge the prima facie validity of the complaint by suspending the member of the academic staff concerned and/or by issuing a less than robust defence of their right to academic freedom. For example, while I was not myself suspended, the University of Bristol and the Law School, nevertheless, made a series of white-flag waving statements more sympathetic to BRISOC's complaint than to me. Senior University management then typically subjects victims to often protracted disciplinary processes which make almost unbearably onerous demands on their time, resources and mental health. As in my case, and that of many others, the universities concerned generally make no attempt to stop the online mob's vicious social media campaigns of vilification, victimization and harassment either during the course of the investigation or thereafter. And even if the inquiry results in the complete exoneration of the accused, other ways will typically be found to placate the complainants, such as, in my case, scrapping the Islam, China and the Far East module on my HRLPS unit, precisely as BRISOC demanded. Finally, even if the victim manages to initiate expensive legal proceedings against their employer, these are likely to take years before a modest out-of-court settlement is reached which leaves the mob unscathed. During this time some colleagues will have taken sides. But most will simply have lost interest. Finally, the victim has to decide whether to tough it out or to seek employment elsewhere. Luckily, just over a year from retirement when the BRISOC crisis began, I was spared having to make such an invidious choice. But, aware of this, both the University and the Law School found it easier to embark on their own head-in-the-sand, tough-it-out policy of denial-and-disregard than might otherwise have been the case.

How should the challenges confronting academic freedom in the UK, discussed in this book, be addressed? To begin with it needs to be acknowledged that every university in the UK already provides abundant opportunities for students to register complaints and/or to make constructive proposals for the modification of curricula and syllabuses. As a result, there will rarely if ever be any justification for social media campaigns such as that launched by BRISOC against me, even when by contrast with theirs, they do not rely upon lies, distortion and misrepresentation. Formal complaints like BRISOC's should, therefore, be firmly rejected where they fail, without good reason, to comply with time limits, where the complainant has no direct personal experience of the alleged misconduct, nor any professional background in relevant academic fields, and which rely instead upon rumour and hearsay allegedly supplied by anonymous third parties. Any campaign, like BRISOC's, should instantly result in any relevant formal complaint being rejected for breach of the duty to act reasonably.

Where a campaign of vilification against an academic has been initiated in the absence of a formal complaint, it should be investigated immediately by the institution concerned. Any campaign for the censorship of teaching materials and/or for the disciplining of its own staff, motivated purely by disagreement with lawful opinion, should result in those involved being required by their host institution to end it forthwith and to apologise to all affected. Formal reprimands, cautions or warnings should also be entered on their records and should be included in any references sought. In the event of non-compliance, more severe sanctions should follow. As far as my own case is concerned, even though BRISOC's social media campaign has retreated to the shadows, the University of Bristol should stop it now. The University should also explain why it has not done so sooner. BRISOC must also be compelled to remove all reference to its campaign from all relevant sites apart from a retraction and apology. Failure to do so should also have legal consequences.

Ideally, all of this should have occurred, in my case and that of others, without external intervention. But the common experience demonstrates that much more needs to be done both inside and outside universities to make it more likely to happen. As in most other fields, as the 20th and 21st centuries have unfolded, self-regulation in the British higher education sector has progressively given way to increased external regulation. This currently takes various forms, with the Office for Students (OfS), established by the Higher Education and Research Act 2017, having become the key agency.

Two other recent pieces of draft legislation are relevant to the ongoing debate. One, the Higher Education (Freedom of Speech) Bill 2022 seeks to strengthen existing obligations upon British universities and students' unions to protect freedom of speech. Although it may be difficult to prove, a proposed new statutory tort would, as a last resort, facilitate claims for compensation regarding a loss which has occurred as a result of an academic institution's failure to protect freedom of expression, including that of 'no platformed' speakers. A statutory duty would be imposed on the OfS to promote free speech and to levy fines on institutions failing to comply with relevant statutory obligations. A new ombudsman – the Director for Freedom of Speech and Academic Freedom, dubbed the 'free speech champion' – would also be responsible for monitoring cases of no-platforming and adverse consequences stemming from the expression of lawful but controversial points of view. A recent report has also recommended the appointment of free speech champions embedded in the senior management of universities themselves.[199] While the Bill is intended to protect academic staff, students and visitors who express controversial opinions, it would also prohibit without good reason, denial of access to the premises of any higher education provider with respect to any group or individual on the basis of their lawfully expressed ideas, belief, or views. The statutory obligation on universities to protect freedom of speech would be extended for the first time to students' unions.

The Bill has had a mixed reception. Some have argued that there is no need for it because academic freedom is not in crisis in the UK and that, in any case, universities can and should be trusted to police themselves without further legal obligations added to the many which already exist. It has also been claimed that the proposed legislation is likely to be ineffective and counterproductive. For example, complaints

---

[199] J. Suissa and A. Sullivan, 'How can universities promote academic freedom? Insights from the front line of the gender wars' (2022) 27 *Impact* 2-61.

to the Office for Students OfS will only be possible once a given institution's own internal complaints mechanisms have been exhausted. This is likely to snarl complaints in protracted bureaucracy, possibly for years. Once it has heard a complaint, the OfS can make 'recommendations' to the higher education provider concerned but will have to take them to court if these are not implemented, providing more opportunity for obfuscation and procrastination. Any academic bringing their own institution to the OfS is likely to be committing professional suicide unless, like me, they're on the verge of retirement. At the very least, they'll certainly not improve their promotion prospects.

However, others – expressing a view I share – have pointed out that there is clear evidence that universities are not defending academic freedom effectively and that it is difficult to see how this is likely to improve without external intervention. One of the most authoritative contributions along these lines comes from Nicola Dandridge, former chief executive of the Office for Students, appointed in the spring of 2022 as Professor of Higher Education Policy at the University of Bristol. She states: 'We've been very clear that we think the bill is needed, that we think there is a serious, evidenced, issue about lack of free speech within universities. We will be working with government as the bill progresses and gets implemented.'[200] Whether the Higher Education (Freedom of Speech) Bill makes matters better or worse remains to be seen. But doing nothing is not a viable option.

The other initiative is the Online Safety Bill 2022 which, although not directly concerned with higher education, may nevertheless have some impact upon it. The proposed legislation is intended to enhance the protection of those victimized or exploited by abuse on the internet and social media. It requires online providers to take action against both legal and illegal harmful content on their platforms. Breach of the proposed duty would expose those concerned to fines of up to 10% of their annual turnover. Ofcom would also be empowered to block offending sites, but not those of news publishers and their readers' comments. Providers would also be obliged by law to ensure that content moderation did not

---

[200] 'Sewell controversy at Nottingham "shows free speech bill needed,"' *Times Higher Education*, 23 March 2022.

arbitrarily remove or infringe access to journalistic material. Large social networks would also be required to protect 'democratically important' content, such as user-submitted posts supporting or opposing particular political parties or policies. The bill has provoked fierce controversy. The proposed power to restrain the publication of 'lawful but harmful' speech, criticized on the grounds that it would effectively create a new form of censorship, was modified during the parliamentary process. As a result, platforms will be legally obliged to protect children from the worst forms of legal but harmful content. But, for adults, they will instead have to identify the type of legal material they will not permit. Meeting these requirements will also have to be demonstrated.

However, regulatory innovation of any kind can, at best, provide only part of the solution. The deeper need is for cultural and managerial change in universities themselves. The prevailing academic culture, particularly in arts, humanities and the social sciences, needs to become much less hospitable to witch hunts and to cancel culture from any part of the political spectrum. Senior university management must also become much less inclined to indulge it. The prospects of this happening any time soon in British universities are not great. But there are, nevertheless, some grounds for hope.

As already indicated in the previous chapter, since the general public is not well-disposed to illiberal leftism, the more the latter is exposed to the cold light of democratic scrutiny, the better. There is also some evidence of a welcome backlash to the kind of risible wokeism which recently led some anti-colonial activists to claim that that the statement '2+2=4' is part of a hegemonic narrative which cannot be objectively true because there are other ways of knowing,[201] and to the University of Bristol permitting its students to use Japanese feline pronouns. Some academics and students, appalled by the lack of intellectual credibility and the suffocating effects of illiberal leftism, are also beginning to organise themselves in free speech societies and in other ways. This might take time to mature. But, as it does, it will offer more compelling counternarratives to the dominant illiberal ones.

---

[201] D. Murray, *The War on the West* (HarperCollins, 2022), pp. 198-99.

While the academic staff in STEM subjects (Science, Technology, Engineering, and Maths) are just as vulnerable as those in other fields to cancellation for comments unrelated to their professional interests, these disciplines themselves otherwise provide a particularly impregnable citadel against woke ideas. The historic contributions of non-western scientists should be more widely known. But the value of seeking to dismiss the discoveries of their seminal long-dead, white, western counterparts on the grounds that they were racist and colonialist is, at best, questionable. For one thing, even if what they said in the past may be offensive by the standards of today, since they are no longer alive they're not going to offend anybody any further. For another, there is no guarantee that, in the past, non-western scientists were any less racist or colonialist. But of greatest importance, all genuine scientific insights remain true no matter what the cultural context, who discovered them, or what their personal virtues and vices were. Attempts to demote science to the status of a mere 'western cultural artefact,' with no greater validity than any discredited traditional western or non-western belief system, are unlikely to fare any better in the long term.[202] Any surgeon conducting a complex, life-saving operation will, for example, have to apply the same understanding of medicine and anatomy no matter whether the procedure is performed in New York, Delhi, or Tehran. And any engineer seeking to construct a safe road or rail bridge will also have to observe universal, not culturally specific, standards. Nor is anyone likely to prefer non-western, pre-modern alternatives in either context.

Proposals to replace British A levels with a continental style baccalaureate consisting of six subjects, including formal training in 'critical thinking,' might help, especially if the latter were genuinely critical. And finally, let us not forget humour. While illiberal leftism is, of course, deadly serious, many of its manifestations, like the Japanese feline pronouns, are overripe for ridicule. Fake news about the emperor's new clothes was exposed by an innocent child unphased by adult complicity in the myth. Let us also hope that, before long, we will all be laughing at the discredited enemies of freedom and truth.

---

[202] Ibid, pp. 196-201.

Chapter 7

Postscript

Introduction

As intimated in the Preface to the paperback edition of this book, a lot has happened in the few months since publication of the hardback in February 2023. The most important development has, without doubt, been global media coverage of my story resulting in a public relations disaster for BRISOC and the University of Bristol. Support for my cause, and concern about the egregious assault upon academic freedom it represents, have also been massively boosted. The free speech and counterterrorism implications of the University of Bristol's mismanagement of the BRISOC scandal have also been laid bare by, respectively, Alumni for Free Speech (AFFS) and the Oxford Institute for British Islam (OIBI). And yet, the University remains stubbornly resistant to addressing this unresolved crisis. The BRISOC scandal has also graphically exposed the extent to which the crime of blasphemy has been subtly resurrected as a socially-sanctioned offence, but only for Islam.

A global public relations disaster for BRISOC and the University of Bristol

To give my book and story the best chance of at least being noticed, I employed the services of a specialist book PR firm, Palamedes.[203] My motives were not egotistical or avaricious. I simply wanted to enhance the prospect of realizing the goals specified in the Preface to the hardback, particularly setting the record straight, naming and shaming

---

[203] https://www.palamedes.co.uk/praise/#portfolio/e7e07018-f6fe-4190-8814-acccf36a022e.

the culpable parties, and making whatever contribution I could to preventing similar misfortunes befalling others. As a result, by late February 2023, news about publication and my story had been covered by outlets with a monthly global distribution of 231 million unique readers, viewers and listeners. This included most of the British print news media. I was interviewed on BBC Radio 4's flagship news programme, *Today*, on the national TV network GB News, and on BBC Bristol's Politics show. Veteran Labour MP, Barry Sheerman, also called for Professor Evelyn Welch, Vice Chancellor and President of the University of Bristol, and the entire senior management team, to resign.[204] Although fully deserved regarding the latter, this was not initially wholly fair with respect to Professor Welch who only took up her post at Bristol in the autumn of 2022. However, as the following account amply demonstrates, the demand has, nevertheless, since become fully warranted.

Shortly after the hardback was published I gave Professor Welch a copy and, in an email, I proposed a face-to-face meeting to explore how the BRISOC scandal might be amicably resolved. She declined on the grounds that it would not be appropriate for us to meet until the letter-before-claim from my solicitors had been withdrawn. Professor Welch's reply also ended with the cryptic statement: 'The University has already reached out to the Bristol SU Society and will take further steps to support its students.' It is not at all clear what this means. But it certainly suggests the opposite of the disciplinary action against BRISOC which remains both deserved and required.

On 17 February I summarized my case on *The Times Red Box* online comment site in an article entitled 'How to solve the campus free speech crisis.'[205] Four days later Professor Welch publicly responded to the developments of the previous week on the same platform with one of her own – 'Bristol University is not defensive or intolerant.' It reads:

> 'I have been vice-chancellor of the University of Bristol for six months and have just passed an important milestone — the first call by a

---

[204] 'Cleared professor fears for academic freedom,' *The Times*, 17 February 2023.
[205] https://www.thetimes.co.uk/article/how-to-solve-the-campus-free-speech-crisis-7d9jr35zg

politician for my immediate resignation in a national newspaper. Given the topic of freedom of speech, it wasn't unexpected, even if it felt a bit precipitous (maybe a phone call in advance next time?)

Universities are central to the success of the UK. How we behave, what we do and what we say matters. I personally welcome the scrutiny. As the Higher Education (Freedom of Speech) Bill makes its way through parliament, I and all UK vice-chancellors can expect much more of this.

At the same time, I have been struck that what should be important debates of principle have become centered on a small number of high-profile cases. This isn't surprising. It is easier to tell a personal story than to write about the fine legal and moral lines between hate speech and freedom of speech. But universities also need to take some responsibility — we know that there are real people involved on all sides, not just abstract ideas. When complaints arise it is important that we have, as Bristol does, fair and balanced processes to address competing perspectives and differing accounts. This takes time, sometimes considerable amounts of it. Due to obligations of confidentiality we cannot and should not give detailed explanations or rebuttals in the media on specific cases either before, during, or after our processes have concluded.

This can and often does lead to assumptions that we have not been robust in our approach to freedom of speech and academic freedom (which are not, by the way, the same thing).

Complexity and confidentiality sit uneasily in a world of social media that wants an instant response. But we do need to give the public more confidence in how we as universities hold ourselves to account. We need to find a way to balance confidentiality with better explanations of what we already do successfully to protect academic freedom and freedom of speech. As it approaches the end of the parliamentary process, the Higher Education (Freedom of Speech) Bill looks set to re-introduce the ability for aggrieved parties to go straight to court rather than use existing internal processes first. I, like many others, believe this approach presents a real risk that we will find ourselves worrying about legal precedents rather than supporting open dialogue.

Good communication is a two-way process. If someone wants to be heard, someone also has to want to listen. It may come as news to many but, for the most part, universities and student unions are not defensive or intolerant. Our student union supports over 350 societies that cover everything from baking to skydiving and includes the Free Speech Society, whose mission is to create a friendly and open environment for students of all backgrounds to explore ideas and viewpoints. Every day at Bristol and other universities across the United Kingdom, staff, students and visitors hold fierce debates about society, politics, religion, race, gender, sexuality, climate change (to name only a few). They do so not because of legislation, but because they have learned to listen carefully, assess evidence thoughtfully, and then to speak with passion and conviction.

In one of its editorials, The Times invites us to 'shout louder' to protect freedom of speech. But shouting is rarely persuasive and hardly helps build better understanding. If we really want to protect academic freedom and freedom of speech, let's put the megaphones down (a technology that betrays my age) and listen better.'[206]

Although there are some positive elements in this contribution, it is mostly riddled with difficulties. For a start, the VC acknowledges the call for her resignation but fails to say why it was made. The claim that 'important debates of principle have become centred on a small number of high-profile cases' because it is 'easier to tell a personal story than to write about the fine legal and moral lines between hate speech and freedom of speech' is also problematic for several reasons. The 'high-profile cases,' such as mine, are the kind of 'lived experiences' by which, in other contexts, the University sets such store. As the flesh and blood perches upon which issues of abstract principle come home to roost, they also graphically illustrate where problems in compliance with relevant principles have arisen. Yet, the VC seems to think they can and should be dismissed with the invocation of vague platitudes and a patrician wave of the hand.

In any case, my book not only explores my 'lived experience' at length; it thoroughly reflects upon the wider issues, including 'the fine legal and moral lines between hate speech and freedom of speech' which the BRISOC scandal raises. It is also true that, in theory, the University of Bristol has 'fair and balanced processes to address competing perspectives and differing accounts.' But, as Chapter 3 and the letter from AFFS discussed below each demonstrate, the University wantonly violated them, apparently confident that they were effectively

---

[206] https://www.thetimes.co.uk/article/bristol-university-not-defensive-intolerant-comment-xz0qrw7g7

unenforceable, a pattern familiar in similar circumstances across the Anglo-sphere.

'Confidentiality' also makes a familiar appearance as an imaginary cloak of invisibility spread over inconvenient truths in order to avoid having to defend them. The fact is that, as a result of BRISOC's social media campaign and the publication of this book, nothing confidential of significance has survived the scandal. The references to 'open dialogue,' and to the Bristol student union supporting over 350 societies including the Free Speech Society, are disingenuous. This is not least because the Law School tried three times to prevent me from taking part in an interview with the Free Speech Society, the very purpose of which was to stimulate 'open dialogue.' Although the interview eventually went ahead, no discussion between me and BRISOC has ever been possible, including at this event, because they declined every opportunity to engage in it.

Support for my cause grows

Not surprisingly, given the publicity it has received, the publication of my book has significantly boosted support for my cause. In addition to the news reportage, I was interviewed by Emma Parks, editor of the distinguished journal, *Freethinker*.[207] On 23 March 2023 I gave a very well-received paper about the BRISOC scandal to the session on 'Islamophobia and Disinformation campaigns: The challenge to policy makers' at Policy Exchange's European Roundtable on Extremism at Hatfield House, Hertfordshire. And on 30 March, I enjoyed a lively conversation with Megan Manson, Head of Campaigns at the National Secular Society, in the company of an online audience of over 100.[208] My book was also officially launched on 6 April at the Art Workers' Guild in London, an event sponsored by the OIBI, the Free Speech Union (FSU) and the Common Sense Society.[209]

---

[207] https://freethinker.co.uk/2023/03/interview-with-steven-greer/
[208] https://www.secularism.org.uk/news/2023/04/academic-hounded-by-islamic-society-speaks-out-at-nss-event
[209] https://www.youtube.com/watch?v=22a8UdmhnBY.

Towards the end of March 2023, the FSU introduced me to AFFS, a campaigning organization which, amongst other things, seeks to encourage alumni and others to suspend donations to British tertiary sector institutions in prima facie breach of their statutory duties to protect academic freedom. The result was a magisterial 14-page letter AFFS sent to the University of Bristol on 11 April 2023.[210]

In a nutshell, AFFS accuses the University of multiple violations of its own free speech guidelines, its staff and student conduct regulations, and relevant statutory obligations. As the letter states: 'The University's failure ... to take all reasonably practicable steps to secure Professor Greer's freedom of speech can only be described as catastrophic, and at the very heart of what went wrong.' AFFS maintains that the University should have prevented BRISOC's potentially criminal and life-threatening social media campaign by warning those concerned of disciplinary consequences when they threatened to 'go public.' And, if the campaign had gone ahead as it in fact did, those involved should have been disciplined rather than having their 'concerns,' which the official inquiry found to be groundless, officially recognised.

AFFS states that the cancellation of the Islam, China and the Far East module, effectively in response to demands from a small group of vocal activists, 'looks like a form of censorship and an unreasonable and unjustified interference with Professor Greer's academic freedom.' They claim it may also amount to a violation of the Public Sector Equality Duty to protect my religious or philosophical beliefs. The letter maintains as well that the University of Bristol's lack of effective management and governance arrangements appear to breach its conditions of registration as an educational charity.

The AFFS recommends that the University of Bristol should now take the following steps.

> '1. Self-report to the OfS ... (Office for Students, the universities' regulator) ... that serious free speech protection failures have occurred, and that it is working to identify what these were and the appropriate remedies, and to set the failures right.

---

[210] https://affs.uk/wp-content/uploads/2023/04/AFFS-letter-to-Bristol-11-04-23.pdf.

2. It should in any event appoint an external and unconflicted person of appropriate seniority and relevant experience to review the events referred to in this letter by reference to the University's relevant internal rules and regulations and existing and future legal obligations ... and make recommendations for changes to its rules, procedures, practices and requirements to ensure its proper compliance with its legal obligations in the future.

3. Implement those recommendations.'

The letter also maintains that:

'The University will need, in any event, to work to improve its free speech protections. In this regard, both Section 43(1) of the Education Act and best free speech practice more generally require all of the following to be done, urgently ... A review and revision of: (a) the University's relevant rules, procedures, practices and requirements relating to free speech ... to ensure that they reflect and properly implement the University's legal and other obligations relating to freedom of speech and academic freedom; and (b) the University's other rules, procedures, practices and requirements to ensure that they are compatible with its legal and other obligations relating to freedom of speech and academic freedom.'

According to AFFS, systems need to be established at all management levels at Bristol to ensure the prompt, firm and effective implementation and enforcement of relevant requirements. Both staff and students need to receive proper training, and regular reminders about the importance of free speech. To ensure compliance with relevant legal obligations, and enforcement of its own rules, an appropriately senior, qualified, adequately empowered, and independent Free Speech Officer should be appointed as its in-house free speech champion. Needless to say, anyone at fault in the mismanagement of the BRISOC scandal should be more eligible for dismissal than consideration as a candidate.

In the letter the AFFS signals its intention to bring the BRISOC scandal to the attention of the OfS and possibly the Charity Commission if the University fails to set up its own independent inquiry into how the controversy was managed. It also recommends that Bristol alumni, and other potential donors, should consider withholding funds until the University demonstrates it has responded satisfactorily to the concerns raised. On 2 June, as a result of having found the University's reply inadequate, AFFS referred the matter to the OfS as promised.

A very welcome contribution to the debate was also received from Eric Barendt, a distinguished Emeritus Professor of Media Law at University College London. In a paper delivered to a conference in France in the spring of 2023, he states:

'.... there can be no doubt that academic freedom may now be seriously threatened by student complaints, backed up by protests on campus (as in Kathleen Stock's case) or social media campaigns which may attract support from people entirely outside the university. Bristol University's decision to delete from Professor Greer's human rights course the module, or element, dealing with Islam and human rights was a clear infringement of a university teacher's academic freedom to determine what topics are covered – though of course it could argue that the freedom to determine the content of its courses and how they are taught is part of its institutional autonomy. There is here a conflict between individual academic freedom and university autonomy.'[211]

Counterterrorism implications of the BRISOC scandal

Media coverage of the publication of my book and story also led to a particularly chilling revelation from a former Bristol colleague, now a professor at another British university, who emailed me as follows.

BRISOC ... 'is really extremist. When I was there, they invited some so-called Islamic scholars to speak to the students about the role of Islam in modern Britain. The large room near the lift was full of students. It was the most threatening experience, they were just attacking verbally students for any question they did not like. I complained to the university but was ignored. One of the speakers was charged a couple of years later with terrorist offences. I do not remember the year, it must have been 2008 or 2009 ... I went there because I was invited by some Muslim LLM students I had. Also, I do not remember the name of the "scholars" other than the guy who was charged had a Greek name. He was English of Greek origin who converted to Islam. If there is any list of people convicted of terrorist offences it will be easy to identify him.'

---

[211] See also E. Barendt, *Academic Freedom and the Law: A Comparative Study* (Bloomsbury, 2010).

Citing this source, the Provost of the OIBI and Imam of the Oxford Islamic Congregation, Dr Taj Hargey, wrote to Professor Welch on 8 June 2023 expressing alarm at 'what appear to be ongoing violations by the University of the legal duty, established by s. 26 of the Counter Terrorism and Security Act 2015, "to have due regard to the need to prevent people from being drawn into terrorism" (the "Prevent duty").'

Dr Hargey acknowledges that nobody claims BRISOC supports terrorism. However, he observes that there is, nevertheless, clear evidence that, in both the recent and more distant past, it has behaved in ways which exhibit extremism, militancy, a dangerous intolerance, and an intention to cause unjustified harm, which could have prompted, and may still prompt others, to attack me physically. As Dr Hargey points out, any such assault would have been, and might still be, an act of terrorism as were the murder of Sir David Amess MP in 2021 and the attempted murder of Stephen Timms MP in 2010. In each case the attackers sought to exact retribution for alleged offences against Muslims, seven years after the initial putative provocation, by stabbing their victims with a knife. The murderer of Sir David Amess claimed to have been motivated by Sir David's support for the bombing of Syria by the UK in 2014 which, in the event, did not go ahead. Mr Timms was attacked for voting in favour of the invasion of Iraq in 2003.

According to Dr Hargey, the University not only failed to prevent or to stop BRISOC's potentially life-threatening social media campaign; in the following ways it materially increased the risk of me becoming the victim of such an attack. It prohibited me from publicly announcing my exoneration when it occurred in July 2021. The Law School then removed the 'Islam, China and the Far East' module from the Human Rights in Law, Politics and Society syllabus exactly as BRISOC demanded and in defiance of the Assessor's verdict that their objections to it were totally unfounded. The University also publicly announced that this was necessary in order, amongst other things, to protect the sensitivities of students. In spite of my unequivocal exoneration, the University also publicly stated in October 2021 that it recognised BRISOC's 'concerns.' It did not say what these were nor how doing so could be reconciled with the inquiry's verdict.

Dr Hargey's letter concludes by claiming that there is at least a prima facie case that the University's mismanagement of the BRISOC scandal constitutes a breach of its statutory duty 'to have due regard to the need to prevent people from being drawn into terrorism.' It adds that OIBI, therefore, joins the AFFS in strongly urging the University to establish an independent investigation along the lines of that recently conducted by former Conservative Attorney General Dominic Grieve KC into compliance and governance failures at Christ Church College, Oxford.[212] As he intimated to the University, having failed to receive a reply, Dr Hargey referred the matter to the OfS on 26 July 2023.

An offence of blasphemy against Islam by the back door?

An issue that has particularly interested secularism campaigners, but which the hardback of this book did not adequately address, concerns the extent to which the BRISOC scandal could be considered part of a wider campaign by some Muslims to replace the defunct criminal offence of blasphemy with a social offence of Islamophobia.

In the late 1980s, reacting to the controversy sparked by the publication of Salman Rushdie's novel *The Satanic Verses*, some Muslims in Britain advocated extending the offence of blasphemy – which then covered only the Christian faith – to include Islam. The campaign failed. Instead, some two decades later, the offence of blasphemy was itself abolished. The Satanic Verses affair nevertheless galvanized, united, and empowered both the typically more traditional older generation of British Muslims and their more westernized offspring. It also led to the establishment in Britain of several institutions including the Muslim Parliament, Jam'iat Ihyaa Minhaaj Al-Sunnah (JIMAS), and Hizb ut-Tahrir. According to Pantucci, it is difficult not to conclude that, in the 1990s, JIMAS and Hizb ut-Tahrir 'played an

---

[212] https://www.chch.ox.ac.uk/news/house/christ-church-publishes-independent-governance-review-dominic-grieve-kc

important role in the radicalization of British Muslim youth,'²¹³ not least through the influence the latter had over university Islamic societies.²¹⁴

The fact that Muslims now have little if any interest in the restoration of the formal criminal offence of blasphemy may be at least partly attributable to the success of the much more subtle attempt to make 'Islamophobia' a 'social offence' punishable by stigmatization, ostracism and the other familiar informal highly punitive sanctions of contemporary cancel culture, not to mention the implicit threat of violent retribution by third parties. The BRISOC scandal could, therefore, indeed be regarded as a manifestation of this strategy.

Conclusion

An otherwise sympathetic reviewer criticized the hardback for having too many repetitive summaries and conclusions.²¹⁵ I will, therefore, resist the temptation to provide yet another here. Instead, I'd like to sign off with a final reflection upon the debate about what should be done to address British academic cancel culture.

Where there is at least a prima facie case of free speech violation, two potentially powerful and mutually supportive options should be considered. One, already pioneered by the AFFS, involves campaigns to encourage alumni and others to withhold donations to recalcitrant institutions until the latter can demonstrate palpable, and not merely rhetorical, improvements in protecting academic freedom. The other would be an OfS policy requiring such providers to set up and fund their own independent investigations. This would save the OfS a huge amount of time, money and effort and would, therefore, enable many more inquiries to be conducted than would otherwise be the case. It would also send a much more effective signal than if the OfS were to conduct all relevant investigations itself. The institutions in question would also receive a sharp and much-deserved taste of their own medicine, turning

---

[213] R. Pantucci, *'We Love Death as You Love Life': Britain's Suburban Terrorists*, (Hurst, 2015), p. 96.
[214] *Ibid.*, p. 167; P. Nesser, *Islamist Terrorism in Europe: A History*, (Hurst & Co., 2015), p. 9.
[215] Daniel Sharp, 'Cancel culture and religious intolerance: "Falsely Accused of Islamophobia," by Steven Greer,' *Freethinker*, 9 May 2023.

on its head the current reality where 'the process is the punishment' for those, like me, subjected to institution-specific cancellation-prompted inquiries. The role of the OfS would, therefore, be limited to approving specific investigations, including personnel, and to supervising the implementation of recommendations. These features should also contribute significantly to neutralizing the familiar complaint that the OfS is simply a tool for the pursuit of the current government's own partisan political agenda in higher education.

Appendix A

Unit Guide for Human Rights in Law, Politics and Society 2019-20

University of BRISTOL

LAWD30125

Human Rights in Law, Politics and Society

Law School
2019/20

Unit Coordinator
Professor Steven Greer

UNIT GUIDE

1. Unit description

This unit covers the following topics and themes: the origins and history of the human rights ideal and its contested status in western debates about law, politics and society; the internationalization and globalization of human rights; arguments about the universality and cultural limits of human rights particularly with respect to Islam, Asia, China, and multicultural societies; attempts to sanction human rights violations through legal and especially judicial processes, particularly by the European Court of Human Rights and the International Criminal Court; and some sharp contemporary debates, including about the profile of human rights in processes of democratization, in relation to poverty and economic development, in response to terrorism, and in armed conflict.

2. Tutor contact details

Professor Steven Greer: Room 3.40. Tel. 954 5337
Steven.Greer@bristol.ac.uk
Office hours: Fridays, 16.00-18.00.

3. Programme

The unit is delivered in a series of nine fortnightly seminars plus a final revision seminar, plus weekly lectures (first term only) in room 3.31 from week 1. Details can be found in the timetable. Power point slides and podcasts of lectures will be available on Blackboard. The programme is as follows:

TOPICS	LECTURE (WEEK)	SEMINARS (WEEKS)
Introduction to unit	1	-
1. Origins and conceptual debate	2	2/3
2. Internationalization and globalization	3	4/5
3. Islam and China	4	6/7
4. Universalism, relativism and multiculturalism	5	8/9
5. Democratization	6	10/11
6. Legal enforcement	7	14/15
7. Poverty and development	8	16/17
8. Terrorism and counterterrorism	9	18/19
9. Armed conflict	10	20/21
10. Revision	Available on Blackboard	22/23

4. Literature

Recommended literature is divided into 'Textbook etc reading' and 'Other.' No single text covers the entire syllabus. However, the closest to unit texts, all but a few chapters in each of which are recommended below, are:
- J. Donnelly and D. Whelan, *International Human Rights* (Westview Press, 6th edn., 2020).
- J. Donnelly, *Universal Human Rights in Theory and Practice* (Cornell University Press, 3rd edn., 2013).

Other texts to which frequent reference is made include:
- I. Bantekas & L. Odette, *International Human Rights Law and Practice* (Cambridge University Press, 3rd edn. 2020).
- K. Larres & R. Wittlinger (eds.), *Global Politics* (Routledge, 2020).
- O. De Schutter, *International Human Rights Law: Cases, Materials, Commentary* (Cambridge University Press, 3rd edn., 2019).
- M. Freeman, *Human Rights: An Interdisciplinary Approach* (Polity, 3rd edn., 2017).
- M. Goodhart, *Human Rights: Politics and Practice* (Oxford University Press, 3rd edn., 2016).
- M. Frezzo, *The Sociology of Human Rights* (Polity, 2015).
- C. Tomuschat, *Human Rights: Between Idealism and Realism* (Oxford University Press, 3rd edn., 2014).

Some particularly useful recent collections of essays covering a range of topics include:
- S. Pinker, *Enlightenment Now: The Case for Reason, Science, Humanism and Progress* (Allen Lane, 2018).
- D. Moeckli et al (eds), *International Human Rights Law* (Oxford University Press, 3rd edn., 2018).
- R. Cruft et al (eds), *Philosophical Foundations of Human Rights* (Oxford University Press, 2015).
- S. Sheeran & Sir N. Rodley (eds), *Routledge Handbook of International Human Rights Law* (Routledge, 2013).
- T. Risse et al (eds), *The Persistent Power of Human Rights* (Cambridge University Press, 2013).

The following dictionary and lexicon may be helpful, particularly for students whose first language is not English:
- C. de la Vega, *Dictionary of International Human Rights Law* (Edward Elgar, 2013).
- S. Marks & A. Clapham, *International Human Rights Lexicon* (Oxford University Press, 2005).

Collections of documents include:
- U. Khaliq, *International Human Rights Documents* (Cambridge University Press, 2018).

- R. Smith, *Core Documents on European and International Human Rights 2017-18* (Palgrave Macmillan, 3rd edn., 2017).
- A. Bisset, *Blackstone's International Human Rights Documents*, 11th edn. (Oxford University Press, 2018).

Students are not expected to read all the listed materials. In any given topic, a great deal, particularly citations to textbooks and edited collections, is intended to provide alternative rather than further sources. As much should be consulted as is required in order to understand any topic fully. Some items can be accessed at https://rl.talis.com/3/bristol/lists/7BA425FE-9F22-9198-24B7-A43CC62EA43D.html?lang=en-US&login=1. See http://www.bristol.ac.uk/library/use/resource-lists/students/ for further information. Particularly useful items are marked with an asterisk. *Students should also seek to cultivate the habits of reading in depth/breadth and reading in preparation for the seminars/for the exam* and are also encouraged to read a quality daily newspaper.

5. Assessment

Summative: Three-hour exam, three answers required. Marks obtained constitute the score for the unit as a whole. Unannotated copies of the following documents, *and no other*, may be taken into the exam: Universal Declaration of Human Rights 1948, International Covenant on Civil and Political Rights 1966, International Covenant on Economic, Social and Cultural Rights 1966 and European Convention on Human Rights 1950 (as amended). Sample exam scripts scored across the range are available on the HRLPS pages on Blackboard under Course Information/Sample Exam Answers. Details of marking scales can be found in LLB guidelines.

Formative: One practice exam-style essay of 1,000 words, word processed, *may be* submitted in answer to any question from the 2019 exam paper, a copy of which can be found at the end of this guide. The deadline is the *end of week 21*. *This exercise is optional not compulsory*. Marks obtained *do not* count towards the unit assessment. Other past LLB exam papers are available on Blackboard (Law Student Information/ Assessment/Past Exam Papers) and in bound volumes in the Wills Library.

6. Intended Learning Outcomes

The unit is intended to cultivate and encourage reflective and creative engagement with issues rather than simply knowledge acquisition and transfer, expectations which are fully conveyed to students in lectures, seminars and revision sessions. By the end of the unit a successful student will be able to:

- Explain the nature of the human rights ideal and its contested status in debates in, and between, western and non-western value systems, and about globalization, international law and international relations.
- Identify and discuss some core debates where human rights are particularly central, eg poverty, counterterrorism, multiculturalism.
- State the various arguments and positions in key debates accurately, assess them critically and come to provisional reasoned conclusions about how the issues might best be understood and problems resolved.
- Demonstrate the following benchmark skills
  - selection of sources from a wide range of suggested literature;
  - reading in depth and in breadth;
  - critical analysis of written texts;
  - written argumentation.

Seminar One

Origins and Conceptual Debate

Textbook etc reading

Pinker (2018), Preface, Chs. 1-4; Freeman (2017), Chs. 1-4; Goodhart (2016), Chs.1, 2, 6 & 7; Bantekas & Odette (2016), Chs. 1 & 2; Cruft et al (2015), Chs 1, 2 & 6; Frezzo (2015), Introduction, Chs 1 & 2, Conclusion; Tomuschat (2014), Chs. 1, 2 & 4; Donnelly (2013) Chs. 1, 2 & 5.

General Edited Collections

Moekli et al (2018), Chs. 1-3; Cruft et al (2015), Introduction, Chs 1 & 6; Sheeran & Rodley (2013), Chs. 3 & 5; Risse et al (2013), Chs. 1, 2 & 15.

Other

T. Mertens, *A Philosophical Introduction to Human Rights* (Cambridge University Press, 2020).

C. Menke, *Critique of Rights* (Polity Press, 2019).

* A. Brysk & M. Stohl (eds.), *Contesting Human Rights: Norms, Institutions and Practice* (Edward Elgar, 2019), Chs 1 & 12.

* A. Brysk, *The Future of Human Rights* (Polity Press, 2018), Chs. 1 & 5.

A. Brysk & M. Stohl (eds.), *Contracting Human Rights: Crisis, Accountability and Opportunity* (Edward Elgar, 2018), Chs. 1 & 18.

A. Brysk & M. Stohl, *Expanding Human Rights: 21st Century Norms and Governance* (Edgaronline, 2017), Ch. 14.

S. Moyn, 'Response to Viewpoint: The End of Human Rights History' (2016) 233 *Past and Present* 307-322.

S-L. Hoffman, 'Human Rights and History' (2016) 232 *Past and Present* 279-310.

* D. Stamos, *The Myth of Universal Human Rights: Its Origin, History, and Explanation, Along with a More Humane Way* (Routledge, 2016), Ch. 1.

* A. Clapham, *Human Rights: A Very Short Introduction* (Oxford University Press, 2nd edn, 2015).

K. Nash, *The Political Sociology of Human Rights* (Cambridge University Press, 2015), Chs. 1 & 8.

* P. Slotte & M. Halme-Tuomisaari, *Revisiting the Origin of Human Rights* (Cambridge University Press, 2015), Foreward, Ch. 1 and Afterword.

C. Douzinas & C. Gearty (eds), *The Meanings of Rights* (Cambridge University Press, 2015), Introduction, Chs. 2 & 3.

* C. McCrudden, 'Human Rights Histories' (2015) 35 *Oxford Journal of Legal Studies* 179-212.

M. Boylan, *Natural Human Rights: A Theory* (Cambridge University Press, 2015), Chs. 1, 2 & Afterward.

W. Edmundson, *An Introduction to Rights*, (Cambridge University Press, 2nd edn., 2013), Chs. 1, 2, 7, 11 & 12.

* S. Greer, 'Being "realistic" about human rights' (2009) 60 *Northern Ireland Legal Quarterly* 147-61.

* E. Kamenka, 'The Anatomy of an Idea' in E. Kamenka & A. Soon Tay (eds.), *Human Rights* (Edward Arnold, 1978), Ch. 1.

Questions

1. Are human rights more guidelines than prescriptions? (May/June 2019).

2. Are 'human rights' really 'natural rights' and does it matter either way? (May/June 2016).

3. 'Human rights are merely a product of modernization.' Discuss. (May/June 2015).

4. 'While there is nothing fundamentally wrong with the idea of human rights there is a great deal wrong with the way some understand and seek to apply them.' Discuss. (May/June 2014).

5. In what sense, if any, do 'human rights' exist and, if they do, why do they exist? (May/June 2013).

Seminar Two

Internationalization and Globalization

General Edited Collections
Moekli et al (2017), Ch. 19; Cruft et al (2015), Chs 11-13; Sheeran (2013), Chs. 6, 7, 8, 38 39, 40; Risse et al (2013), Chs. 5, 6 & 7.

Textbook etc reading on International Law/International Relations
Donnelly & Whelan (2017), Chs. 1, 5 & 6; Freeman (2017), Chs, 3 & 7; Goodhart (2016), Chs. 3 & 4; Bantekas & Odette (2016), Chs. 2-6; Clapham (2015), Chs. 2 & 3; Tomuschat (2014), Chs. 6-8; Donnelly (2013) Chs. 2 & 11; De Shutter (2014), Chs. 1, 9 & 10.

Other: International Law/International Relations
S. Egan, 'Transforming the UN Human Rights Treaty System' (2020) 42 *Human Rights Quarterly* 762-89.

A. Moses, M. Duranti, R. Burke, *Decolonization, Self-Determination, and the Rise of Global Human Rights Politics* (Cambridge University Press, 2020).

P. Taylor, *A Commentary on the International Covenant on Civil and Political Rights: The UN Human Rights Committee's Monitoring of ICCPR Rights* (Cambridge University Press, 2020).

* T. Weiss, *Would the World Be Better without the UN* (Polity, 2018), Chs. 4 & 7.

* N. Rodley, 'International Human Rights Law' in M. Evans (ed.) *International Law* (Oxford University Press, 5th edn., 2018).

G. Dancy & C. Fariss, 'Rescuing Human Rights Law from International Legalism and Its Critics' (2017) 39 *Human Rights Quarterly* 1-36.

* D. Forsythe, *Human Rights in International Relations* (Cambridge University Press, 4th edn., 2017), Chs. 1-3, 5 & 10.

C. Roberts, *The Contentious History of the International Bill of Human Rights* (Cambridge University Press, 2015), Introduction, Chs. 1 & 2, Epilogue.

A. Føllesdal, J. Schaffer & G. Ulfstein (eds), *The Legitimacy of International Human Rights Regimes: Legal, Political and Philosophical Perspectives* (Cambridge University Press, 2015), Chs. 1 & 2.

* E. Posner, *The Twilight of Human Rights Law* (Oxford University Press, 2014), Chs. 3-5.

* J. Hopgood, *The End Times of Human Rights* (Cornell University Press, 2013), Preface, Chs. 1 & 8.

B. Simmons, *Mobilizing for Human Rights: International Law and Domestic Politics* (Cambridge University Press, 2009), Chs. 1 & 9.

Textbook etc reading on Globalization

Donnelly & Whelan (2017), Ch.11; Goodhart (2016), Chs. 9 & 13; Bantekas & Odette (2016), Ch. 17; S. Joseph & A. McBeth (eds), *Research Handbook on International Human Rights Law* (Edward Elgar, 2010), Ch. 6.

Other: Globalization

* C. Crouch, *The Globalisation Backlash* (Polity Press, 2018), Ch. 4.

* C. Gopinath, *Globalisation: A Multi-Dimensional System* (SAGE Publications, 3rd edn. 2018), Chs. 1 & 11.

C. Lafont, 'Neoliberal globalization and the international protection of human rights' (2018) 25 *Constellations* 315-28.

J. Michie, *Advanced Introduction to Globalisation* (Edward Elgar, 2017), Chs. 1 & 11.

* M. Steger, *Globalization: A Very Short Introduction* (Oxford University Press, 4th edn. 2017).

A. de Smet, J. Dirix, L. Diependaele, & S. Sterckx, 'Globalization and Responsibility for Human Rights' (2015) 14 *Journal of Human Rights* 419-438.

A. Brysk & A. Jimenez, 'The Globalization of Law: Implications for the Fulfilment of Human Rights' (2012) 11 *Journal of Human Rights* 4-16.

J. Addicott, M. Bhuiyan & M. Chowdhury, *Globalization, International Law and Human Rights* (Oxford University Press, 2011), Ch. 8.

Questions

1. 'The great unsung success story of the human rights ideal concerns its achievements in the west.' Discuss. (May/June 2018).

2. Is international human rights law fit for the 'era of globalization'? (May/June 2017).

3. How, if at all, might the core problems of the international human rights regime be solved? (May/June 2016).

4. 'There is little evidence that human rights treaties have improved the wellbeing of people' (Posner, 2014). If this is true, what if anything should be done about it? (May/June 2015).

5. 'Globalization presents more of a threat to, than an opportunity for, the effective protection of human rights.' Discuss.

Seminar Three

Islam and China

Textbook etc Reading

Donnelly (2013), Chs. 9 & 10.
See also 'Core Differences: Islam etc' on Blackboard/Course Documents

General Edited Collections

Sheeran (2013), Chs. 26 & 27; Risse et al (2013), Chs. 9 & 10.

Other

Islam

* E. Karagiannis (ed.), *The New Political Islam: Human Rights, Democracy and Justice* (University of Pennsylvania Press, 2018), Introduction and Conclusion.
* A. Saeed, *Human Rights and Islam: An Introduction to Key Debates between Islamic Law and International Human Rights Law* (Elgaronline, 2018), Introduction and Conclusion.
M. A. Baderin, *International Human Rights and Islamic Law* (Oxford University Press, 2nd edn., 2017), Chs. 1 & 6.
A. Ibrahim, 'A Not-So-Radical Approach to Human Rights in Islam' (2016) 96 *Journal of Religion* 346-77.
D. Johnston, 'Islam and Human Rights: A Growing Rapprochement?' (2015) 74 *American Journal of Economics and Sociology* 113-48.
J. Edmunds, 'Human rights, Islam and the failure of cosmopolitanism' (2013) *Ethnicities* 671-88.
A. Emon, M. Ellis & B. Glahn (eds), *Islamic Law and International Human Rights* (Oxford University Press, 2012), Editors' Introduction.
* M. Ruthven, *Islam: A Very Short Introduction* (Oxford University Press, 2nd edn. 2012).
* A. E. Mayer, *Islam and Human Rights: Tradition and Politics* (Westview Press, 5th edn., 2012), Chs.1, 3 & 10.
K. Dalacoura, *Islam, Liberalism and Human Rights* (I.B. Taurus, 3rd edn., 2007), Chs. 2 & 6 & 'Conclusion.'
* M. Rishmawi, 'The Revised Arab Charter on Human Rights: A Step Forward?' (2005) 5 *Human Rights Law Review* 361-376.

China

* S. Biddulph and J. Rosenzweig (eds.), *Handbook on Human Rights in China* (Edward Elgar, 2019), Ch. 1.

* T. Wright (ed.), *Handbook of Protest and Resistance in China* (Edward Elgar, 2019), Introduction, Chs. 1-3.

J. Mauldin, 'Introduction to the Special Issue on Human Dignity, Religion, and Rights in Contemporary China' (2019) 20 *Political Theology* 361-68.

* R. Shepherd, 'Human Rights, modernization theory and China' (2018) 50 *Critical Asian Studies* 484-92.

L. Jun, 'Human Rights Lawyers' Role in Rights NGOs in China: History and Future' (2018) 41 *Fordham International Law Journal* 1197-1214.

Y. Zhengqing, L. Zhiyong, & Z. Xiaofei, 'China and the Remoulding of International Human Rights Norms' (2017) 38 *Social Sciences in China* 25-46.

* E. Pils, *Human Rights in China* (Polity, 2017), Introduction and Conclusion.

J. Na, 'China as an "International Citizen": Dialogue and Development of Human Rights in China' (2016) 14 *China: An International Journal* 157-77.

S. Biddulph, *The Stability Imperative: Human Rights and Law in China* (University of British Columbia Press, 2016), Chs. 1 & 7.

J. Zhao, 'China and the Uneasy Case for Universal Human Rights' (2015) 37 *Human Rights Quarterly* 29-52.

B. Ahl, 'The Rise of China and International Human Rights Law' (2015) 37 *Human Rights Quarterly* 637-61.

P. Chan, 'Human Rights and Democracy with Chinese Characteristics?' (2013) 13 *Human Rights Law Review* 645-89.

Questions

1. 'The key to reconciling human rights with Islam and "Asian values" lies less in the modernization of Islamic and Asian states and societies themselves, and more in greater flexibility in the application of the human rights ideal.' Discuss. (May/June 2019).

2. 'A "Chinese conception of human rights" is more credible and legitimate than an Islamic equivalent.' Discuss. (May/June 2017).

3. Has globalization finally resolved the universalism/relativism debate about human rights, and if it has, what are the likely consequences, especially for the 'Islamic world' and China? (May/June 2016).

4. 'The "relative universality" of human rights is no longer in doubt. But answers to the questions– how relative and relative to what? – are far from clear.' Discuss. (May/June 2015).

5. 'Islamic, Asian and Western conceptions of human rights are simply mutually incompatible.' Discuss. (May/June 2014).

Seminar Four

Universalism, Relativism and Multiculturalism

Textbook etc Reading

Donnelly & Whelan (2017), Ch. 3; Freeman (2017), Ch. 6; Bantekas & Odette (2016), Ch. 10; Tomuschat (2014), Ch. 3; Donnelly (2013), Chs. 6 & 7.

General Edited Collections

Moekli et al (2018), Chs. 14 & 18; Sheeran (2013), Ch. 4.

Other: 'Universalism/Cultural Relativism'

* R. Howard-Hassmann, *In Defence of Universal Human Rights* (Polity, 2018), Chs 1 & 2.

A. Fagan, *Human Rights and Cultural Diversity: Core Issues and Cases* (Edinburgh University Press, 2017), Chs. 1 & 2.

* S. Greer, 'Universalism and Relativism in the Protection of Human Rights in Europe' in P. Agha (ed.), *Human Rights between Law and Politics: The Margin of Appreciation in Post-national Contexts* (Hart, 2017), Ch. 1.

R. Afashari, 'Relativity in Universality: Jack Donnelly's Grand Theory in Need of Specific Illustrations' (2015) 37 *Human Rights Quarterly* 854-512.

F. Lenzerini, *The Culturalization of Human Rights Law* (Oxford University Press, 2014), Chs, 4 & 5.

C. Walsh, 'Compliance and Non-compliance with International Human Rights Standards: Overplaying the Cultural' (2010) 11 *Human Rights Review*, 45-64.

* J. Donnelly, 'Human Rights: Both Universal and Relative (A Reply to Michael Goodhart)' (2008) 30 *Human Rights Quarterly* 194-204.

Other: Multiculturalism

A. Mohiuddin, 'Muslims in Europe: Citizenship, Multiculturalism and Integration' (2017) 37 *Journal of Muslim Minority Affairs* 393-412.

* R. Chin, *The Crisis of Multiculturalism in Europe: A History* (Princeton University Press, 2017), Introduction, Ch. 5 & Epilogue.

* C. Joppke, *Is Multiculturalism Dead? Crisis and Persistence in the Constitutional State* (Polity, 2016), Chapters 1 & 6.

G. Crowder, *Theories of Multiculturalism* (Polity, 2013), Chs. 1 & 9.

T. Modood, *Multiculturalism* (Polity, 2nd edn., 2013), Chs. 1 & 8.

D. Newman, *Community and Collective Rights: A Theoretical Framework for Rights Held by Groups* (Hart Publishing, 2011), Ch. 1.

* A. Rattansi, *Multiculturalism: A Very Short Introduction* (Oxford University Press, 2011).
* D. McGoldrick, 'Multiculturalism and its Discontents' (2005) 5 *Human Rights Law Review* 27-56.

B. Parekh, *Rethinking Multiculturalism: Cultural Diversity and Political Theory*, 2nd edn. (Macmillan, 2005), Chs. 3 & 7.

B. Barry, *Culture and Equality* (Blackwell, 2001), 'Introduction' & Ch 7.

W. Kymlicka, *Multicultural Citizenship* (Clarendon Press, 1996), Ch 4.

Questions

1. 'To be viable "liberal multiculturalism" must be more "liberal" than "multicultural."' Discuss. (May/June 2019).

2. 'While human rights are universal, including in non-western states and societies, one size does not necessarily fit all.' Discuss with particular reference to Islamic and Asian contexts (May/June 2018).

3. In what ways, if any, does the idea of 'minority rights' conflict with and/or contribute to the realization of human rights? (May/June 2018).

4. 'The recent rise of right-wing populism in the west suggests that protecting minorities from prejudice should be a much more compelling priority for public policy than the official affirmation of their distinctive identities.' Discuss. (May/June 2017).

5. Has globalization finally resolved the universalism/relativism debate about human rights, and if it has, what are the likely consequences, especially for the 'Islamic world' and China? (May/June 2016).

Seminar Five

Democratization

Textbook etc Reading

Pinker (2018), Ch. 14; Goodhart (2016), Chs. 5, 14 & 22; Frezzo (2015), Ch 3.

General Edited Collections

Cruft et al (2015), Chs. 25 & 26; Sheeran (2013), Ch. 41.

Other

Democracy and democratization

* R. Pildes, 'Supranational Courts and The Law of Democracy: The European Court of Human Rights' (2018) 9 *Journal of International Dispute Settlement* 154-79.

* D. Runciman, *How Democracy Ends* (New York: Basic Books, 2018), Preface, Introduction, Conclusion & Epilogue.

* W. Galston, *Anti-Populism: The Populist Threat to Liberal Democracy* (Yale University Press, 2018), Introduction, Chs. 3 & 8.

* S. Levitsky & D. Ziblatt, *How Democracies Die: What History Reveals About Our Future* (Viking, 2018), Introduction, Chs. 1 & 9.

Z. Öniş, 'The Age of Anxiety: The Crisis of Liberal Democracy in a Post-Hegemonic Global Order' (2017) 52 *International Spectator* 18-35.

J. Schaffer, 'The co-originality of human rights and democracy in an international order' (2015) 7 *International Theory* 94-124.

C. Douzinas & C. Gearty (eds), *The Meanings of Rights* (Cambridge University Press, 2015), Ch 10.

K. Armingeon & K. Guttmann, 'Democracy in crisis? The declining support for national democracy in European countries, 2007-2011' (2014) *European Journal of Political Research* 423-442.

* D. Runciman, *The Confidence Trap: A History of Democracy in Crisis from World War One to the Present* (Princeton University Press, 2013), pp. xi-xxiii, 1-34, 263-336.

C. Haerpfer et al (eds), *Democratization* (Oxford University Press, 2009), Chs. 1 & 24.

C. Tilly, *Democracy* (Cambridge University Press, 2007), Chs. 1 & 8.

D. Held, *Models of Democracy* (Polity, 3rd edn, 2006), 'In sum' to each chapter.

M. Goodhart, *Democracy as Human Rights: Freedom and Equality in the Age of Globalization* (Routledge/Cavendish, 2005), Chs. 7-9.
B. Crick, *Democracy: A Very Short Introduction* (Oxford University Press, 2002).

Democracy, Islam, and the Arab spring

I. al-Shatti, 'The state of democracy and human rights in the Arab ummah (nation)' (2016) 9 *Contemporary Arab Affairs* 523-35.
* J. Esposito, T. Sonn & J. Voll, *Islam and Democracy After the Arab Spring* (Oxford University Press, 2016), Chs. 1 & 9.
J. Brownlee, T. Masoud & A. Reynolds, *The Arab Spring: Pathways of Repression and Reform* (Oxford University Press, 2015), Introduction, Chs 1 & 6.
* J. Gelvin, *The Arab Uprisings: What Everyone Needs to Know* (Oxford University Press, 2nd edn. 2015), Chs. 1 & 5.
A. Stepan & J. Linz, 'Democratization Theory and the "Arab Spring"' (2013) 24 *Journal of Democracy* 15-30.
J. Davis (ed.), *The Arab Spring and Arab Thaw: Unfinished Revolutions and the Quest for Democracy* (Ashgate, 2013), Introduction & Ch. 10.
A. Abdelali, 'Wave of change in the Arab world and chances of a transition to democracy' (2013) 6 *Contemporary Arab Affairs* 198-210.
A. Bayat, 'The Arab Spring and its Surprises' (2013) 44 *Development and Change* 587-601.
N. Hashemi, *Islam, Secularism and Liberal Democracy: Towards a Democratic Theory for Muslim Societies* (Oxford University Press, 2009), Concluding chapter.

Questions

1. 'Democracy is good for human rights and human rights are good for democracy. But not always.' Discuss. (May/June 2019).
2. Are democracy and human rights really in crisis? (May/June 2018).
3. What, if anything, might be done to improve the prospects of democratization and transitional justice in the Arab world? (May/June 2017).
4. 'In any significant conflict between democracy and human rights, the former will, and should, always prevail over the latter. The key challenge lies instead in determining what constitutes a "significant conflict," and in deciding which public institution should have the final say in the matter.' Discuss. (May/June 2016).

5. 'Modernization transformed both the prospect and meaning of democracy and transitional justice in the 19th and 20th centuries. The 21st century is likely to present as many, if not more, challenges for democracy, but fewer for transitional justice.' Discuss. (May/June 2015).

Seminar Six

Legal Enforcement

Textbook etc Reading

Tomuschat (2014), Chs. 9 & 12; De Schutter (2014), Ch. 8.

General Edited Collections etc

Moeckli et al (2018), Chs. 20 & 22; Cruft et al (2015), Chs 15 & 16; Sheeran (2013), Ch. 13.

Other

National

* G. Webber, P. Yowell, R. Ekins, M. Köpcke, B. Miller, and F. Urbina, *Legislated Rights: Securing Human Rights through Legislation* (Cambridge University Press, 2018), Introduction.

R. Leckey, *Bills of Rights in the Common Law* (Cambridge University Press, 2015) Introduction, Ch. 2 & Conclusion.

A. Bhagwat, *The Myth of Rights: The Purposes and Limits of Constitutional Rights* (Oxford University Press, 2012), Chs. 1 & 4.

W. Sandholtz, 'Treaties, Constitutions, Courts and Human Rights' (2012) 11 *Journal of Human Rights* 17-32.

* M. Volcansek & C. Lockhart, 'Explaining Support for Human Rights Protections: A Judicial Role' (2012) 11 *Journal of Human Rights* 33-50.

J. Lewis, 'The Constitutional Court of South Africa' (2009) *Law Quarterly Review* 440-67.

International: General

J. Haglund, *Regional Courts, Domestic Politics, and the Struggle for Human Rights* (Cambridge University Press, 2020).

C. Hillebrecht, 'Normative Consensus and Contentious Practice: Challenges to Universalism in International Human Rights Courts' (2019) 41 *Human Rights Quarterly* 190-94.

A. Huneeus & M. Madsen, 'Between universalism and regional law and politics: A comparative history of the American, European, and African human rights systems (2018) 16 *International Journal of Constitutional Law* 136-160.

* A. Buyse & M. Hamilton, 'Human Rights Courts as Norm-Brokers' (2018) 18 *Human Rights Law Review* 205-32.

* S. Greer, J. Gerards & R. Slowe, *Human Rights in the Council of Europe and the European Union: Achievements, Trends and Challenges* (Cambridge University Press, 2018), Chs. 1, 2 & 6.

C. Ovey & R. C. A. White, *Jacobs & White, The European Convention on Human Rights*, 7th edn. (Oxford University Press, 2017), Chs. 1 & 25.

M. Scheinin, H. Krunke & M. Aksenova (eds.), *Judges as Guardians of Constitutionalism and Human Rights* (Edward Elgar, 2016), Chs. 15 & 16.

J. Kirkpatrick, 'A Modest Proposal: A Global Court of Human Rights' (2014) 13 *Journal of Human Rights* 230-48.

* Y. Shany, 'The Effectiveness of International Courts: A Goal-Based Approach' (2012) 106 *The American Journal of International Law* 225-70.

International Criminal Courts

* E. P Mendes, *Peace and Justice at the International Criminal Court: A Court of Last Resort* (Edward Elgar, 2nd edn., 2019), Chs. 1 & 5.

* B. McGonigle Leyh, 'Pragmatism over Principles: The International Criminal Court and a Human Rights-Based Approach to Judicial Interpretation' (2018) 41 *Fordham International Law Journal* 697-736.

C. Rossi, 'Hauntings, Hegemony and the Threatened African Exodus from the International Criminal Court' (2018) 40 *Human Rights Quarterly* 369-405.

* M. de Hoon, 'The Future of the International Criminal Court. On Critique, Legalism and the Strengthening of the ICC's Legitimacy' (2017) *International Criminal Law Review* 592-614.

* A. Prorok, 'The (In)Compatibility of Peace and Justice? The International Criminal Court and Civil Conflict Termination' (2017) 71 *International Organization* 213-43. Anon, 'The International Criminal Court on Trial: A Conversation with Fatou Bensouda' (2017) 96 *Foreign Affairs* 48-53.

* I. Hurd, *International Organizations: Politics, Law, Practice* (Cambridge University Press, 3rd edn, 2017), Ch. 9.

W. Schabas, *An Introduction to the International Criminal Court* (Cambridge University Press, 5th edn, 2017), Chs. 1 & 2.

L. E. Carter, M. S. Ellis and C. C. Jalloh, *The International Criminal Court in an Effective Global Justice System* (Edward Elgar, 2016), Ch 1 & Conclusion.

H. Jo & B. Simmons, 'Can the International Criminal Court Deter Atrocity?' (2016) 70 *International Organization* 443-75.

* D. Bosco, *Rough Justice: The International Criminal Court in a World of Power Politics* (Oxford University Press, 2014), Introduction & Conclusion.

Questions

1. What lessons can and should be learned from the attempt to protect human rights through international judicial processes? (May/June 2019).

2. Should the International Criminal Court be replaced by ad hoc tribunals? (May/June 2018).

3. 'The failure of the International Criminal Court, and the limited success of the European Court of Human Rights, vividly illustrate that human rights can only be effectively judicially enforced by national courts in functional liberal democracies.' Discuss. (May/June 2017).

4. Assess the contribution made by courts to the effective protection of human rights. (May/June 2015).

5. 'The adjudication of alleged human rights violations will never be more than a partial success.' Discuss. (May/June 2013).

Seminar Seven

Poverty and Development

Textbook etc Reading

Pinker (2018), Chs. 6-9; Freeman (2017), Ch. 8; Bantekas & Odette (2016), Chs. 9 & 12; Cruft et al (2015), Chs. 29 & 30; Frezzo (2015), Chs. 4 & 5; Donnelly (2013), Chs. 3, 13 & 14.

General Edited Collections

Moeckli et al (2018), Ch. 30; Risse et al (2013), Ch. 12; Sheeran (2013), Chs. 15, 16, 30 & 33.

Other

Social and economic rights

A. Pillay, 'Revisiting the Indian Experience of Economic and Social Rights Adjudication: the Need for a Principled Approach to Judicial Activism and Restraint' (2014) 63 *International and Comparative Law Quarterly* 385-408.

C. Gearty & V. Mantouvalu, *Debating Social Rights* (Hart, 2011), pp. 54-84 & 107-53.

* P. O'Connell, 'The Death of Socio-Economic Rights' (2011) 74 *Modern Law Review* 532-554.

D. Whelan & J. Donnelly, 'The West, Economic and Social Rights, and the Global Human Rights Regime: Setting the Record Straight' (2007) 29 *Human Rights Quarterly* 908-949.

Poverty and development

N. Schrijver, 'A new Convention on the human right to development' (2020) 38 *Netherlands Quarterly of Human Rights*, 84-93.

* C. Armstrong, *Why Global Justice Matters: Moral Progress in a Divided World* (Polity Press, 2019), Chs. 1-3.

* H. Miller, 'Human rights and development: the advancement of new campaign strategies' (2019) 23 *International journal of human rights* 719-739.

* P. Nelson & E. Dorsey, 'Who practices rights-based development? A progress report on work at the nexus of human rights and development' (2018) 104 *World Development* 97-107.

* M. Broberg & Hans-Otto Sano, 'Strengths and weaknesses in a human rights-based approach to international development – an analysis of a

rights-based approach to development assistance based on practical experiences (2018) 22 *International journal of human rights* 664-80.
P. Hopper, *Understanding Development* (Polity, 2nd edn., 2018), Introduction, Chs. 1, 13 and Conclusion.
I. Goldin, *Development: A Very Short Introduction* (Oxford University Press, 2018), Chs. 1 & 6-8.
* E. Posner, 'Should Human Rights Play a Role in Development?' (2017) 30 *World Bank Economic Review* S16-S33.
G. MacNaughton, 'Vertical inequalities: are the SDGs and human rights up to the challenges? (2017) 21 *International Journal of Human Rights* 1050-72.
H. Miller, 'Rejecting "rights-based approaches" to development: Alternative engagements with human rights' (2017) 16 *Journal of Human Rights* 61-78.
D. Cahill & M Konings, *Neoliberalism* (Polity, 2017), Introduction, Chs. 1 & 6.
I. Hurd, *International Organizations: Politics, Law, Practice* (Cambridge University Press, 3rd edn, 2017), Chs. 3 & 4.
T. Pogge & M. Sengupta, 'Assessing the sustainable development goals from a human rights perspective' (2016) 32 *Journal of International and Comparative Social Policy* 83-97.
* D. Kennedy, *Decolonization: A Very Short Introduction* (Oxford University Press, 2016).
M. Langan & J. Scott, 'The Aid for Trade Charade' (2014) 49 *Cooperation and Conflict* 143-61.
* A. Vandenbogaert, 'The Right to Development in International Human Rights Law: A Call for Its Dissolution' (2013) 31 *Netherlands Quarterly of Human Rights* 187-209.
E. M. Hafner-Burton, *Forced to Be Good: Why Trade Agreements Boost Human Rights* (Cornell University Press, 2009), Ch. 7.
* J. Stiglitz, *Fair Trade For All: How Trade Can Promote Development* (Oxford University Press, 2007), Chs. 1 & 5.

Questions

1. What contribution, if any, does and could the human rights ideal make to achieving sustainable development in developing countries? (May/June 2019).
2. 'The effective realization of economic and social rights presents much greater challenges than those associated with their civil and political

counterparts, particularly in the developing world.' Discuss. (May/June 2018).

3. 'At best human rights can play only a secondary role in addressing the problem of global poverty.' Discuss. (May/June 2017).

4. 'Improving the prospects of sustainable development in less developed countries does not lie primarily in economics but in good governance.' Discuss. (May/June 2016).

5. What does the 'right to sustainable development' imply for aid and trade? (May/June 2013).

Seminar Eight

Terrorism and Counterterrorism

Textbook etc Reading
Pinker (2018), Ch. 13; Donnelly & Whelan (2017), Ch. 12; Bantekas & Odette (2016), Ch. 15.

General Edited Collections
Moeckli et al (2018), Ch. 29; Sheeran (2013), Ch. 32.

Other

United Kingdom
* S. Greer, 'Terrorism and Counter-Terrorism in the UK: From Northern Irish Troubles to Global Islamic Jihad' in G. Lennon, C. McCartney and C. King (eds.), *Justice, Counter Terrorism, and Miscarriages of Justice: A Festschrift for Clive Walker* (Oxford: Hart, 2018).
* S. Greer and L. Bell, 'Counter-Terrorist Law in British Universities: A Review of the "Prevent" Debate' (2018) *Public Law* 83-104.
F. Foley, *Countering Terrorism in Britain and France: Institutions, Norms and the Shadow of the Past* (Cambridge University Press, 2015), Introduction and Conclusion.
* K. Roach (ed.), *Comparative Counter-Terrorism Law* (Cambridge University Press, 2015), Ch. 6.
* D. Bonner, 'Counter-Terrorism and European Human Rights since 9/11: The United Kingdom Experience' (2013) 19 *European Public Law* 97-128.
D. Anderson QC, 'Shielding the compass: how to fight terrorism without defeating the law' [2013] *European Human Rights Law Review* 233-46.

International
* S. Greer, Is the Prohibition against Torture, Cruel, Inhuman and Degrading Treatment Really "Absolute" in International Human Rights Law? A Reply to Graffin and Mavronicola' (2018) 18 *Human Rights Law Review* 297-307.
* M. Nowak and A. Charbord (eds.), *Using Human Rights to Counter Terrorism* (Edward Elgar, 2018), Chs. 1 & 2.
Lord Dyson, 'Protecting Human Rights in and Age of Terrorism' (2017) 50 *Israel Law Review* 251-64.
* S. Pinker, *The Better Angels of Our Nature: A History of Violence and Humanity* (Penguin, 2012), 414-34.

C. Townshend, *Terrorism: A Very Short Introduction* (Oxford University Press, 3rd edn., 2018, 2nd edn., 2011).

B. Nacos, *Terrorism and Counterterrorism* (Routledge, 5th edn., 2016), Chs 1, 12 & 17.

* G. Lennon & C. Walker (eds), *Routledge Handbook of Law and Terrorism* (Routledge, 2015), Chs. 1, 6 & 30.

M. Volcansek & J. F. Stack Jr, *Courts and Terrorism: Nine Nations Balance Rights and Security* (Cambridge University Press, 2014), Introduction and Conclusion.

A. Masferrer & C. Walker (eds.), *Counter-terrorism, Human Rights and the Rule of Law* (Edward Elgar, 2013) Ch. 3.

F. de Londras & F. Davis, 'Controlling the Executive in Times of Terrorism: Competing Perspectives on Effective Oversight Mechanisms' (2010) 30 *Oxford Journal of Legal Studies* 19-47.

Questions

1. 'The most convincing implications of "human rights realism" concern the struggle against terrorism.' Discuss. (May/June 2019).

2. How should the UK tackle terrorism? (May/June 2018).

3. Has the western response to 'jihadi terrorism' primarily enhanced public safety or violated human rights? (May/June 2015).

4. 'While the West has largely observed the proportionality principle in the struggle against terrorism at home, it has not done so abroad.' Discuss. (May/June 2014).

5. To what extent, if at all, is it true to say that the 'war on terror' has brought the 'age of human rights' to an end? (May/June 2013).

Seminar Nine

Armed Conflict

Textbook etc Reading

Pinker (2018), Ch. 11; Donnelly & Whelan (2017), Ch. 10; Bantekas & Odette (2016), Ch. 14; Tomuschat (2014), Ch. 11.

General Edited Collections etc

Moeckli et al (2018), Ch. 25; Sheeran (2013), Ch. 12; Iriye et al (2013), Chs. 3 & 4.

S. Pinker, *The Better Angels of Our Nature: A History of Violence and Humanity* (Penguin, 2012), xix-xxviii, 355-86.

Other

Humanitarian intervention/responsibility to protect

* P. Dixon, 'Endless wars of altruism? Human rights, humanitarianism and the Syrian war' (2019) 23 *International Journal of Human Rights* 819-42.

* C. Finlay, *Is Just War Possible?* (Polity Press, 2018), Chs. 1 & 5.

* A. J. Bellamy & E. C. Luck, *The Responsibility to Protect: From Promise to Practice* (Polity Press, 2018), Ch. 7 & Conclusion.

B. Falk & S. Skinner, 'Review Article: The Responsibility to Protect: A Normative Shift from Words to Action?' (2016) 23 *International Peacekeeping* 493-512.

A. Bellamy & T. Dunne (eds), *The Oxford Handbook of the Responsibility to Protect* (Oxford University Press, 2016), Chs. 1, 52 & 53.

T. Weiss, *Humanitarian Intervention* (Polity Press, 3rd edn, 2016), Chs. 1, 2 & 5.

* J. Baziraki & P. Bukuluki, 'A Critical Reflection on the Conceptual and Practical Limitations of the Responsibility to Protect' (2015) 19 *International Journal of Human Rights* 1129-89.

G. Evans, R. Thakur, R. Pape, 'Humanitarian Intervention and the Responsibility to Protect' (2013) 37 *International Security* 199-214.

E. Talal & R. Schwarz, 'The Responsibility to Protect and the Arab World: An Emerging International Norm?' (2013) 34 *Contemporary Security Policy* 1-15.

T. Alkopher, *Fighting for Rights: From Holy Wars to Humanitarian Military Interventions* (Ashgate, 2013), Introduction & Conclusions.

* C. Guthrie & M. Quinlan, *Just War: The Just War Tradition – Ethics in Modern Warfare* (Walker Books, 2007).

International Humanitarian Law – The Law of War

* M. Sassoli, *International Humanitarian Law: Rules, Controversies and Solutions to Problems Arising in Warfare* (Edward Elgar, 2019), Chs. 1 & 11.

A. Clapham, 'Human Rights in Armed Conflict: Metaphors, Maxims, and the Move to Interoperability' (2018) 12 *Human Rights & International Legal Discourse* 9-22.

O. Swed, 'Promoting human rights under fire: INGOs' mitigating effect on human rights violations during armed conflict' (2018) 75 *Social Science Research* 1-12.

* B. van Dijk, 'Human Rights in War: On the Entangled Foundations of the 1949 Geneva Convention' (2018) 112 *American Journal of International Law* 553-582.

* D. Turns, 'The Law of Armed Conflict (international humanitarian law),' in M. Evans (ed.), *International Law* (Oxford University Press, 5th edn., 2018), Ch. 27.

C. Sriram, O. Martin-Ortega, J. Herman, *War, Conflict and Human Rights: Theory and Practice* (Routledge, 3rd edn., 2017), Chs. 1, 4 & 15.

G. Solis, *The Law of Armed Conflict: International Humanitarian Law in War* (Cambridge University Press, 2nd edn., 2016), Ch. 1 and summaries to every other chapter.

S. Weill, *The Role of National Courts in Applying International Humanitarian Law* (Oxford University Press, 2014), Introduction and Conclusion.

* A. Orakshelashvili, 'The Interaction between Human Rights and Humanitarian Law: Fragmentation, Conflict, Parallelism, or Convergence' (2008) *European Journal of International Law* 161-182.

Questions

1. When, if ever, is the killing of non-combatants in armed conflict a violation of human rights? And, if it is, what could and should be done about it? (May/June 2019).

2. Should the attempt to humanize warfare be based upon international humanitarian law, international human rights law, both, or neither? (May/June 2018).

3. How, if at all, might human rights be better protected, both in decisions to go to war, and in the conduct of contemporary armed conflicts? (May/June 2016).

4. 'While the attempt to humanize warfare through legal codes is laudable, bringing those who violate them to justice will always be "political."' Discuss. (May/June 2015).

5. Has the attempt to humanize war failed? (May/June 2014).

UNIVERSITY OF BRISTOL

Examination in the Law School

May / June 2019

HUMAN RIGHTS IN LAW, POLITICS AND SOCIETY
LAWD30125

Time allowed: 3 hours

This paper contains **EIGHT** questions.

Answer **THREE** questions.

Only **THREE** answers will be marked. If you attempt a question and do not wish it to be marked, delete it clearly, otherwise your first **THREE** answers will be marked.

Erasmus students should answer **TWO** questions.

Candidates may take into the examination **unannotated** copies of the following, *and no other* documents: Universal Declaration of Human Rights 1948, International Covenant on Civil and Political Rights 1966, International Covenant on Economic, Social and Cultural Rights 1966, and the European Convention on Human Rights 1950 (as amended).

PLEASE TURN OVER ONLY WHEN TOLD TO START WRITING

1. Are human rights more guidelines than prescriptions?
2. 'The key to reconciling human rights with Islam and "Asian values" lies less in the modernization of Islamic and Asian states and societies themselves, and more in greater flexibility in the application of the human rights ideal.'
Discuss.
3. 'To be viable "liberal multiculturalism" must be more "liberal" than "multicultural."'
Discuss.
4. 'Democracy is good for human rights and human rights are good for democracy. But not always.'
Discuss.
5. What lessons can and should be learned from the attempt to protect human rights through international judicial processes?
6. What contribution, if any, does and could the human rights ideal make to achieving sustainable development in developing countries?
7. 'The most convincing implications of "human rights realism" concern the struggle against terrorism.'
Discuss.
8. When, if ever, is the killing of non-combatants in armed conflict a violation of human rights? And, if it is, what could and should be done about it?

END OF PAPER

Appendix B

Lecture 3: Islam, China and the Far East

Overview of lecture

- See Core Differences in Course Documents on Blackboard

- Three questions
  - Why Islam, China and the Far East?
    - The only self consciously asserted alternatives to western liberalism with significant political implications for contemporary world, although existence and identity of 'Asian values' disputed.
  - Challenges posed by international human rights ideal for Islam, China and Far East: universalism?
  - Challenges posed by Islam, China and Far East for international human rights ideal: relativity?

- Part One: Human rights and Islam
- Part Two: Human rights, China and the Far East
- Part Three: Conclusion

Part One: human rights and Islam – overview

1. What is Islam?
2. Political history of Islam
3. Contemporary political profile of Islam
4. Islam and human rights
   1. Key human rights challenges
   2. The Arab Charter on Human Rights 2004

1.1. The Qur'an, hadith and sunnah

- 'Islam': 'submission to the will of the one true God'.

- Founded in Arabia by Mohammad (570-632 CE)
  - Monotheistic religion
  - One of three Abrahamic faiths: Judaism and Christianity: 'people of the book': regarded as authentic, though less complete, sources of religious truth than Islam.

- Qur'an: 'the recitation' (610-632 CE)
  - dictated by God to Mohammad via Archangel Gabriel.
  - contains God's final flawless revelation to humanity
  - non-narrative; non-chronological; non-systematic
  - style is allusive and elliptical: addressed to people already familiar with its message
  - open to interpretation: understanding requires ref to context/external sources.

- Hadith and sunnah (not sharply distinguished):
  - Hadith: traditions about life of Mohammad
    - Authenticity of some disputed
    - Others unclear or mutually contradictory
  - Sunnah: rules or norms derived from hadith but not straightforwardly
    - Mohammad's tastes in food.
    - Prohibition on alcohol or merely fermented grape and date juice?

1.2. Sharia and the Five Pillars

- Sharia: 'path', 'way', 'well-trodden path', 'the way to a watering place' – Islamic law
    - derives from Qur'an, hadith, sunnah, 'ijma' (consensus amongst Muslims), 'qiyas' (reasoning by analogy).
    - Principles or rules?Natural or positive law?
    - applies to:
        - social order: ie crime, business, marriage, trial procedure etc.
        - personal religious observance, eg food and drink, worship, rites of passage etc.
    - uncompromisingly individualistic: no sense of corporate entities subject to law
    - no Islamic society has ever been governed by Sharia alone
        - Delivered by tribal and client-patron systems
        - Supplemented by local law and custom
        - And responsive to political expediency.

- The 'Five Pillars' of Islam
    - Shahadah (the 2 testimonies)
        - 'there is no God but Allah and Mohammad is his prophet'
    - Salat: praying 5 times a day.
    - Zakat: alms giving/taxation.
    - Sawm: fasting during Ramadan.
    - Hajj: pilgrimage to Mecca during month of Dhu-al-Hijah

University of BRISTOL

1.3. Sunnism, Shiaism, Sufism

- Mohammad was religious, political and military leader - 'Caliph' ('Caliphate' – territory governed by Caliph)
- Debate about succession following Mohammad's death in 632 caused rift between Sunnis and Shias: M's death created 'a crisis of authority that has never been resolved' (Ruthven).
  - Husayn ibn Ali, grandson of M, killed by forces of Abbassid empire at battle of Karbala 680CE
- Lack of any institution ('church') with authority to interpret the faith:
  - Tension between tribal leadership and leadership based on religious scholarship.
  - 'The crisis of modern Islam ... is not so much a 'spiritual crisis' as a 'crisis of authority – political, intellectual and legal as well as spiritual'. (Ruthven)
- Sunnism
  - favour succession endorsed by Muslim community ('charismatic' not democratic).
  - traditional sunnah accorded central place.
  - recognise four legal traditions: main differences concern marriage and guardianship.
- Shi'ism
  - favour hereditary succession (Immam).
  - reject first three Caliphs post-Mohammad
  - acknowledge different sunnah from Sunnis
  - distinct legal traditions.
- Sufism
  - mystical and peace-loving tradition followed by some Sunnis and Shias
  - emphasises subordination of ego to will of God.
  - Less dogmatic than other traditions and more sympathetic to modernization and inter-faith dialogue.

2. 1. Political history

- Core and periphery
  - Islam spread rapidly through war, conquest, trade, and conversion.
  - Within century of Mohammad's death, first Caliphate extended from Atlantic to Himalayas.
  - Rival Byzantine and Persian empires defeated.
  - Muslim empires: Umayyad (Damascus), 661-750; Abbasid (Baghdad), 750-1258; Ottoman (Istanbul), 1299-1920; Mogul (16th-19th centuries, Northern India); Seljuk Turks (11th-14th centuries: Turkey and middle east); Safavid (16th-18th centuries, Persia)
  - Spread of Islam in south-east Asia more gradual, complex and (apart from Mogul empire in northern India), less imperialistic
  - Diaspora in modern west

- Political theory of Islam in core is 'imperial authoritarianism':
  - Caliph exercises absolute power, delegated by God on sacred trust for welfare of all (particularly Muslims), legitimized by, and subject to, Qur'an and Sharia.
  - Core normative concept – obligation not rights.
  - No separation of religious from other spheres of interest, authority, and power:
    - little room for distinction between civil society and state
    - Little scope for idea of formal constitutional limits on exercise of public power
  - Key site/context for exercise of power: 'Ummah' (the 'community'/'nation' of Muslims) rather than race, ethnicity, territory

University of BRISTOL

2. 2. Political history (continued)

- Ottoman empire: 1299-1920
  - Decline in 19th century: 'sick man of Europe'.

- Post 1st World War: end of Ottoman empire
  - Defeat, humiliation, schism - modernize or return to tradition?
  - Mandate system – colonization.

- Post 2nd World War challenges and opportunities
  - Modernization and materialism
  - Decolonization/'re-colonization': Israel and oil
  - Secular 'nationalist' pan-Arabism: 1950s-70s
  - Religious 'Islamist' internationalism: 1980s-
    - Iranian revolution: 1979-82
    - Soviet invasion of, and war in Afghanistan: 1979-89
    - National and international jihad: 1979-

3. Contemporary political profile of Islam

- 1.4 billion adherents worldwide.
    - 2nd largest religion in world (20%); Christianity (33%)
    - 2nd largest religion in UK and in many other European countries.
    - 20% of Muslims are Arabs
    - 85% of Muslims are Sunnis; (15%) Shia (majority in Iran)
- Types of state with Muslim majorities
    - 'Secular' republics/democracies (no shari'a): eg Turkey, Caucasian and central Asian republics.
    - Secular dictatorships (no/limited shari'a), eg Egypt, Syria, Iraq (pre-2003), Libya (pre-2011)
    - Constitutional monarchies (no/limited shari'a), eg Malaysia, Morocco.
    - 'Hybrid republics/democracies' (some shari'a), eg Islamic Republic of Pakistan
    - Traditional authoritarian kingdom(s) ('full' shari'a), Saudi Arabia.
    - Islamic republic(s) ('full' shari'a), eg Iran, ISIS (pre-2018).

4. Islam and human rights: key challenges

- Source of political values in Islam is revelation not reason:
  - how open are Qur'an and Sharia to 'human rights interpretations'?
  - what 'human rights interpretation(s)' are appropriate? 'global, 'western', 'Islamic'?
- Interpretation of 'grand narratives' driven by internal & external factors
  - Internal: technical debates amongst scholars.
  - External: economic, political, military exigencies.
- Pressure for Islam to address human rights caused by external forces of globalization, westernization & modernization.

4.1. Key human rights challenges

- Freedom of expression
  - insult to Islam punishable by death, eg Charlie Hebdo.
- Freedom of thought, conscience and religion
  - apostasy punishable by death
- Position of non-Muslims and other minorities in Islamic states:
  - only Muslims are full citizens
  - some rights limited to citizens
- Position of women:
  - polygamy, divorce, custody of children on divorce, inequality of legal testimony, physical chastisement by husband, dress (women who wear hijab less likely to work outside home or be involved in higher education).
- Hadd punishments:
  - unlawful intercourse; false accusations of unlawful intercourse; highway robbery; drinking alcohol.

4. 2. The Arab Charter on Human Rights 2004

- Islamic human rights statements: each less conservative than predecessor
  - Universal Islamic Declaration on Human Rights 1981
  - Cairo Declaration of Human Rights in Islam 1990
  - Arab Charter of Human Rights 2004
- 'Arab' not 'Muslim': most difficulties stem from Islamic influence
- Achievements
  - Milestone in formal recognition of human rights by (one branch of) Islam
  - Outside experts and NGOs consulted
  - Faithfully reproduces many international human rights
  - Establishes monitoring process similar to UN human rights treaties
- Core problems: omits several central international human rights or reproduces them in manner which conflicts with international standards, eg
  - No obligation on states to provide effective national remedies
  - Some core economic and social rights limited to citizens
  - States obliged to protect from torture, inhuman or degrading *treatment* but not *punishment:* no prohibition on use of statements extracted by torture.
  - Subordinates gender equality to Sharia.
  - Permits national legal limitations on rights to freedom of movement
    - significant limitations on women's freedom of movement in laws of, eg, Saudi Arabia

Part Two: China and South East Asia

- Religious map of Asia
- The 'Asian values' debate
- Confucianism
- Human rights in post-Maoist China

1. 1. The case for 'Asian values'

- 1990s: argument that Asia has distinct path to modernization, industrialization, capitalism, economic growth etc where primacy is given to collective good over individual rights
  - Mahathir bin Mohamad (PM of Malaysia)
  - Lee Kuan Yew (PM of Singapore).
  - Bangkok Declaration 1993
- 'Orientalism' and 'Occidentalism'
  - 'Orientalism': stereotypes of 'east' (mostly by 'west')
  - 'Occidentalism': stereotypes of 'west' (by 'east' and anti-western westerners)
- Key 'Asian values':
  - Willing subordination of personal freedom to family, corporation, nation.
  - Social prioritization of public order/social harmony over individual fulfilment.
  - Respect for hierarchy, tradition, authority, obligation.
  - Work ethic, thrift, pursuit of academic and technological excellence
- Influence of Confucianism
  - some confusion over whether relevant values pertain to 'Asia', 'China', or to 'societies with Confucian culture', ie China, Japan, Korea, Taiwan, Singapore and Vietnam.

1. 2. The critique of Asian values

- Leading (Asian) critics of 'Asian values':
  - Lee Teng-hui (former President of Taiwan)
  - Kim Dae Yung (former President of S. Korea)
  - Amartya Sen (Noble prize-winning Indian economist).
- Asia has many value systems in addition to Confucianism
  - eg Islam, Taoism, Buddhism, Hinduism, Shintoism
- Pre-modern precursors to modern idea of human rights found in east as well as west
  - Kautulya (4th century BCE); Asoka (3rd century BCE); Akbar (1556-1605)
- Arguments about Asian values also applied to pre-modern west
- Economic growth (aggregation) ≠ realization of soc/econ rights (distribution): can often be disproportionately to benefit of elites
- No evidence authoritarianism is more conducive to economic success than liberal constitutionalism
  - free press is key to preventing famine (Sen)

2. 1. Confucianism

- Confucius (K'ung Fu Tzu) 551-479 BCE
    - Sage, teacher, and middle-ranking government official
    - Remembered for aphorisms collected in no particular order by disciples in the *Analects of Confucius* (also huge secondary literature)
    - Confucius claimed these derived from already ancient sources

- The *Analects*
    - often bland, vague, obtuse.
    - address politics, morality, duty, etiquette, familial responsibility.
    - political/moral/legal method not political/moral/legal code
        - non-dogmatic, flexible.
        - seek to cultivate moral character not prescribe fixed rules of conduct.
    - basis of Chinese civil service exam from 165BCE- early 20th century.
    - embodiment of essence of Chinese, and related, cultures - 2,000 years.

2. 2. Confucianism (continued)

- Central goals
  - Identify qualities of good personal and public conduct
  - maintain social equilibrium by preserving 'natural' social hierarchies
  - loyalty and deference expressed in highly formalized conduct
  - discharge of obligations appropriate to each level of hierarchy
  - 'rites' not 'rights'.
- Centrality of virtue and benevolence in all moral individual and public action
  - Virtue: cultivated inclination to act for common good rather than personal advancement .
  - 'Junzi': 'exemplary person' – acts instinctively for common good.
  - 'Xio-ren' – 'petty person' – acts only on basis of personal advancement.
- Five cardinal social relationships (all but last hierarchical)
  - Ruler/subject; Father/son; husband/wife; elder/younger brother; friends
- 'Mandate of heaven' (theory of political stewardship):
  - Power of emperor formally absolute
  - But conditional upon benevolent governance in common interest
  - Popular acquiescence: rebellion = loss of mandate of heaven

University of BRISTOL

- **Similarities**
  - Everyone entitled to dignity and respect
  - Benevolence and respect for individual dignity limit exercise of public power and pursuit of individual self interest
- **Differences**

Confucianism	Human Rights
1. Addresses duty-bound agent	1. Addresses rights-holder
2. Control public power by cultivating moral character of powerful	2. Control public power through clear, detailed, formally-stated norms and separation of powers
3. Vague general principles	3. Detailed rights and obligations
4. Appeals to moral sensibilities of officials to remedy injustice	4. Remedies for rights violations provided by independent courts
5. Dignity stems from obligation	5. Dignity stems from autonomy/individual rights
6. Hierarchical	6. Egalitarian

3. 1. Human rights in modern China

- Pre-Communist China (1912-49)

    - Chaos, fragmentation, Japanese occupation, civil war
    - Competing models of modernization
    - Chinese contribution to UDHR 1948

- Maoist China (1949-1976)
    - Distinctive interpretation of Marxism
    - Hostility to
        - 'bourgeois imperialist values', including human rights,
        - Confucianism and Chinese tradition

University of BRISTOL

3. 2. Human rights in post-Maoist China: official ideology

- Quest for legitimacy in alternative post-Maoist ideology

  - Mix of communism, state-controlled capitalism, nationalism, revival of traditional Chinese belief systems (Confucianism, Daoism, Buddhism)
  - Strong commitment to national sovereignty, economic development, political and territorial stability, and collective rights over individual needs/rights
  - 19th Congress of Communist Party of China, 2017: Xi Jinping Thought on Socialism with Chinese Characteristics for the New Era:
    - Enhanced formal commitment to rule of law
    - Significant strengthening of personal power of President Xi Jinping.

- Role of human rights: antagonistic trends

3.3. Human rights in post-Maoist China: positives

- Increasing official engagement with international human rights/hr organizations
  - White papers on human rights and Human Rights Action Plans, 1991-: self congratulatory and defensive.
  - Art. 33, 2004 constitutional amendment: state 'respects and safeguards human rights' providing, inter alia, this doesn't infringe upon interests of state.
  - Ratifying hr treaties; drafting new instruments; engaging in dialogue etc
  - Official affirmation of 'human rights with Chinese characteristics'
  - Increasing scholarly interest in human rights

- Affirmation of 'human rights with Chinese characteristics'

- Some improvements in due process rights, eg curbs over confessions induced by torture, rights of defence lawyers, correcting miscarriages of justice, limitation to pre-trial detention and scope of death penalty.

- Social and economic rights: 600m people taken out of poverty in 30 years

University of BRISTOL

3. 3. Human rights in post-Maoist China: negatives

- Increasingly authoritarian party-state.
    - 2015-: crackdown on human rights lawyers, academics and activists.
    - 2018: millions of Uighurs (Xinjiang) detained in counter-terrorist 're-education camps'.

- Enduring gap between commitment to standards and effective implementation: : non-justiciability of rights.

- Weak civil and political rights, eg expression, belief, protest and dissent.
    - Compare Falun Gong with Christianity

- Weak rule of law: systematic use of torture, arbitrary detention, death penalty.

Part three: Conclusion

- As pre-modern ideologies Islam and Chinese/'Asian values' emphasise obligations not rights.
- Islam and Asian/Chinese values are each open to interpretations which reject international human rights as inappropriate for Islamic/Asian societies.
- But over past decade or so there have been countervailing trends
  - Anti-human rights ideas have increasingly lost ground to others in these contexts which take international human rights standards more seriously, though selectively **EITHER**
    - 'Human rights scepticism': less than full commitment to human rights. **OR**
    - 'Weak cultural relativism': full commitment to human rights but with legitimate emphasis on adaptation to specific cultural context.
  - Profile of anti-human rights policy and practice have also increased
    - Eg Islamic state; Rohingya; repression in Turkey

Part three: Conclusion

- Human rights-sensitive interpretations of Islam and Chinese/Asian values emerged because
    - of global social and political processes not logic of 'internal' debates
    - (some) leading exponents of Islam and Asian values recognised need to respond to external processes

- Multi-layered debates: between and within each paradigm

- Key contemporary issues
    - Are distinctive 'Islamic', 'Chinese/Asian' models of human rights possible/desirable?
        - According to whose judgment?
    - Will further modernization close gap between Islamic/Asian/western models?
    - Is accommodation *on specific human rights issues* between Islam/China/SE Asia and international human rights a matter of principle or pragmatic compromise?
        - According to whose judgment and according to what criteria?
        - What happens in practice?

Appendix C

Core Differences Between IHRL, Traditional Political Islam and Traditional 'Asian values'

ISSUE	IHRL	ISLAM	'ASIAN VALUES'
Dignity	Inherent	God-given Linked to obligation	Linked to obligation and tradition
Source	Modernity	Revelation/Koran Pre-modern tradition	Pre-modern tradition
Primary normative concept	Rights	Obligations	Obligations
Social model	Equality Freedom	Hierarchy Submission	Hierarchy Subordination to collective
Canonical text	Treaties etc	Koran	Various, eg Analects
Lists	Yes	No	No
Openness to interpretation	Yes	Yes	Yes
Institutionalization	Yes Constitutional rights Democracy Rule of Law	No	No
Implementation	Partial	Even more partial	
Areas of difficulty	Proportionality Margin of Appreciation	Expression Thought etc Women Minorities	Subordination to collective punishment

Appendix D

Steven Greer: Evidence Report

Abstract

This evidence file has been collated by the University of Bristol Islamic Society where we have gathered our discoveries of islamophobic hate speech as well as colonial, bigoted views being taught at the university in the name of freedom of expression. Whilst we honour free speech, we must not let it transgress to the point where it promotes anti-muslim rhetoric and justifies discrimination and hate crime towards muslims. This goes against the rights of freedom of religion, basic human dignity and respect towards others in our democracy. This evidence file is by no means exhaustive but we aim to highlight Greer's lecture notes, videos, articles, blogs and publications that we have found to be anti-muslim and derogatory in nature towards muslims and their faith. Not only are they dehumanising but the knowledge of Islam he teaches are wholly incorrect. Greer, who has no formal education on Islamic Studies or Islamic Law and Ethics, is therefore unfit to be teaching a human rights course which places large emphasis on Islam. Please note: All sources mentioned are widely publicly available.

Professor Steven Greer

Table of contents

Lectures	**3-4**
Video/Audio	**5**
Articles	**6**
Blogs	**6**
Publications	**7**
Events	**7**

Lectures

2020/21 Academic year: https://bit.ly/2LRBnHI, https://bit.ly/3rQLtbc
2018/2019 Academic year: https://bit.ly/3qnG23a, https://bit.ly/2ZluSA4

- "No typical jihadi terrorist, however, overwhelmingly young, male & Muslim"
- "Islam is hostile to the modern conception of democracy"
- "Pressure for Islam to address human rights caused by external forces of globalisation, westernisation & modernisation"
- "Women who wear hijab less likely to work outside home or be involved in higher education"
- "Women in Islam are not formally equal to men, all the ideologies benefit men"
- "The Qur'an also permits the physical chastisement by a husband of his wife"
- "If a particular piece of legislation impacts disproportionately against a group, it looks 'superficially' like it is discrimination...this is the case with China – Muslims in re-education camps"
- "Most difficulties stem from Islamic influence upon it"
- "Islamic law is uncompromisingly individualistic – big contrast to Western Society"
- "Islam spread rapidly through war, conquest, trade & conversion"
- "Islam was a progressive faith insofar as its open to all"
- "Core normative concept here is obligation, not rights – Islam is fundamentally based on submission and the performance of obligations."
- "An issue for Islam is the lack of an institution to interpret the faith"
- "This is typical of non-western ideologies – non-narrative, non-systematic, and non-chronological. The style is elusive and elliptical, addressed to people already familiar with its message"
- "Several other well-documented areas of friction in traditional political Islam with regards to human rights: position of women – divorce, custody of children, inequality in legal testimony (woman's testimony in Sharia court is worth half that of a man), position of non-Muslims and other minorities in Islamic states – only Muslims are full citizens."

Videos

Talk: "Human Rights and Islam: A non-muslim perspective"
- 12:19: Argues that HR & Islam conflict
- 15:45: Argues that "the source of political authority in islam is relevation not reason" suggesting Islam is illogical and irrational
- 16:45: Argues "Islam does not recognise human rights at all"
- 20:15: Argues that Islam promotes gender inequality
- 21:30: Argues HR and islam are very different and thus largely incompatible
- Argues PREVENT is 'human rights compliant' and the campaign against it is based on 'myths and misconceptions.'
- Further arguing that the fact that muslims are mostly targeted is 'a reflection of the fact that islamist terrorism is the principle terrorist threat UK faces'

Articles

- Argues against those who advocate for 'decolonising the curriculum'
- Defends PREVENT and agrees muslims must be targeted in order to be deradicalised

Blogs

- In favour of PREVENT and freedom of speech whilst ignoring the irreversible damaging effects it has upon the muslim population
- Argues that the "UCU boycott is not only illegal, illegitimate and deeply flawed, but also potentially dangerous and irresponsible."
    - For context, the UCU boycott was "to boycott the requirements of the Act and the wider 'Prevent strategy' of which it is a part, on the grounds that they seriously threaten academic freedom, stifle campus activism, require staff to engage in racial profiling, legitimize Islamophobia, and jeopardize safe and supportive learning environments."
- Argues that Islamophobia and racism don't really exist

Publications

- Argues that counter-terrorism is not discriminatory or islamophobic
- Argues that counter-terrorism is not islamophobic stating that PREVENT does not 'inherently conflict with democracy, human rights' despite data from HR organisations arguing the contrary
- Defends PREVENT strategy and dismisses its negative effects rather than rationally addressing the implications of a political strategy that targets muslims
- Argues that 'neither the Prevent duty nor the relevant legislation violates human rights nor do they have any of the other negative characteristics alleged by the anti-Prevent movement.'

Events

- Greer chaired the banned islamophobic talk led by Bristol's Free Speech society with Emma Fox

Appendix E

Lecture 8: Terrorism and counter-terrorism

Overview

1. Non-state terrorism
   1. What is it?
   2. Key characteristics
   3. Risks and harms
   4. The European experience: 1970s-2019.
   5. Key characteristics of post-9/11 'jihadi' terrorism
      1. International
      2. UK
2. Counterterrorism
   1. What is it?
   2. UK counterterrorism: CONTEST
   3. Counterterrorism and international human rights law
   4. Counterterrorism and human rights as risk management
   5. Key counterterrorism and human rights issues
3. Conclusion

1. 1. What is non-state terrorism?

- No agreed definition
  - 'one person's "terrorist" is another person's "freedom fighter"'
- Historical
  - Jacobin terror, 1793
- Some distinctions
  - War or crime?
  - Instrumental or symbolic?
    - Macabre theatre of lethal protest/asymmetric armed conflict?
    - Contrast IRA & jihadi terrorism.
  - Normative or descriptive?
    - Does deliberate targeting of non-combatants as matter of strategy itself render terrorism illegitimate in all/most/some circumstances?

University of BRISTOL

1. 2. Key characteristics of non-state terrorism

- Engagement in violent conflict with states:
  - by militarily and politically weak, but ideologically committed, non-state organisations and individuals;
  - typically involving attacks on state officials, on public and private institutions, and on civilian targets;
  - in order to create a climate of fear and insecurity;
  - intended to undermine the credibility of the state in defending itself and civil society;
  - to provoke counter-productive over-reaction by state/aggravate social division;
  - and, in the ensuing crisis, to exploit whatever opportunities might arise for the advancement of other terrorist goals, eg destabilization, propaganda, recruitment etc.
- 'Terrorism' is, therefore, inherently incompatible with human rights

1. 3. Risks and harms: death and personal injury

	US	W.Europe	World
Deaths in 2015 from......................			
• Terrorism	44	175	38,422
• War	28	5	97,496
• Homicide	15,696	3,962	437,000
• Road traffic accidents	35,398	19,219	1.25m
• All accidents	136,053	126,482	5m
• All deaths	2.6m	3.9m	56.4m

(Pinker, 2018, 192)

Globally

- Death from homicide — 11 times more likely than from terrorism

- Death from road traffic accident — 30 times more likely than from terrorism

- Death from accident — 125 times more likely than from terrorism

- Potential casualties for biological, chemical, nuclear terrorism: x 1,000s, 100,000s.

1. 3. Other risks and harms

- Damage to
  - social systems, eg transport, economic, information (cyber attacks)
    - Eg Tunisian tourist industry severely damaged by recent terrorist incidents
  - sense of public security
  - credibility of state as protector of national security & public safety
- So far, terrorism rarely succeeds: those primarily targeting civilians have always failed.

1. 4. The European experience: 1970s-2019

- Ideological terrorism (left & right):1970s-1980s
  - Germany, Italy, Turkey, France
- Secessionist struggles/nationalist terrorism: 1970s-2000
  - eg UK (N. Ireland); Spain (Basque country); France (Corsica); Turkey (Kurds – still continues)
  - Also civil wars: Balkans, Chechnya (1990s-2000s), Ukraine (2014)
- Jihadi and far-right terrorism: 2001-2019

University of BRISTOL

1. 5. 1. Key characteristics of post-9/11 jihadi terrorism (international)

- Inspired by a global *ideal*, but there is no global *organization*.
  - Those involved are motivated by the shared goal of establishing and extending the reach of an Islamic caliphate, governed by a particularly harsh and uncompromising form of sharia law, which would include, amongst other things, death sentences for apostates, for having sex outside marriage, for gays, and for those deemed to have insulted the faith, and which would also, at best, be intolerant of other minorities, including adherents to other Muslim traditions and sects.

- 'Alt-imperialism' rather than anti-imperialism.

- These shared objectives are typically complicated, and sometimes compromised, by tribal and sectarian rivalries in regional or national contexts and conflicts, not least the wars in Syria and Iraq.

1.5.1. Key characteristics of post-9/1 jihadi terrorism (international)

- As a result, jihadi terrorism has divided Muslims themselves around the world at least as much as it has divided Muslims from non-Muslims. Muslims are also much more likely to be victims than non-Muslims.
  - For example, world-wide fatalities due to terrorism rose from 6,000 in 2005 (the year of the London bombings) to 33,000 in 2014, declining slightly over the past five years.

- Since 2005 more fatalities have occurred in Nigeria, Syria, Iraq, Afghanistan, and Pakistan than in the rest of the world combined, a pattern which largely remains.
  - Four of these countries are overwhelmingly Muslim, and in the fifth, Nigeria, Muslims account for about 40% of the population.
  - In 2013 alone, 82% of global terrorist fatalities were in these five states.

- Yet in spite of these statistics, no country is entirely safe.

- In addition to the UK, high profile attacks have already occurred across the world in places as diverse as Russia, Spain, Kenya, India, France, Australia, China, and Egypt.

1. 5. 2. Key characteristics of jihadi terrorism (UK)

- First, Britain has, so far, suffered comparatively few casualties from this kind of terrorism on its own territory.

- From 9/11-2019, an annual average of just under 8 people have been killed in terrorist incidents, all but a handful from jihadi attacks, significantly fewer than, for example, the annual average killed in road traffic incidents, about 2,500.

- Second, as already indicated casualty figures don't tell the whole story.

- For example, scores of terrorist plots, most of them jihadi, have, for example, been thwarted in the UK since 2005, any one of which could have had catastrophic consequences.

- While it may not be wholly convincing to describe jihadi terrorism as posing an 'existential threat' to the UK, it certainly poses such a threat in other places, and it is difficult to argue that the risk the UK faces is one which government and society can, or should, ignore.

1. 5. 2. Key characteristics of jihadi terrorism (UK)

- Third, there's no single route into jihadi terrorism in the UK, and no 'typical' jihadi terrorist.

- Apart from the fact that such terrorists are overwhelming young, male, under 30, and Muslim, they come from a wide variety of experiences and backgrounds.

- Some are privileged, privately and university educated, British-born, and from apparently well-integrated Muslim families.

- Others are converts from other faiths and none, some from economically deprived and/or criminal backgrounds.

- Yet all acquire a sense of personal, socio-political and/or religious injustice, real or imagined.

- This comes from various sources. But the internet and charismatic preachers have proved particularly influential.

- Many are also personally vulnerable in various ways and/or undergoing an existential crisis at the time of recruitment or simply relish the thrill of being the ultimate rebel..

1. 5. 2. Key characteristics of jihadi terrorism (UK)

- Fourth, except for the fact that each is a manifestation of terrorism, jihadi terrorism differs from the terrorism associated with Northern Ireland in almost every respect.

- There are huge differences, for example in ideology, grievances, goals, targets, methods of recruitment, type of organisation, national and international profile etc.

- But one of the most significant differences is that no political party, and no organisation of any kind, represents UK jihadis, with whom negotiations might be conducted leading to a counterpart of the 1998 Belfast Agreement, which brought a the violent element in the conflict in Northern Ireland almost entirely to an end.

- Finally, the differences between the two contexts mean that CT policies which were used in Northern Ireland cannot be straightforwardly revived to deal with the current challenge, nor can criticisms to which they were subjected simply be resurrected.

2. 1. What is counter-terrorism?

- 'Counter-terrorism' is anything and everything, official and unofficial, lawful and unlawful, legitimate and illegitimate, intended to address, respond to, or to tackle terrorism.

- The 'who-threw-the-first-stone' problem.

- Relationship between 'non-state terrorism' and 'counter-terrorism' is symbiotic and interactive: one side delivers a blow, the other responds, the other reacts, etc.

- But, for liberal democracies, the suite of possible responses is limited, not only by what is logistically, but also by what is politically, constitutionally and normatively possible within a regulatory environment framed by democracy, human rights and rule of law, ultimately managed by the courts.

2. 2. UK counterterrorism: CONTEST

- Terrorism Act 2000: consolidates mostly NI 'Troubles'-related CT law

- Post-9/11: CONTEST
  - PREPARE: to mitigate the impact of terrorist attacks by bringing them to an end as swiftly and effectively as possible and by increasing capacity to recover in the aftermath ('resilience').

  - PROTECT: intended to reduce vulnerability to terrorism largely as far as national border security, transport systems, national infrastructure, crowded places both public and private, and British interests overseas are concerned.

  - PREVENT: aims to stop people from becoming terrorists, or from supporting those who already are, by countering terrorist ideology and challenging those who promote it ('counter-radicalization'), steering vulnerable individuals away from it ('de-radicalization'), and working with sectors and institutions where these risks are considered high.

2. 2. UK counterterrorism: CONTEST

- PURSUE: detect, prosecute, punish, control, and/or disrupt those who engage in terrorism both at home and abroad.

- While the four 'Ps' may be more memorable than other less alliterative alternatives, arguably, they do not clearly distinguish functions or objectives as clearly as they might. *Prepare* is, for example, the only one with no preventive element.

- Nor is it always entirely clear to which stream a specific counterterrorist law and policy, for example stop and search, belongs. Some may indeed belong to more than one.

University of BRISTOL

2. 3. Counter-terrorism and international human rights law

- States have domestic political and international legal and political responsibilities to combat terrorism including counter-radicalization and de-radicalization.

  - UN, EU, Council of Europe unanimously emphasise duty of states to tackle terrorism effectively respecting human rights, refugee and humanitarian law.

  - But lack of consensus on details of human rights constraints.

  - UNSC sets up Counter-terrorism Committee (Res. 1373(2001))
    - mandates all states to criminalize assistance for terrorist activities, deny financial support and safe haven to terrorists and share information about groups planning terrorist attacks.
    - no sanctioning powers.

- Subject to certain conditions, IHRL (eg ECHR) permits human rights to be suspended or restricted without being violated in struggle against terrorism.

2. 3. Counterterrorism and human rights: non-derogable rights

- Non-derogable rights can never ever be suspended (derogated from), nor are most subject to any express restriction for any express reason including struggle against terrorism (Art. 15 ECHR).
    - Not to be tortured, inhumanly or degradingly treated or punished
    - Not to be held in slavery or servitude
    - No retrospective criminalization or imposition of heavier sentence
    - Not to be killed except by lawful acts of war and where no more force than absolutely necessary is used for specific law enforcement objectives provided by Art. 2 ECHR.

University of BRISTOL

2. 3. Counterterrorism and human rights: derogable rights

Derogable rights (all other rights):

- Typically subject to express limitations subject to rule of law and democratic necessity, including, eg national security, prevention of disorder or crime.
    - Eg Art 8 ECHR: right to respect for private and family life, home and correspondence

An infringement of an expressly limited human right, in pursuit of a legitimate restriction, only becomes a violation if it cannot be justified according to the legality and democratic necessity tests which embody principles of proportionality, non-discrimination and the doctrine of national margins of appreciation.

Also capable of being suspended (derogated from) 'in time of war or public emergency threatening the life of the nation ... to the extent strictly required by the exigencies of the situation' – Art. 15(1) ECHR (a triple high-threshold proportionality test)

2. 3. Implications of human rights for counterterrorism

- no interference with non-derogables in any circumstance (except Art. 2, right to life) including counterterrorism.

- if relevant tests are satisfied, derogables can be infringed or suspended for various purposes including counterterrorism without this amounting to violation.

2. 4. Counter-terrorism and human rights as risk management

- Problems presented by non-state terrorism, and the appropriate responses to it, can best be conceived in terms of the effective management of three risks.

- First, there's the risk posed by terrorism to life, limb, property, public institutions and systems and, often, to community cohesion.

2. 4. Counter-terrorism and human rights as risk management

- Second, there's the risk potentially posed by CT to human rights and civil liberties, eg

    - arrest and detention without reasonable suspicion or prompt access to courts.
    - excessive limitations on rights to privacy, freedom of expression etc

- Third, there's the risk posed by CT to community cohesion, integration and confidence in the state, particularly as far as jihadi terrorism and Muslim communities are concerned.

- The challenge is effectively to manage all these risks on several dimensions simultaneously: political; policing; criminal justice; social justice; ideological; cultural; educational; communal, etc

University of BRISTOL

2. 4. Counter-terrorism and human rights as risk management

- Key to effective national action is accurate targeting based on reliable intelligence
    - This is both a matter of protection of rights and efficient use of resources

- Secret surveillance permitted under Art. 8 provided (Klass v Germany 1978)

    - Enshrined in law
    - Decisions taken by senior police officers
    - Independent official scrutiny of surveillance systems

    - Intelligence obtained presents choices between
        - pre-emption/disruption
        - prosecution
        - 'coercive executive control', eg house arrest

2.5. Key CT and human rights issues

- Killing by state officials: permitted under Art 2 ECHR where
  - 'No more force than absolutely necessary' in defence of any person from unlawful violence, to effect lawful arrest or prevent escape of someone lawfully detained, or in action lawfully taken to quell riot or insurrection
    - lack of other viable alternatives
    - imminence of risk of harm

  - Distinction between selective assassination (not permitted) and killing suspected suicide bomber to prevent detonation of bomb (permitted).

  - Official investigation by independent agencies afterwards.

  - No impunity where force unjustified.

- Torture or inhuman or degrading treatment or punishment prohibited in all circumstances without exception: including 'ticking bomb scenario'? (Art. 3):
  - Extraordinary rendition
  - Ticking bomb

University of BRISTOL

2. 5. Key CT and human rights issues

- Asylum and immigration
  - Non-refoulment (Art. 3): prohibition on repatriation of aliens where real risk of torture etc
  - Memoranda of Understanding

- Detention without trial
  - Permitted with valid derogation under Art. 15 (*Ireland v UK; Lawless v Ireland*)
  - UK's brief re-introduction of detention without trial in Pt IV of the Anti-Terrorism, Crime and Security Act 2001: declared discriminatory and disproportionate by HoL and ECtHR.

- Restrictions on movement
  - UK's Control Orders upheld in principle by HoL but recent decisions require tighter regulation, eg greater disclosure of reasons.
  - Replaced by less stringent TPIMs 'terrorism prevention and investigation measures'
  - Stop and search: privacy and discrimination?

2. 5. Key CT and human rights issues

- Terrorism-related offences
- Restrictions on freedom of expression and association, eg banning organisations
  - Permitted under Arts. 9, 10 & 11 without derogation provided necessary in democratic society in interests of public safety, national security, prevention of disorder or crime, protecting rights and freedoms of others, etc. (proportionality, pressing social need, margin of appreciation)
- Freezing and seizure of assets
  - permitted under Art. 1, Protocol No. 1 'in the public interest and subject to the conditions provided for by law and by the general principles of international law.'

University of BRISTOL

2. 5. Key CT and human rights issues

- Prevent and 'securitized Muslim communities'? a deeply flawed thesis for UK though less so elsewhere, eg China.

    - Superficially appears to be true.

    - Suffers from problems at every level including conceptual, methodological, evidential, analytical, logical and implications for public policy.

    - Yet, in spite of having failed to address these problems it continues to dominate the NGO and social science perspectives.

University of BRISTOL

2. 5. Key CT and human rights issues

- Three central weaknesses
    - Crude and one-dimensional when the reality is complex and multidimensional

    - No credible evidence that being a Muslim is enough systematically to attract attention of policing and security agencies in UK.

    - Very unclear what kind of counter terrorist law and policy directed against jihadi terrorism would not impact disproportionately upon Muslims since only Muslims (albeit a tiny minority) will be involved in it

    - By the same token any counter terrorist law and policy directed against right wing terrorism will impact disproportionately upon white non-Muslims. Yet no one claims this has turned them into a securitized community.

University of BRISTOL

3. Conclusion

- Terrorism and counter-terrorism each pose challenges for human rights
    - Terrorism is inherently a violation of human rights
    - Counterterrorism is only a violation of human rights if it fails to meet relevant IHRL criteria

- Key issue is risk management. Depends upon

    - Nature of threat posed by particular type of terrorism

    - Reliability of intelligence

    - Responsible use of intelligence
        - Pre-emption
        - Prevention
        - Prosecution

3. Conclusion

- CT and human rights scepticism

    - Focuses on threats terrorism poses to human rights and much less upon threat potentially posed by CT to human rights

- CT and human rights perfectionism

    - Tends to regard every limitation upon right in pursuit of CT as violation.

3. Conclusion

- Human rights realism observes

    - IHRL permits interferences with/restrictions or limitations upon human rights for purposes of CT provided certain conditions are met.

    - But whether they have been violated often depends upon

        - distinction between derogable and non-derogable rights

        - non-objective judgment hinging largely upon context-specific proportionality.

    - Extent to which human rights have been legitimately infringed or violated varies from state to state.

Appendix F

Chronology

2020

30 October	Date of formal complaint to the University of Bristol by the University's Islamic Society (BRISOC) alleging multiple counts of Islamophobia in my teaching and other public output.
11 December	I'm informed by the Law School's senior management that a formal complaint has been lodged with the University by BRISOC. But I'm told no further details are yet available.

2021

15 February	Coinciding with the launch of BRISOC's social media campaign, I'm officially informed by the University about the details of the formal complaint. BRISOC's campaign includes an online petition to have the unit scrapped. The University is also called upon to dismiss me from my employment if I don't apologise for multiple alleged counts of Islamophobia. The petition eventually garners over 4,100 signatures and BRISOC's campaign over 7,000 'likes' on its various social media sites.
19 February	Two University of Bristol student newspapers, *Epigram* and *The Bristol Tablet*, publish stories about the campaign together with my photo, implying that the accusations are true. Other than denying the charges, I'm rendered powerless by the University's insistence that, in spite of BRISOC's violation of theirs, I remain bound by my duty of confidentiality regarding the investigation of the complaint.
25 February	I submit my full, formal response to the Assessor appointed by the University. The international, Qatar-based, news network, *Al Jazeera*, publishes an online story about the

	controversy. The same evening, I encounter a suspicious stranger outside my home. They give an implausible excuse and leave. An unlikely coincidence or a reconnoitre?
26 February	Conscious of the Samuel Paty murder in France, and fearful for my safety, I flee Bristol with my wife to stay somewhere safer a long way away.
3 March	Having referred the issue of my personal safety to the University of Bristol police officer, I'm informed that an investigation has been launched by the Avon and Somerset Constabulary into all aspects of the complaint and its consequences.
13 March	I discover that, at a public protest in Bristol in December 2020, I was named as an Islamophobe by a member of BRISOC, a medical student and one of the University's own student anti-racism advisers. She proudly announced this on her Facebook page on 19 February 2021 just days after BRISOC's campaign began.
15 February - 14 March	BRISOC continues to pump out defamatory material on social media including lies from 'anonymous students.'
	I receive a number of hostile and threatening emails which I refer to the police.
14 March	I learn that the Avon and Somerset Constabulary has emailed BRISOC and the University of Bristol Jewish Society informing them that an investigation has been launched into allegations of anti-Semitism and Islamophobia at the University of Bristol.
	I email the University of Bristol to ask why it has not acted more decisively to stop BRISOC from continuing its defamatory and potentially life-threatening campaign. I'm informed that BRISOC will be reminded of the confidentiality of the University's investigation into the complaint which BRISOC has irretrievably broken since the campaign began on 15 February.
22 March	I'm informed by the police that their investigation into my alleged misconduct has been dropped due to lack of evidence and the unwillingness of BRISOC to pursue a criminal complaint.

24 March	I learn from the University Assessor that BRISOC has yet to respond to my reply to their formal complaint.
12 May	The Assessor tells me that the complainant has been given until 16 May to respond to my reply to the complaint– two and a half months after I had submitted it.
2/3 June	I send the Assessor two emails indicating that I intend to instruct lawyers to contest the University's failure to discharge the duty of care it owes me as an employee by failing to exonerate me from the allegations promptly and by apparently stalling the inquiry indefinitely in the apparent hope that things will sort themselves out.
10 June	I instruct a solicitor with a London firm.
23 July	Having considered the merits, the University inquiry concludes with my complete, unequivocal and unreserved exoneration from all BRISOC's allegations. My 'duty of confidentiality' is said to include not telling anyone apart from close family about this result pending a joint public statement between me, the complainant and the University following any appeal. I indicate to the Assessor that I'm willing to engage in mediation, and to cooperate with the production of a joint statement, provided the complainant publicly apologises and retracts the false allegations. But no such statement ever materializes.
2 August	I report the news of my exoneration to the Law School's senior management and ask when colleagues will be informed. I point out that there is disturbing evidence that some members of the Law School, have been involved in the campaign to discredit me. For example, the University of Bristol Unity and Diversity in Law, and University of Bristol Women in Law Society, each of which is supported by the School, signed BRISOC's petition to have me sacked. I suggest that these are matters of the utmost seriousness which require further investigation by the Law School's senior management. I receive no reply.

18 August	I discover that BRISOC has uploaded a false and potentially dangerous TikTok video to their Instagram account. Having passed this information to the police, I decide not to tell the University on account of its failure to do anything effective about my predicament thus far.
4 September	Having reached stalemate in negotiations with two junior colleagues, now coordinators of the undergraduate and postgraduate units in HRLPS, about my teaching commitments in 2021-22, I propose that I deliver the lecture and conduct all the seminars in the Islam, China and the Far East module.
6 September	I receive a reply from the coordinators indicating that they have decided that they 'will not be running a cycle on "Islam, China, and the Far East" either on the UG or PG units …. for a number of reasons' including 'the likelihood of recurrence of complaints.' They add that 'it is important that Muslim students in particular do not feel that their religion is being singled out or in any way "othered" by the class material…' Their decision is immediately endorsed by the Law School.
10 September	I'm signed off work by my doctor on account of the stress caused by the BRISOC crisis. I lodge a formal complaint against BRISOC with the police.
12 September	The *Mail on Sunday* publishes my story.
8 October	A panel of three senior Bristol academics rejects BRISOC's appeal against the inquiry's decision.
11 October	Following publication of the University's statement regarding my case the student newspaper, the *Bristol Tab*, publishes a statement from me followed a few days later by *Epigram*.
1 December	Only a few hours before an online interview with me about Islamophobia and academic freedom, hosted by the Bristol Free Speech Society is due to take place, the Law School's senior management emails me to 'insist' that I do 'not attend … pending the outcome of an Occupational Health report.' They add that, 'depending on the OH report and future circumstances, it may be possible for you to attend such an event in the future.'

5 December	I notify the Law School to the effect that I look forward to cooperating with Occupational Health and Human Resources in facilitating my return to work on 3 January 2022 when my fit note expires. I also identify several issues which, in my opinion, need to be resolved first.
15 December	I'm informed by her former firm, that my solicitor no longer works for them and that they will appoint another to represent me. I reply to the effect that I will be instructing another solicitor from a different firm.
21 December	The Free Speech Union finds, and provides initial funding for, a new team of lawyers.

2022

3 January	The fit note from my doctor, officially signing me off work, expires without any attempt having been made by the University or senior management of the Law School to facilitate my phased return.
18 January	My appointment as the first Visiting Research Fellow at the Oxford Institute for British Islam (OIBI), a new liberal Muslim think tank, is formally announced.
24 January	An Occupational Health consultation is conducted on the phone. The report which follows focuses almost entirely upon the need for the workplace issues, to which I'd already drawn the attention of the University and the Law School, to be addressed before I can safely physically return to work on campus. It makes no reference to working from home which, in the consultation, I emphasised, had never raised any health-related concerns.
21 February	I receive an email from senior management at the Law School insisting that I do not participate in the Free Speech Society interview, postponed from 1 December to 24 February, on the grounds that 'the OH advice states very clearly that you should not be undertaking any work activities at this time, in any place, because the work issues you have raised need to be resolved to prevent further exacerbation of stress … For the avoidance of doubt, that includes work activities conducted at home and externally, not just on University premises.'

8 March	Another OH consultation unequivocally resolves any doubt about my immediate return to working from home, and if and when I please, at the Law School. This expressly includes participation in speaking events.
30 March	Senior Law School management 'instructs' me not to participate in the Free Speech Society interview scheduled for that evening on the grounds that the issues raised in the first OH report which they themselves have refused to address remain unresolved. The event goes ahead with my full involvement anyway.
1 April	I email the Law School to inform it that as a result of its failure to protect my best interests I have lost confidence in senior management and would like the last few months of my full-time working life to be managed by somebody else.
28 April	At their invitation, I meet senior University officials to discuss how the University has mismanaged my case.
13 May	A letter-before-claim is sent by my legal team to the University of Bristol.
24 May	The Oxford Institute for British Islam (OIBI) is officially launched at St Peter's College, Oxford.
26 July	I deliver a farewell speech at the end of session Law School party which includes a celebration of my retirement and that of other colleagues.
19-21 August	The OIBI holds its inaugural conference at St John's College, Oxford.
1 September	I'm appointed OIBI's first Research Director.
1 October	Retirement begins.
20 December	Riddled with mistakes and claiming not to understand the case against their client, the University's solicitors reply to the letter-before-claim sent by my solicitors on 13 May.

2023

13 February	*Falsely Accused of Islamophobia* is published. According to Palamedes, within a week or so, media outlets with a global readership/audience of 231 million have covered my story.

Appendix F

17 February	Veteran Labour MP, Barry Sheerman, calls for the Vice Chancellor and President of the University of Bristol, Professor Evelyn Welch, and the entire senior management team, to resign. I publish, 'How to solve the campus free speech crisis,' on *The Times Red Box* online comment site.
21 February	On *The Times Red Box* site Professor Welch publicly responds to developments the previous week with an article entitled, 'Bristol University is not defensive or intolerant.'
23 February	Professor Welch rejects my invitation for a face-to-face meeting until my solicitor's letter-before-claim is withdrawn.
23 March	I present a paper about my book at Policy Exchange's European Roundtable on Extremism.
29 March	An interview with me, conducted by the editor, Emma Parks, is published in *The Freethinker*.
30 March	Megan Manson, Head of Campaigns at the National Secular Society, and I have an online conversation in the company of an audience of over 100.
6 April	*Falsely Accused of Islamophobia* is officially launched at the Art Workers' Guild in London, an event sponsored by the Oxford Institute for British Islam, the Free Speech Union, and the Common Sense Society.
11 April	Alumni for Free Speech (AFFS) sends a 14-page letter to the University of Bristol detailing how its mismanagement of the BRISOC scandal constitutes multiple violations of its own codes of conduct and its statutory obligations. An independent investigation is proposed.
2 June	Following the University of Bristol's failure to respond adequately to its letter of 11 April, AFFS reports the matter to the Office for Students (OfS), the universities' regulator.
8 June	OIBI writes to the University of Bristol asking why its response to the BRISOC scandal does not constitute an ongoing violation of the statutory duty to have due regard to the need to prevent people from being drawn into terrorism. It also proposes that the University should appoint an independent inquiry.
26 July	OIBI refers BRISOC scandal to OfS.

www.ingramcontent.com/pod-product-compliance
Ingram Content Group UK Ltd.
Pitfield, Milton Keynes, MK11 3LW, UK
UKHW021324220625
6518UKWH00033B/634